BROODHOLLOW

CURIOUS LITTLE THING

BY KRIS STRAUB

To Marlo, whom I have loved for a thousand holidays

Broodhollow: Curious Little Thing

Contains material originally published at *broodhollow.com*.

Thank you to all the Kickstarter backers without whom this would not have been possible.

ISBN-13: 978-0-9898165-0-2
First printing: September 2013. Printed in China.

Published by Chainsawsuit Studios
studios.chainsawsuit.com

OUR PAST OUR FOUNDATION

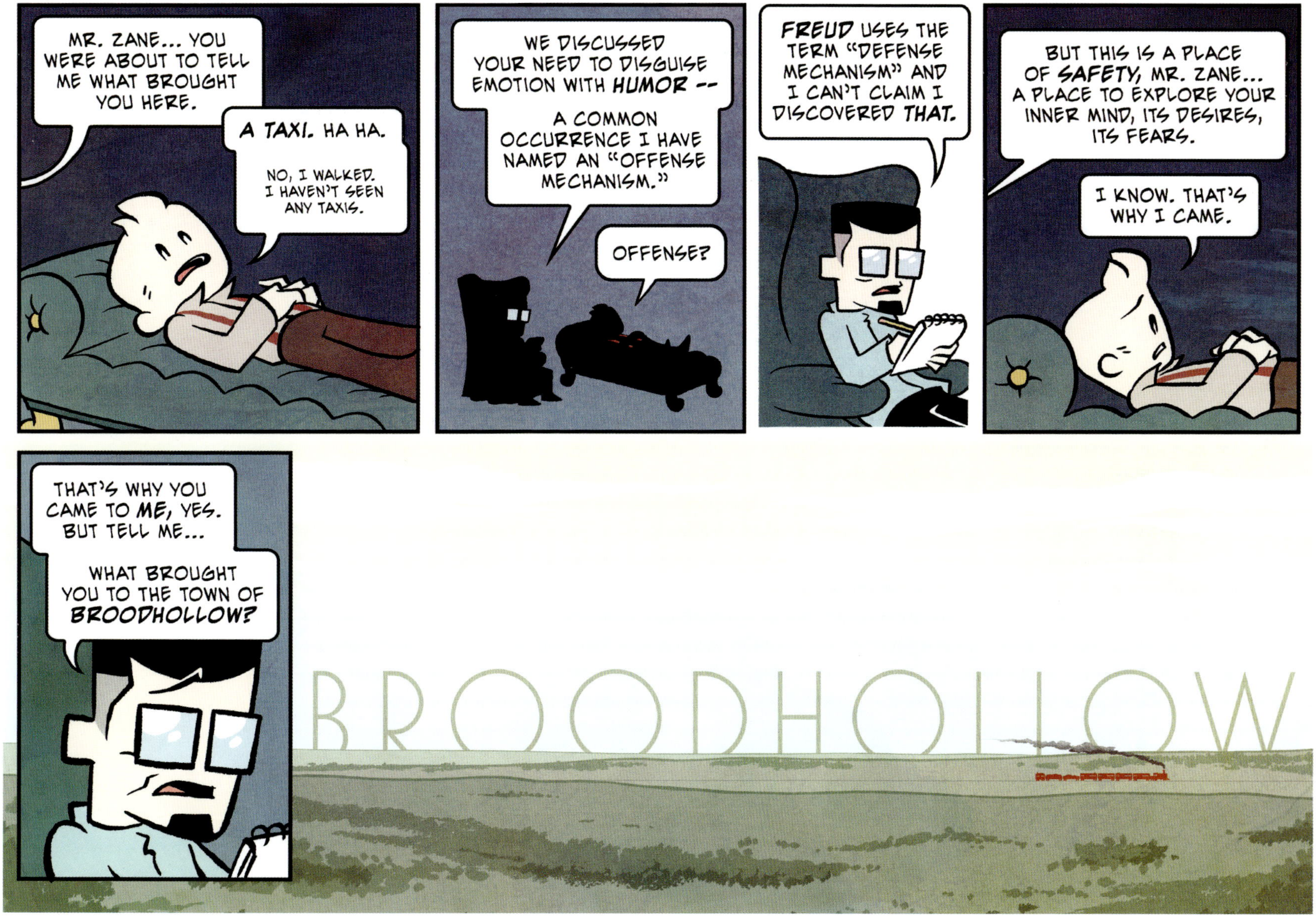
MR. ZANE... YOU WERE ABOUT TO TELL ME WHAT BROUGHT YOU HERE.
A TAXI. HA HA.
NO, I WALKED. I HAVEN'T SEEN ANY TAXIS.
WE DISCUSSED YOUR NEED TO DISGUISE EMOTION WITH HUMOR --
A COMMON OCCURRENCE I HAVE NAMED AN "OFFENSE MECHANISM."
OFFENSE?
FREUD USES THE TERM "DEFENSE MECHANISM" AND I CAN'T CLAIM I DISCOVERED THAT.
BUT THIS IS A PLACE OF SAFETY, MR. ZANE... A PLACE TO EXPLORE YOUR INNER MIND, ITS DESIRES, ITS FEARS.
I KNOW. THAT'S WHY I CAME.
THAT'S WHY YOU CAME TO ME, YES. BUT TELL ME...
WHAT BROUGHT YOU TO THE TOWN OF BROODHOLLOW?
BROODHOLLOW

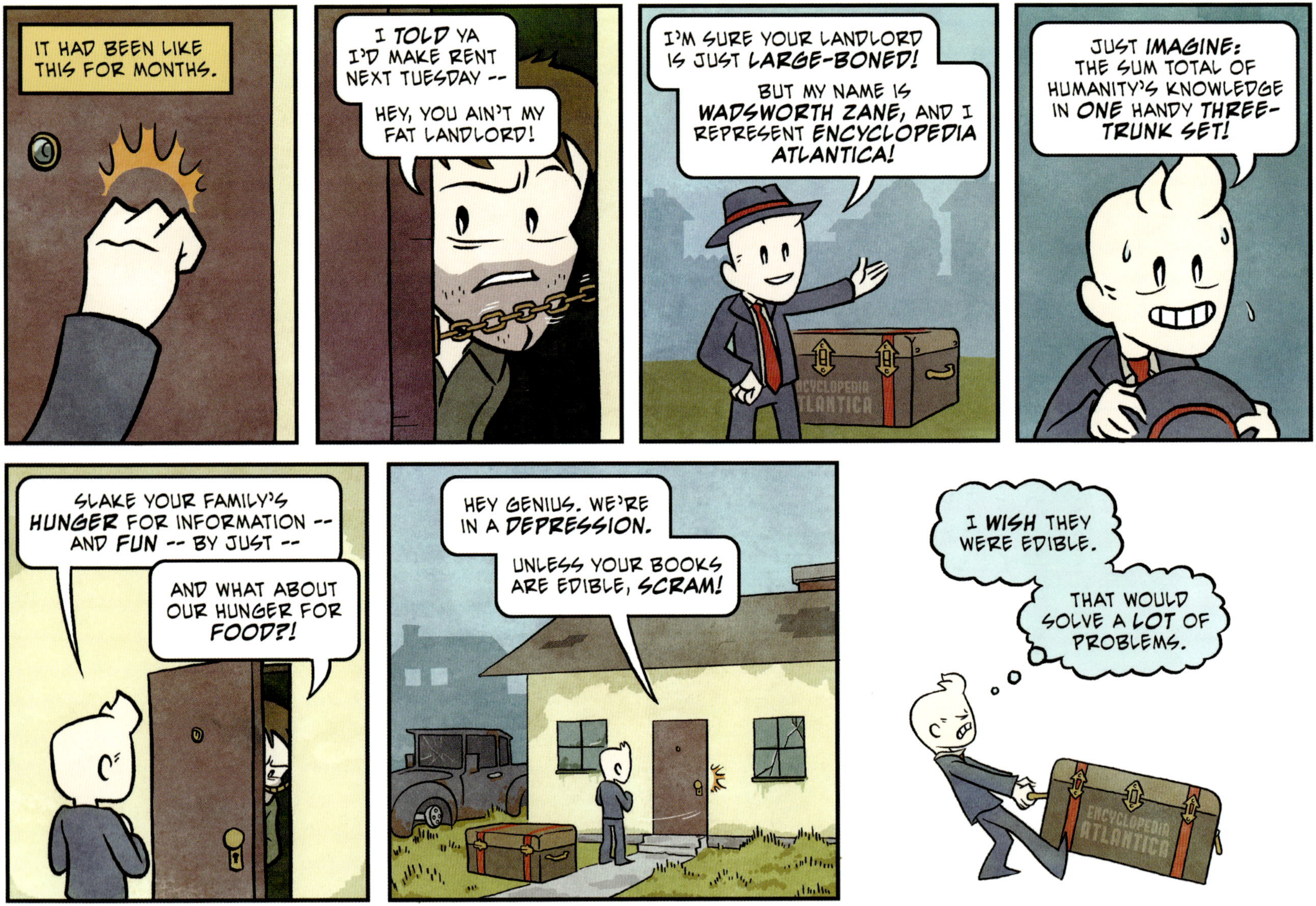
IT HAD BEEN LIKE THIS FOR MONTHS.
I TOLD YA I'D MAKE RENT NEXT TUESDAY --
HEY, YOU AIN'T MY FAT LANDLORD!
I'M SURE YOUR LANDLORD IS JUST LARGE-BONED!
BUT MY NAME IS WADSWORTH ZANE, AND I REPRESENT ENCYCLOPEDIA ATLANTICA!
ENCYCLOPEDIA ATLANTICA
JUST IMAGINE: THE SUM TOTAL OF HUMANITY'S KNOWLEDGE IN ONE HANDY THREE-TRUNK SET!
SLAKE YOUR FAMILY'S HUNGER FOR INFORMATION -- AND FUN -- BY JUST --
AND WHAT ABOUT OUR HUNGER FOR FOOD?!
HEY GENIUS. WE'RE IN A DEPRESSION.
UNLESS YOUR BOOKS ARE EDIBLE, SCRAM!
I WISH THEY WERE EDIBLE.
THAT WOULD SOLVE A LOT OF PROBLEMS.
ENCYCLOPEDIA ATLANTICA

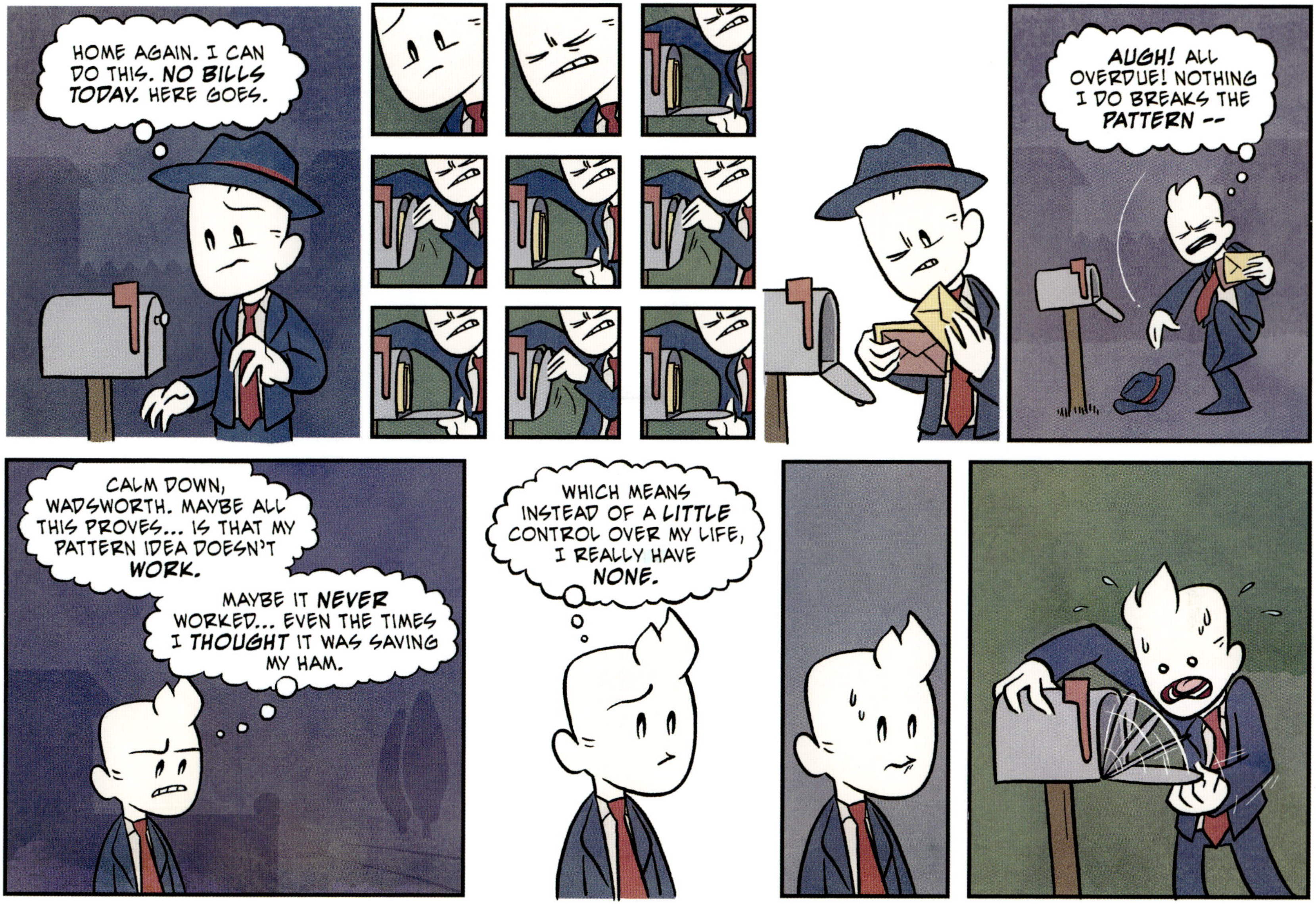
HOME AGAIN. I CAN DO THIS. NO BILLS TODAY. HERE GOES.
AUGH! ALL OVERDUE! NOTHING I DO BREAKS THE PATTERN --
CALM DOWN, WADSWORTH. MAYBE ALL THIS PROVES... IS THAT MY PATTERN IDEA DOESN'T WORK.
MAYBE IT NEVER WORKED... EVEN THE TIMES I THOUGHT IT WAS SAVING MY HAM.
WHICH MEANS INSTEAD OF A LITTLE CONTROL OVER MY LIFE, I REALLY HAVE NONE.

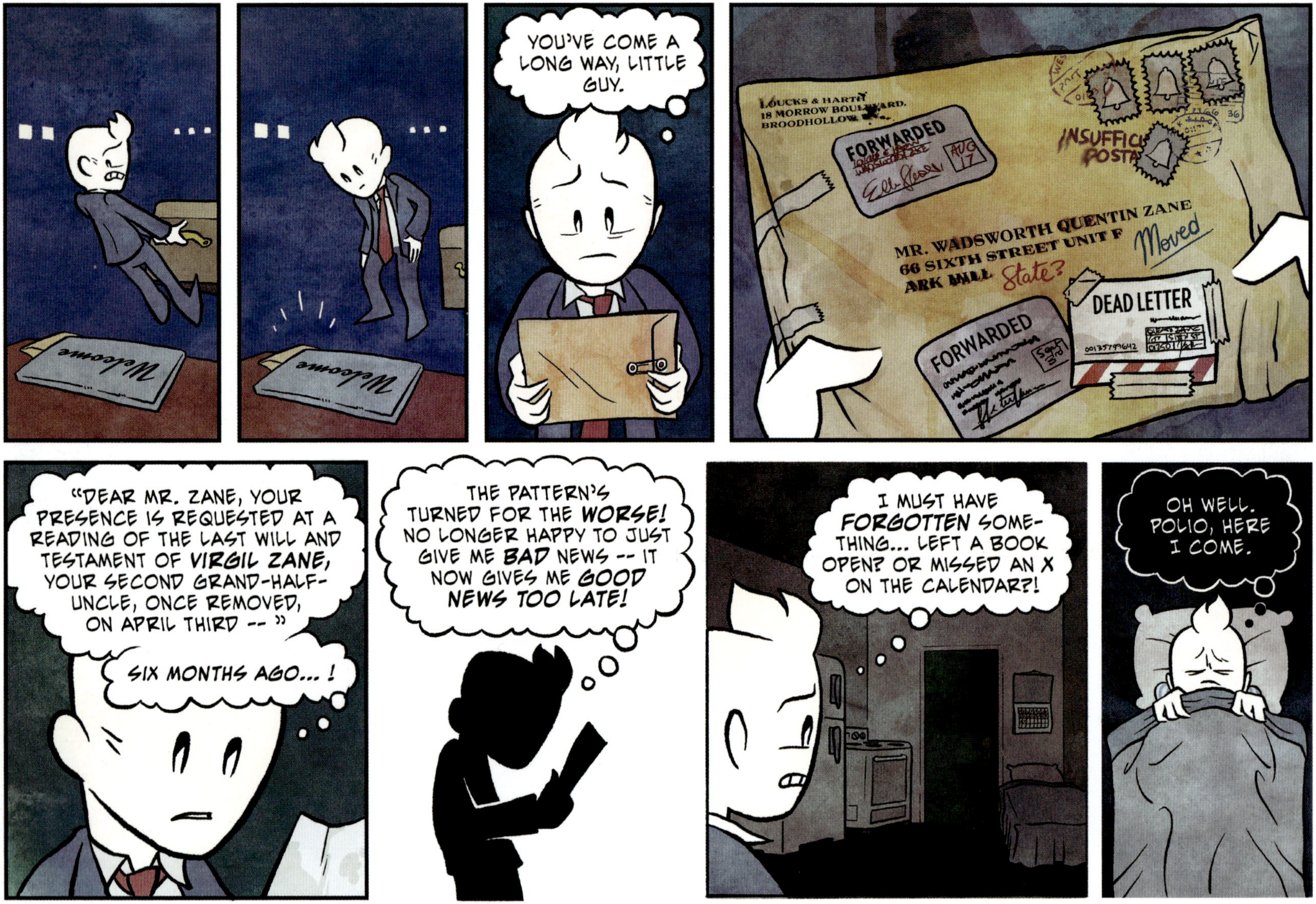
YOU'VE COME A LONG WAY, LITTLE GUY.
FORWARDED
MR. WADSWORTH QUENTIN ZANE
66 SIXTH STREET UNIT F
Moved
State?
DEAD LETTER
FORWARDED
"DEAR MR. ZANE, YOUR PRESENCE IS REQUESTED AT A READING OF THE LAST WILL AND TESTAMENT OF VIRGIL ZANE, YOUR SECOND GRAND-HALF-UNCLE, ONCE REMOVED, ON APRIL THIRD -- "
SIX MONTHS AGO... !
THE PATTERN'S TURNED FOR THE WORSE! NO LONGER HAPPY TO JUST GIVE ME BAD NEWS -- IT NOW GIVES ME GOOD NEWS TOO LATE!
I MUST HAVE FORGOTTEN SOMETHING... LEFT A BOOK OPEN? OR MISSED AN X ON THE CALENDAR?!
OH WELL. POLIO, HERE I COME.

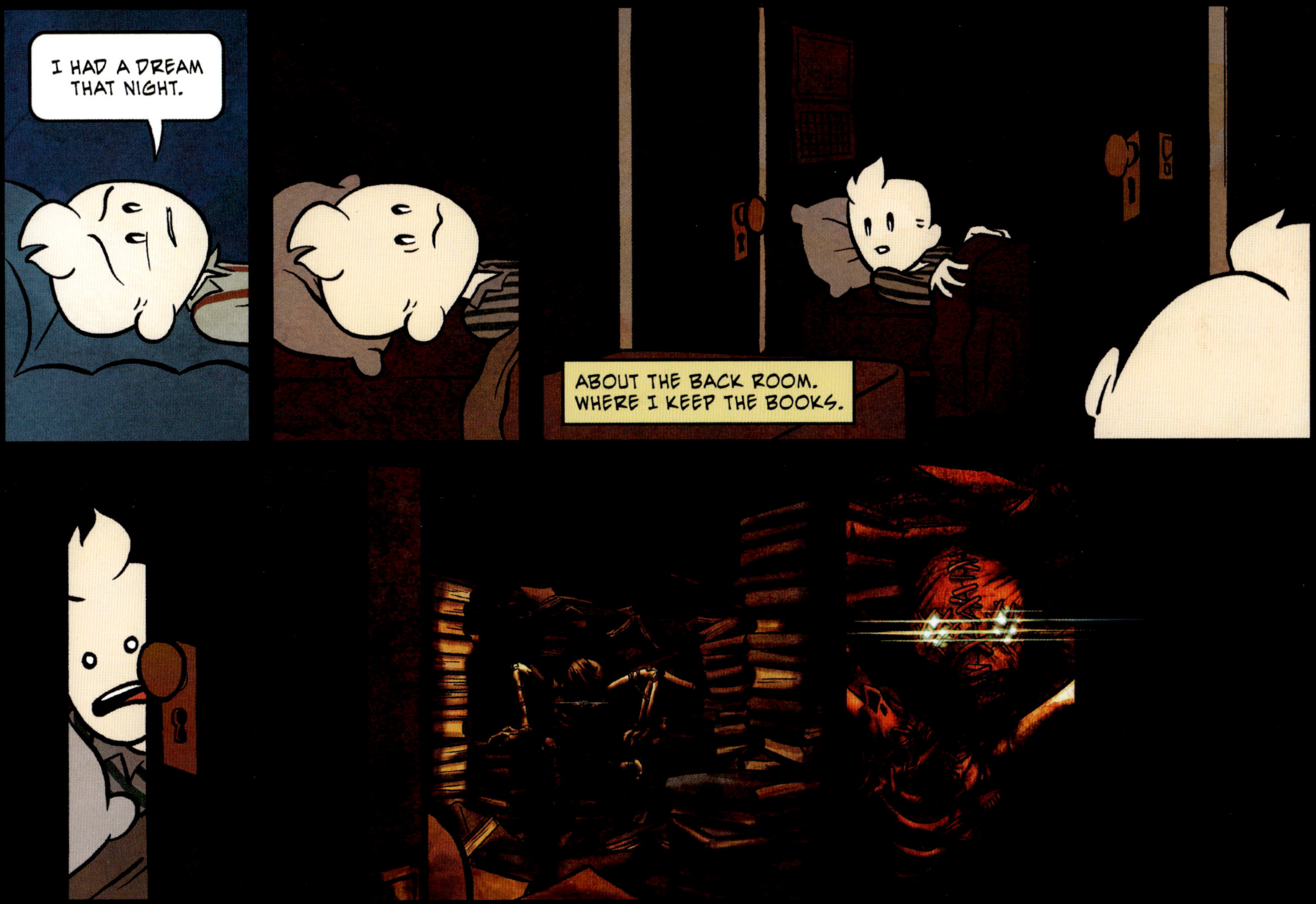
I HAD A DREAM THAT NIGHT.
ABOUT THE BACK ROOM. WHERE I KEEP THE BOOKS.

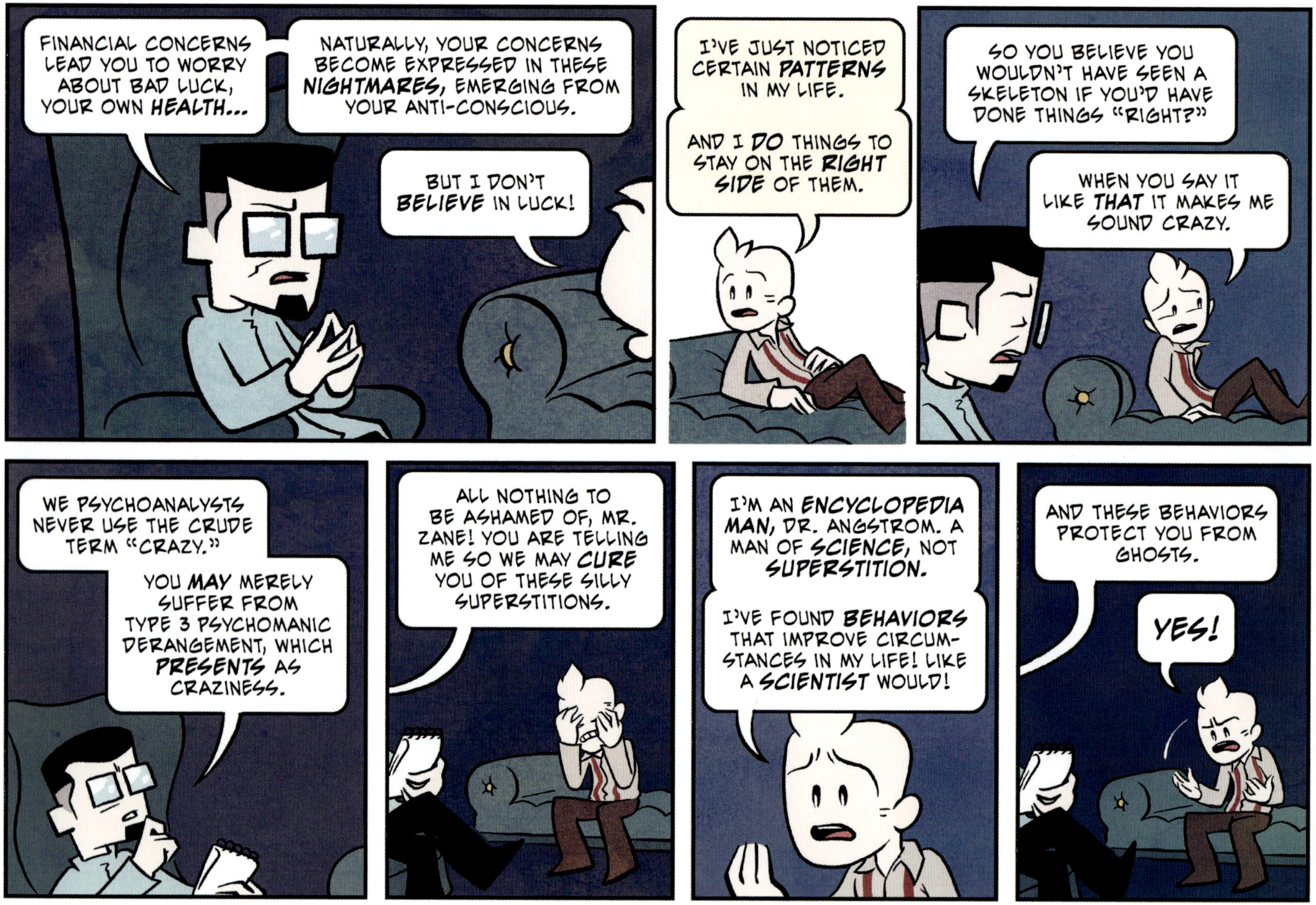
FINANCIAL CONCERNS LEAD YOU TO WORRY ABOUT BAD LUCK, YOUR OWN HEALTH...
NATURALLY, YOUR CONCERNS BECOME EXPRESSED IN THESE NIGHTMARES, EMERGING FROM YOUR ANTI-CONSCIOUS.
BUT I DON'T BELIEVE IN LUCK!
I'VE JUST NOTICED CERTAIN PATTERNS IN MY LIFE.
AND I DO THINGS TO STAY ON THE RIGHT SIDE OF THEM.
SO YOU BELIEVE YOU WOULDN'T HAVE SEEN A SKELETON IF YOU'D HAVE DONE THINGS "RIGHT?"
WHEN YOU SAY IT LIKE THAT IT MAKES ME SOUND CRAZY.
WE PSYCHOANALYSTS NEVER USE THE CRUDE TERM "CRAZY."
YOU MAY MERELY SUFFER FROM TYPE 3 PSYCHOMANIC DERANGEMENT, WHICH PRESENTS AS CRAZINESS.
ALL NOTHING TO BE ASHAMED OF, MR. ZANE! YOU ARE TELLING ME SO WE MAY CURE YOU OF THESE SILLY SUPERSTITIONS.
I'M AN ENCYCLOPEDIA MAN, DR. ANGSTROM. A MAN OF SCIENCE, NOT SUPERSTITION.
I'VE FOUND BEHAVIORS THAT IMPROVE CIRCUMSTANCES IN MY LIFE! LIKE A SCIENTIST WOULD!
AND THESE BEHAVIORS PROTECT YOU FROM GHOSTS.
YES!

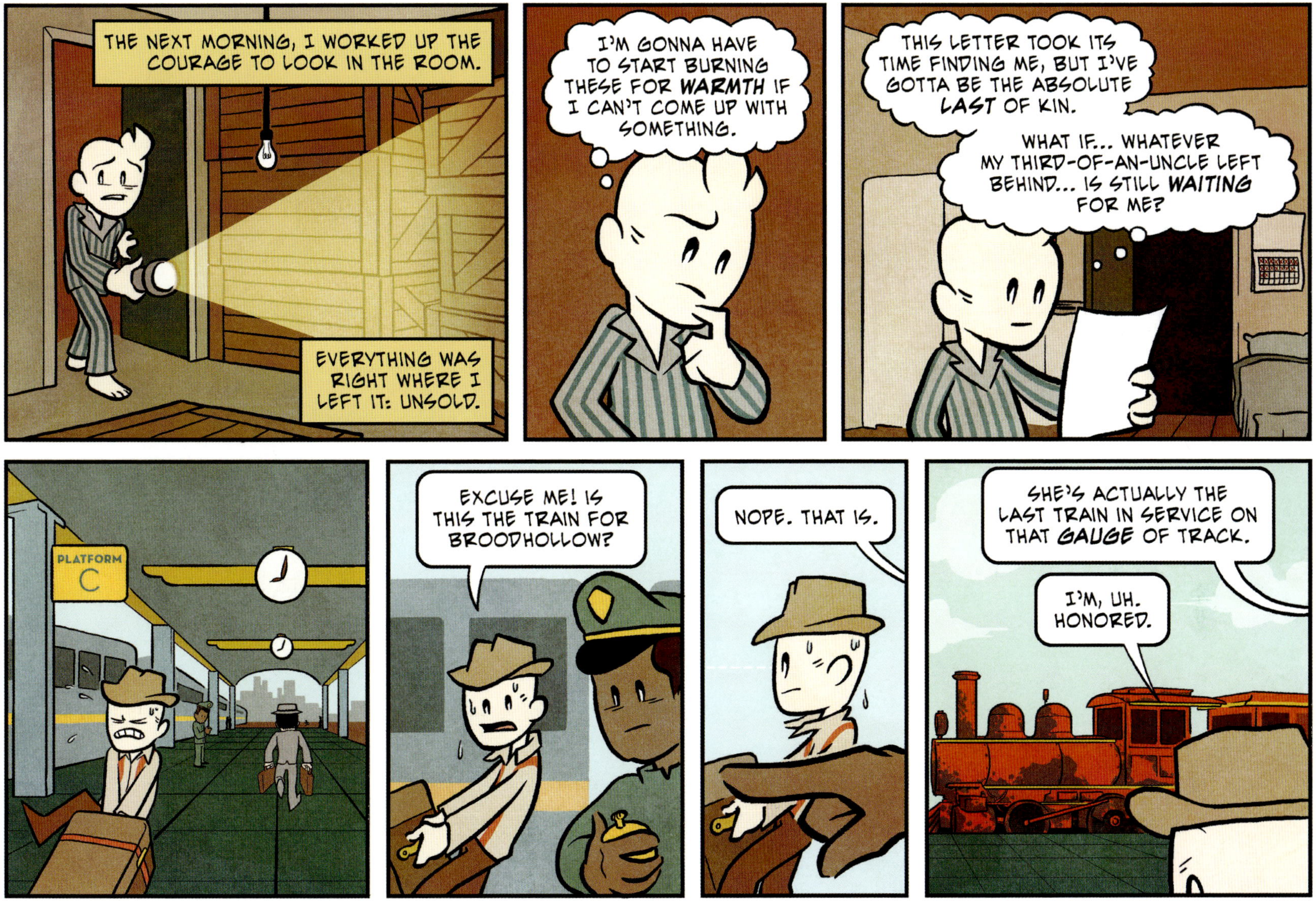
THE NEXT MORNING, I WORKED UP THE COURAGE TO LOOK IN THE ROOM.
EVERYTHING WAS RIGHT WHERE I LEFT IT: UNSOLD.
I'M GONNA HAVE TO START BURNING THESE FOR WARMTH IF I CAN'T COME UP WITH SOMETHING.
THIS LETTER TOOK ITS TIME FINDING ME, BUT I'VE GOTTA BE THE ABSOLUTE LAST OF KIN.
WHAT IF... WHATEVER MY THIRD-OF-AN-UNCLE LEFT BEHIND... IS STILL WAITING FOR ME?
PLATFORM C
EXCUSE ME! IS THIS THE TRAIN FOR BROODHOLLOW?
NOPE. THAT IS.
SHE'S ACTUALLY THE LAST TRAIN IN SERVICE ON THAT GAUGE OF TRACK.
I'M, UH. HONORED.

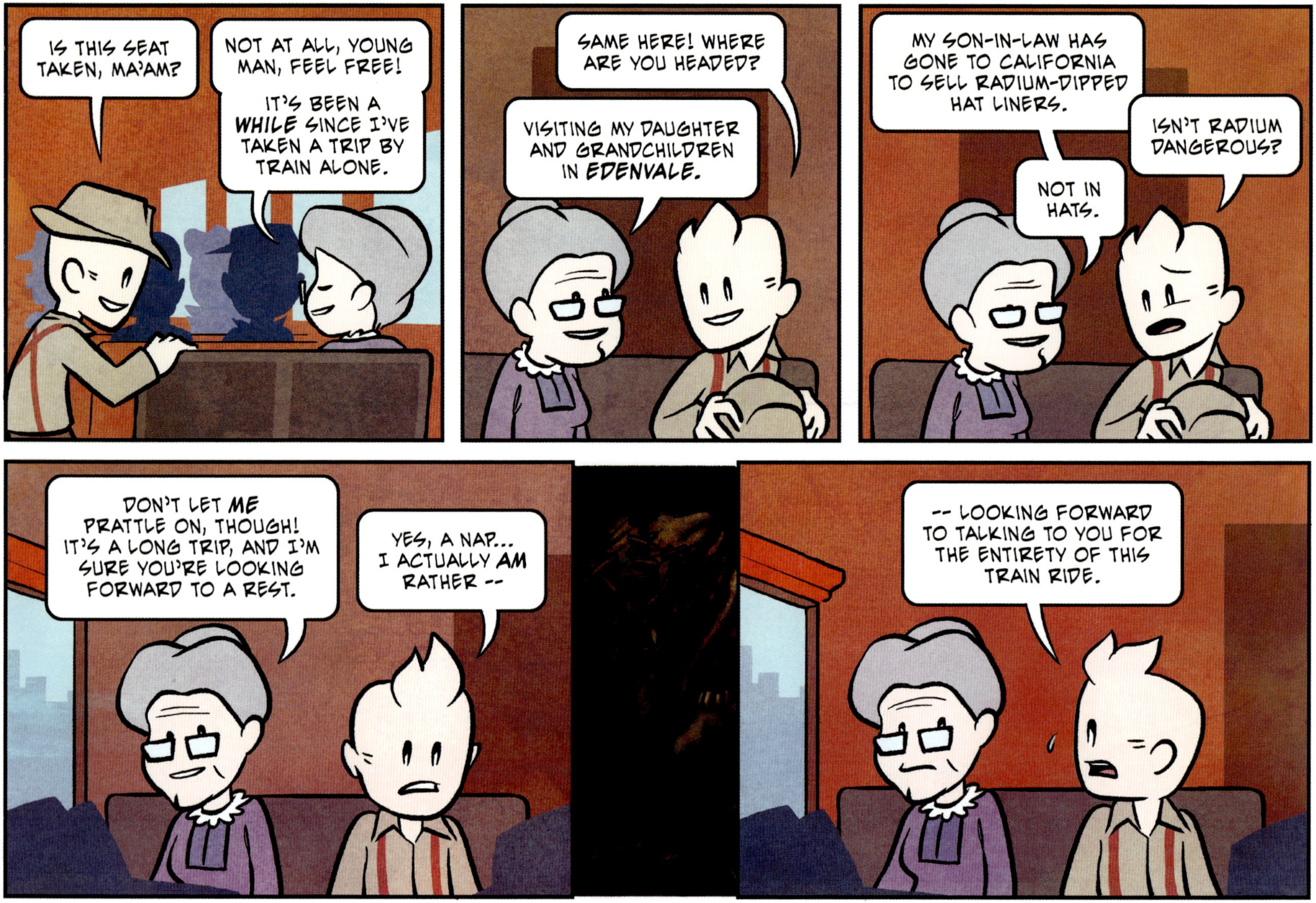

IS THIS SEAT TAKEN, MA'AM?
NOT AT ALL, YOUNG MAN, FEEL FREE!
IT'S BEEN A *WHILE* SINCE I'VE TAKEN A TRIP BY TRAIN ALONE.
SAME HERE! WHERE ARE YOU HEADED?
VISITING MY DAUGHTER AND GRANDCHILDREN IN *EDENVALE.*
MY SON-IN-LAW HAS GONE TO CALIFORNIA TO SELL RADIUM-DIPPED HAT LINERS.
ISN'T RADIUM DANGEROUS?
NOT IN HATS.
DON'T LET *ME* PRATTLE ON, THOUGH! IT'S A LONG TRIP, AND I'M SURE YOU'RE LOOKING FORWARD TO A REST.
YES, A NAP... I ACTUALLY *AM* RATHER --
-- LOOKING FORWARD TO TALKING TO YOU FOR THE ENTIRETY OF THIS TRAIN RIDE.

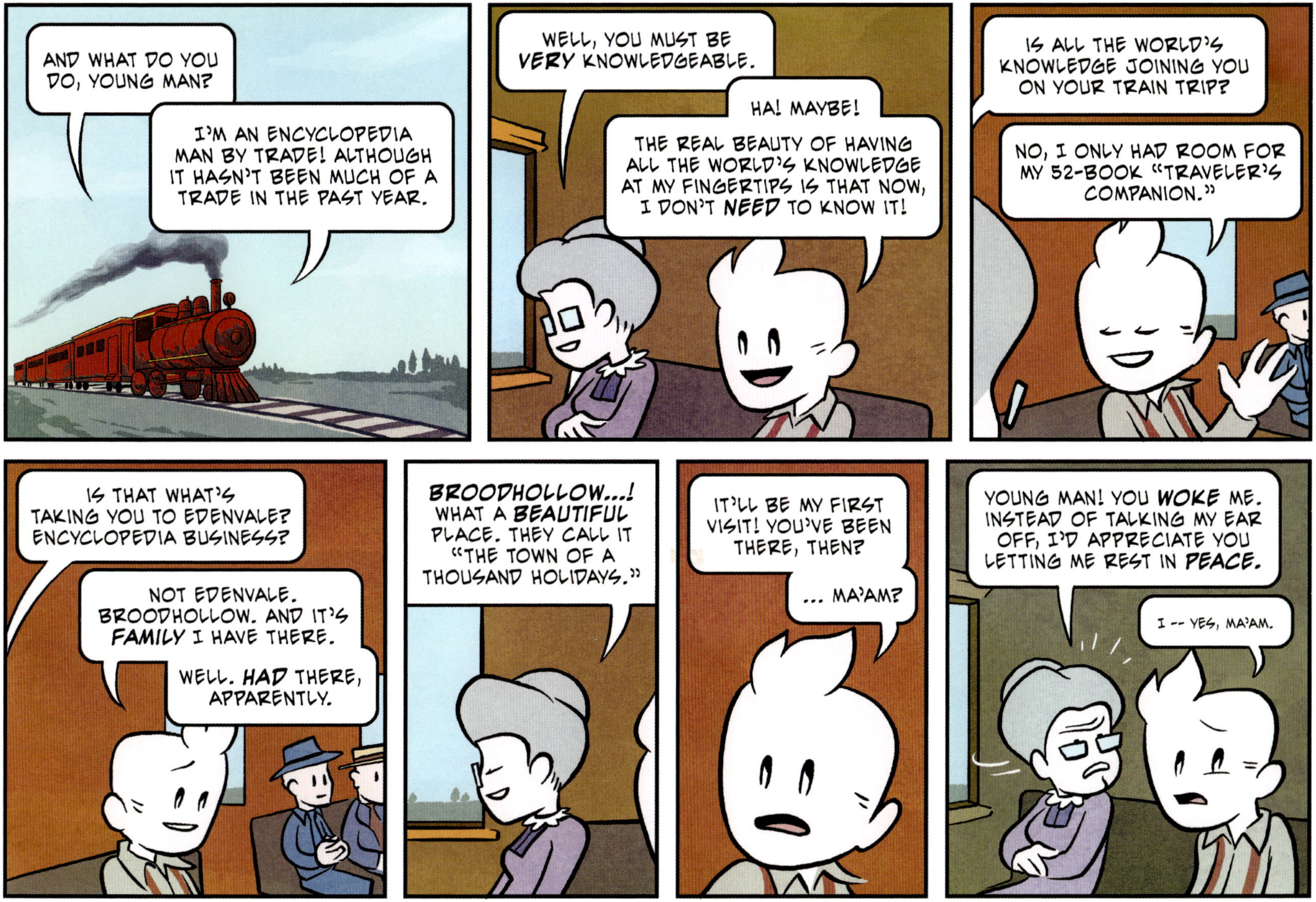
AND WHAT DO YOU DO, YOUNG MAN?
I'M AN ENCYCLOPEDIA MAN BY TRADE! ALTHOUGH IT HASN'T BEEN MUCH OF A TRADE IN THE PAST YEAR.
WELL, YOU MUST BE VERY KNOWLEDGEABLE.
HA! MAYBE!
THE REAL BEAUTY OF HAVING ALL THE WORLD'S KNOWLEDGE AT MY FINGERTIPS IS THAT NOW, I DON'T NEED TO KNOW IT!
IS ALL THE WORLD'S KNOWLEDGE JOINING YOU ON YOUR TRAIN TRIP?
NO, I ONLY HAD ROOM FOR MY 52-BOOK "TRAVELER'S COMPANION."
IS THAT WHAT'S TAKING YOU TO EDENVALE? ENCYCLOPEDIA BUSINESS?
NOT EDENVALE. BROODHOLLOW. AND IT'S FAMILY I HAVE THERE.
WELL. HAD THERE, APPARENTLY.
BROODHOLLOW...! WHAT A BEAUTIFUL PLACE. THEY CALL IT "THE TOWN OF A THOUSAND HOLIDAYS."
IT'LL BE MY FIRST VISIT! YOU'VE BEEN THERE, THEN?
... MA'AM?
YOUNG MAN! YOU WOKE ME. INSTEAD OF TALKING MY EAR OFF, I'D APPRECIATE YOU LETTING ME REST IN PEACE.
I -- YES, MA'AM.

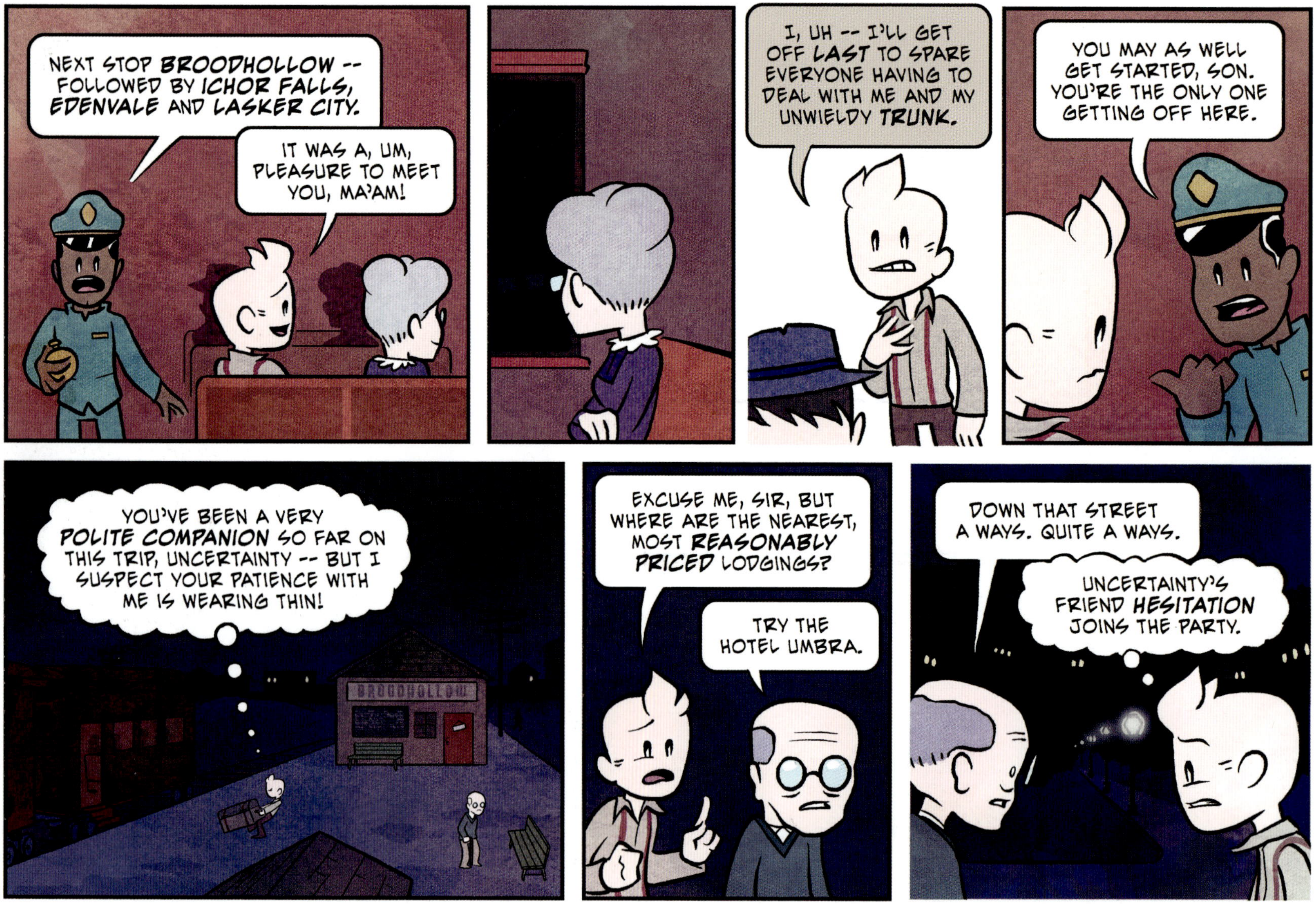

NEXT STOP BROODHOLLOW -- FOLLOWED BY ICHOR FALLS, EDENVALE AND LASKER CITY.
IT WAS A, UM, PLEASURE TO MEET YOU, MA'AM!
I, UH -- I'LL GET OFF LAST TO SPARE EVERYONE HAVING TO DEAL WITH ME AND MY UNWIELDY TRUNK.
YOU MAY AS WELL GET STARTED, SON. YOU'RE THE ONLY ONE GETTING OFF HERE.
YOU'VE BEEN A VERY POLITE COMPANION SO FAR ON THIS TRIP, UNCERTAINTY -- BUT I SUSPECT YOUR PATIENCE WITH ME IS WEARING THIN!
BROODHOLLOW
EXCUSE ME, SIR, BUT WHERE ARE THE NEAREST, MOST REASONABLY PRICED LODGINGS?
TRY THE HOTEL UMBRA.
DOWN THAT STREET A WAYS. QUITE A WAYS.
UNCERTAINTY'S FRIEND HESITATION JOINS THE PARTY.

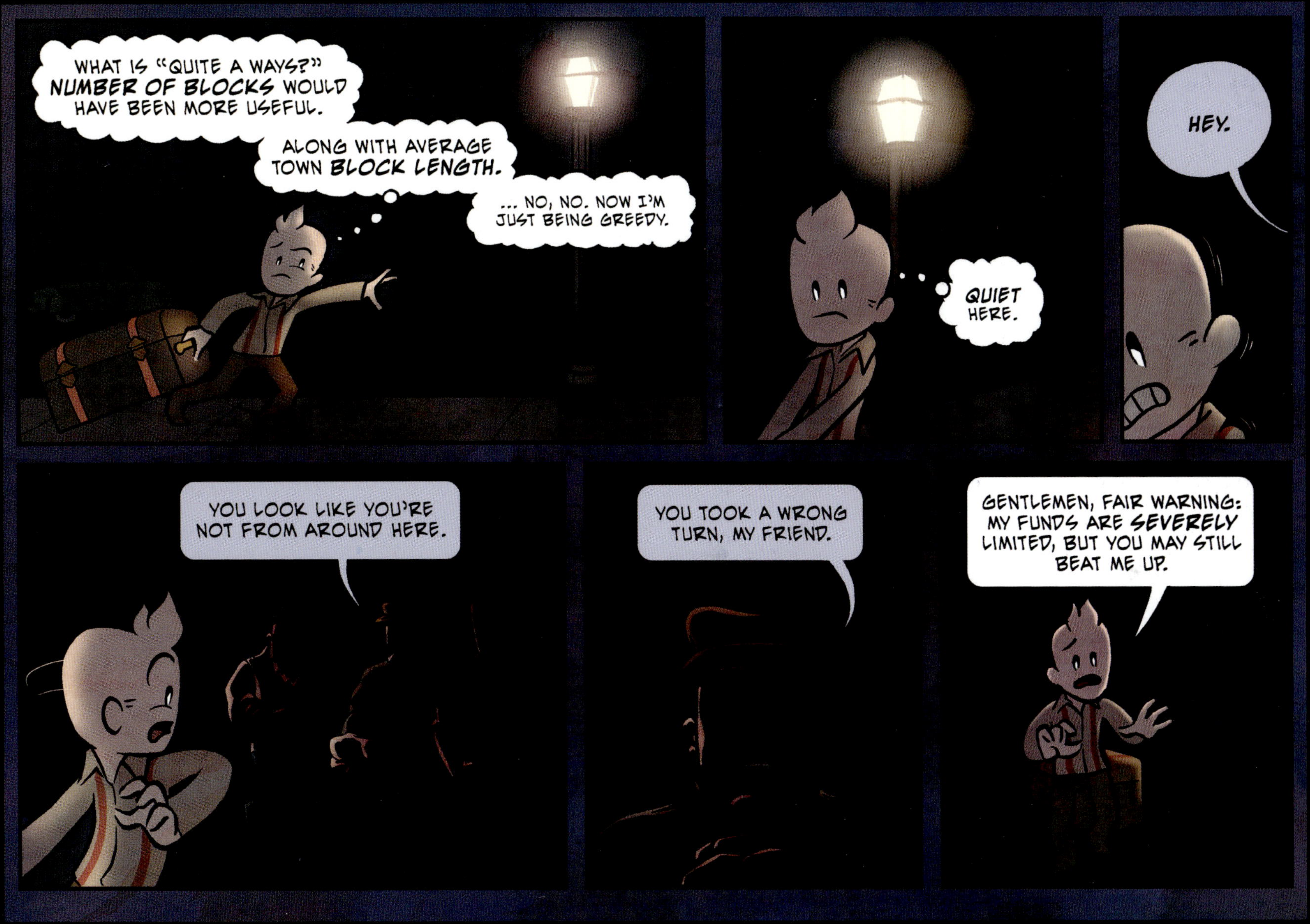
WHAT IS "QUITE A WAYS?" NUMBER OF BLOCKS WOULD HAVE BEEN MORE USEFUL.
ALONG WITH AVERAGE TOWN BLOCK LENGTH.
... NO, NO. NOW I'M JUST BEING GREEDY.
QUIET HERE.
HEY.
YOU LOOK LIKE YOU'RE NOT FROM AROUND HERE.
YOU TOOK A WRONG TURN, MY FRIEND.
GENTLEMEN, FAIR WARNING: MY FUNDS ARE SEVERELY LIMITED, BUT YOU MAY STILL BEAT ME UP.

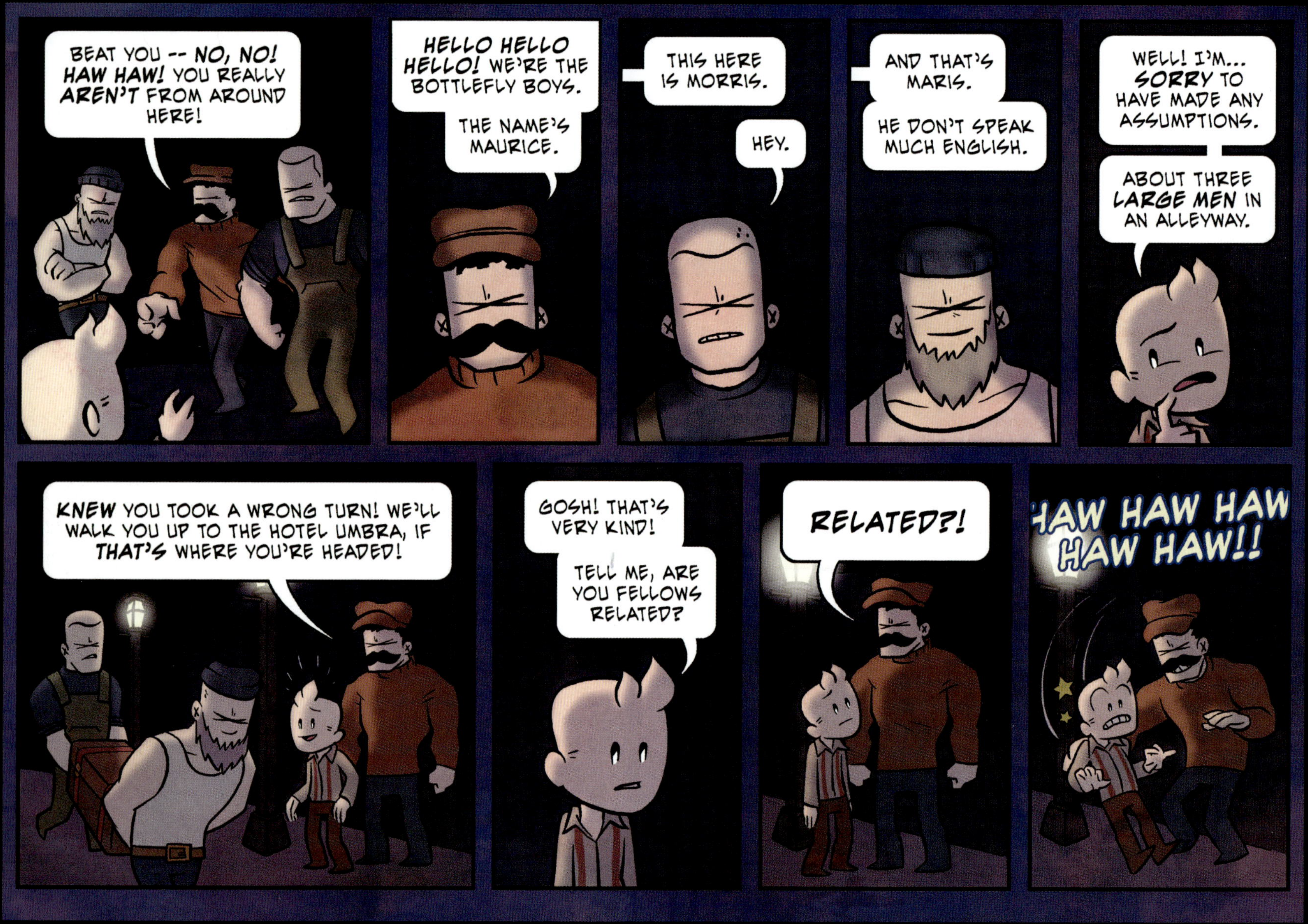
BEAT YOU -- NO, NO! HAW HAW! YOU REALLY AREN'T FROM AROUND HERE!
HELLO HELLO HELLO! WE'RE THE BOTTLEFLY BOYS.
THE NAME'S MAURICE.
THIS HERE IS MORRIS.
HEY.
AND THAT'S MARIS.
HE DON'T SPEAK MUCH ENGLISH.
WELL! I'M... SORRY TO HAVE MADE ANY ASSUMPTIONS.
ABOUT THREE LARGE MEN IN AN ALLEYWAY.
KNEW YOU TOOK A WRONG TURN! WE'LL WALK YOU UP TO THE HOTEL UMBRA, IF THAT'S WHERE YOU'RE HEADED!
GOSH! THAT'S VERY KIND!
TELL ME, ARE YOU FELLOWS RELATED?
RELATED?!
HAW HAW HAW HAW HAW!!

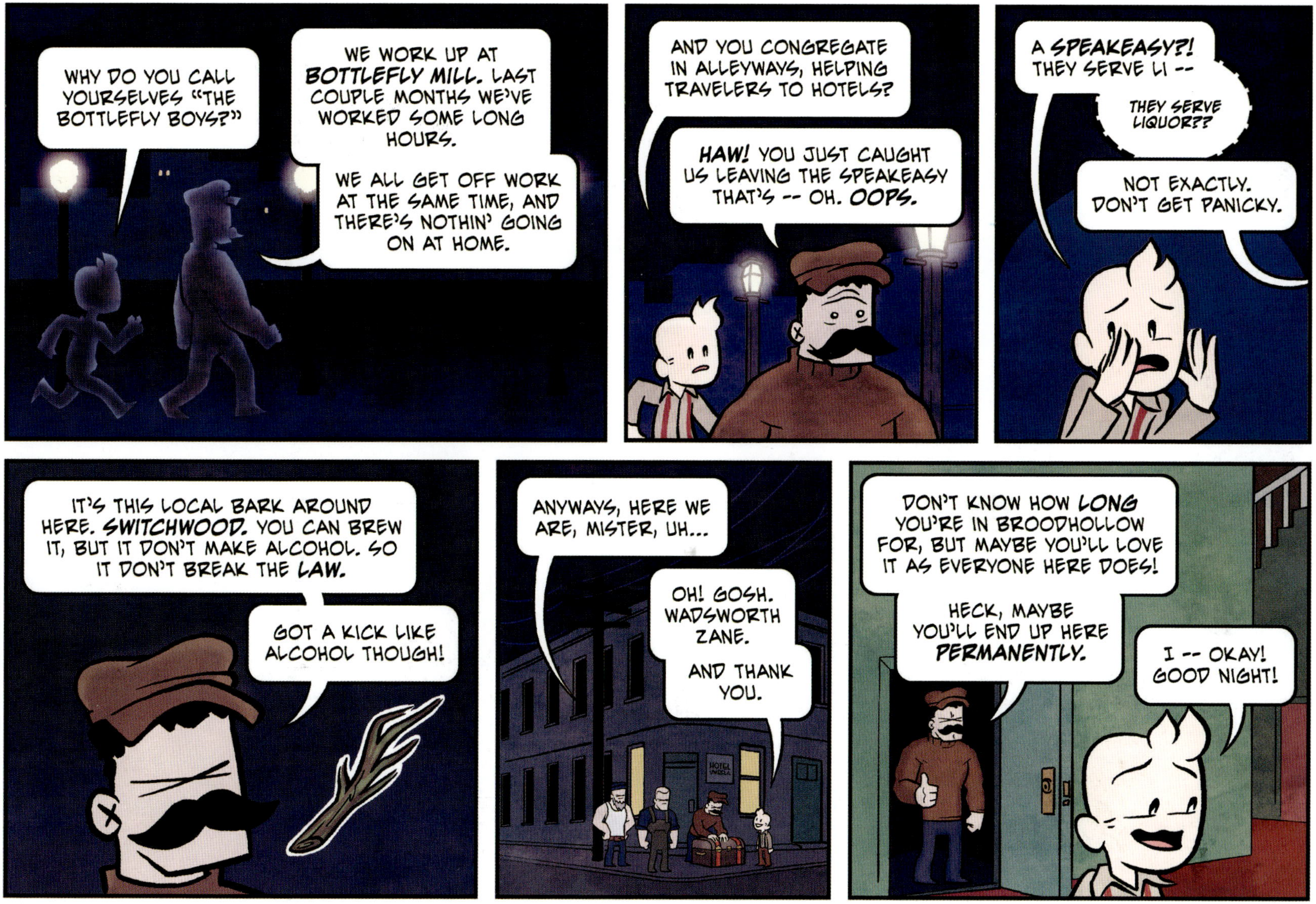
WHY DO YOU CALL YOURSELVES "THE BOTTLEFLY BOYS?"
WE WORK UP AT BOTTLEFLY MILL. LAST COUPLE MONTHS WE'VE WORKED SOME LONG HOURS.
WE ALL GET OFF WORK AT THE SAME TIME, AND THERE'S NOTHIN' GOING ON AT HOME.
AND YOU CONGREGATE IN ALLEYWAYS, HELPING TRAVELERS TO HOTELS?
HAW! YOU JUST CAUGHT US LEAVING THE SPEAKEASY THAT'S -- OH. OOPS.
A SPEAKEASY?! THEY SERVE LI --
THEY SERVE LIQUOR??
NOT EXACTLY. DON'T GET PANICKY.
IT'S THIS LOCAL BARK AROUND HERE. SWITCHWOOD. YOU CAN BREW IT, BUT IT DON'T MAKE ALCOHOL. SO IT DON'T BREAK THE LAW.
GOT A KICK LIKE ALCOHOL THOUGH!
ANYWAYS, HERE WE ARE, MISTER, UH...
OH! GOSH. WADSWORTH ZANE.
AND THANK YOU.
DON'T KNOW HOW LONG YOU'RE IN BROODHOLLOW FOR, BUT MAYBE YOU'LL LOVE IT AS EVERYONE HERE DOES!
HECK, MAYBE YOU'LL END UP HERE PERMANENTLY.
I -- OKAY! GOOD NIGHT!

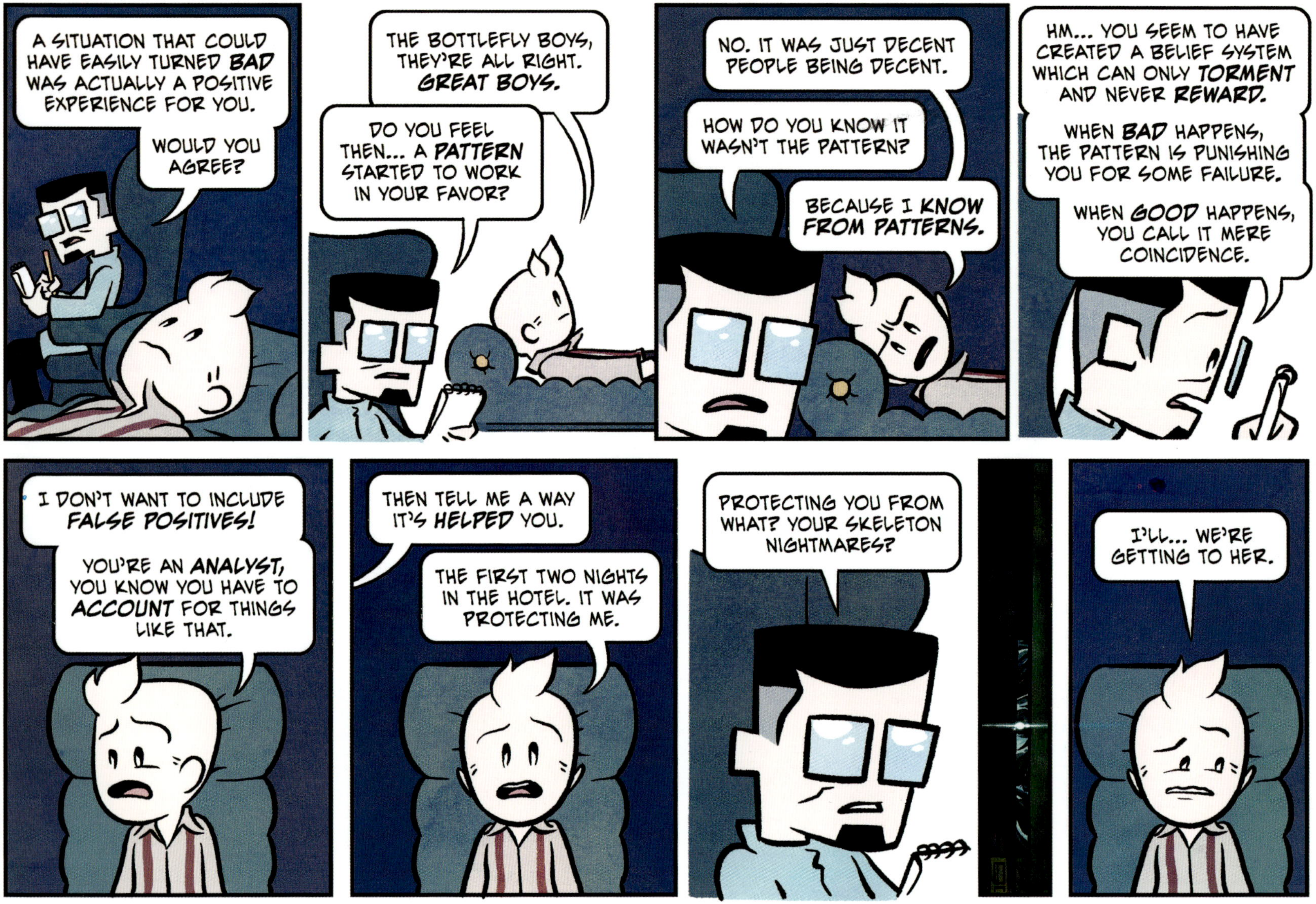
A SITUATION THAT COULD HAVE EASILY TURNED BAD WAS ACTUALLY A POSITIVE EXPERIENCE FOR YOU.
WOULD YOU AGREE?
THE BOTTLEFLY BOYS, THEY'RE ALL RIGHT. GREAT BOYS.
DO YOU FEEL THEN... A PATTERN STARTED TO WORK IN YOUR FAVOR?
NO. IT WAS JUST DECENT PEOPLE BEING DECENT.
HOW DO YOU KNOW IT WASN'T THE PATTERN?
BECAUSE I KNOW FROM PATTERNS.
HM... YOU SEEM TO HAVE CREATED A BELIEF SYSTEM WHICH CAN ONLY TORMENT AND NEVER REWARD.
WHEN BAD HAPPENS, THE PATTERN IS PUNISHING YOU FOR SOME FAILURE.
WHEN GOOD HAPPENS, YOU CALL IT MERE COINCIDENCE.
I DON'T WANT TO INCLUDE FALSE POSITIVES!
YOU'RE AN ANALYST, YOU KNOW YOU HAVE TO ACCOUNT FOR THINGS LIKE THAT.
THEN TELL ME A WAY IT'S HELPED YOU.
THE FIRST TWO NIGHTS IN THE HOTEL. IT WAS PROTECTING ME.
PROTECTING YOU FROM WHAT? YOUR SKELETON NIGHTMARES?
I'LL... WE'RE GETTING TO HER.

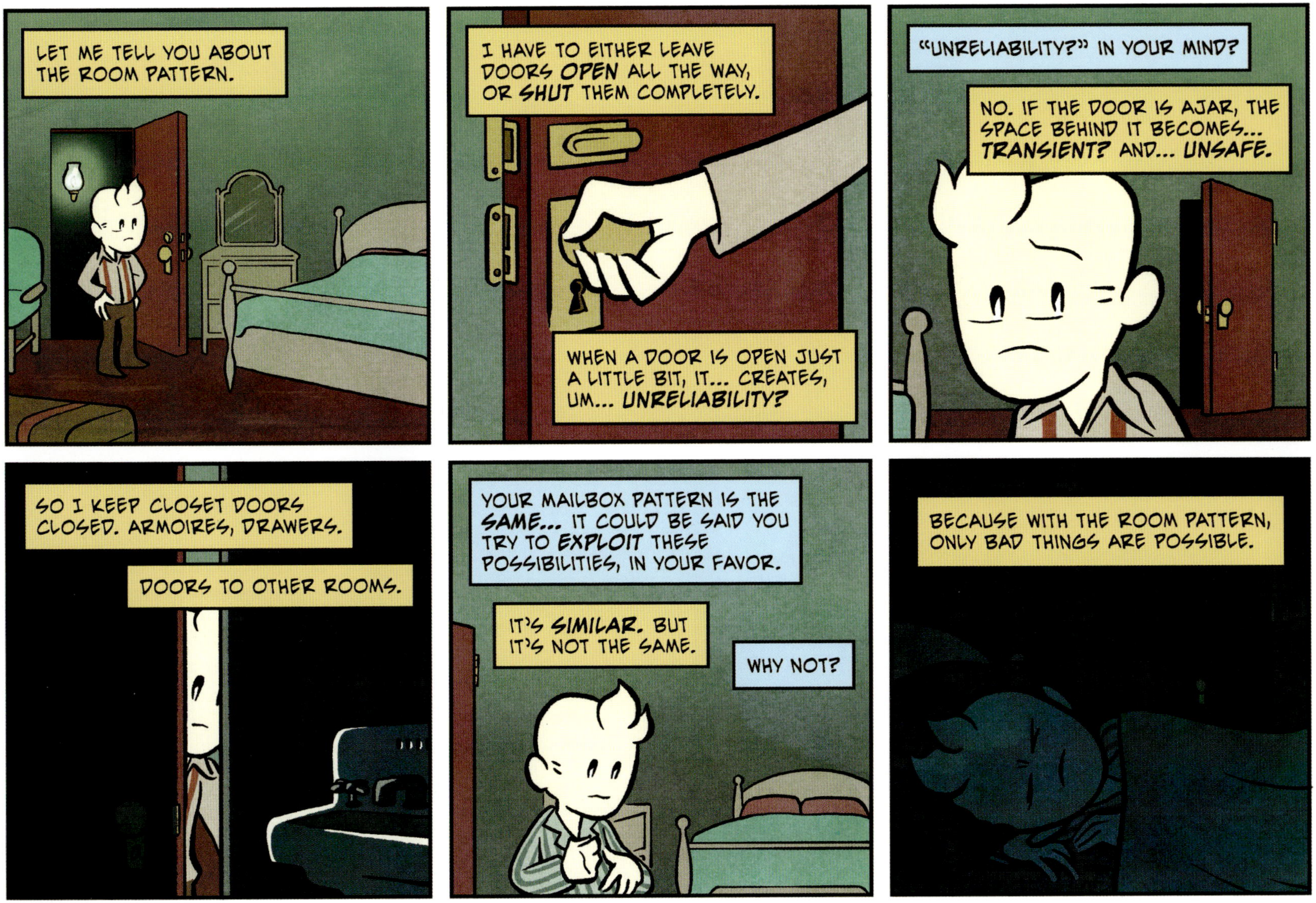
LET ME TELL YOU ABOUT THE ROOM PATTERN.
I HAVE TO EITHER LEAVE DOORS OPEN ALL THE WAY, OR SHUT THEM COMPLETELY.
WHEN A DOOR IS OPEN JUST A LITTLE BIT, IT... CREATES, UM... UNRELIABILITY?
"UNRELIABILITY?" IN YOUR MIND?
NO. IF THE DOOR IS AJAR, THE SPACE BEHIND IT BECOMES... TRANSIENT? AND... UNSAFE.
SO I KEEP CLOSET DOORS CLOSED. ARMOIRES, DRAWERS.
DOORS TO OTHER ROOMS.
YOUR MAILBOX PATTERN IS THE SAME... IT COULD BE SAID YOU TRY TO EXPLOIT THESE POSSIBILITIES, IN YOUR FAVOR.
IT'S SIMILAR. BUT IT'S NOT THE SAME.
WHY NOT?
BECAUSE WITH THE ROOM PATTERN, ONLY BAD THINGS ARE POSSIBLE.

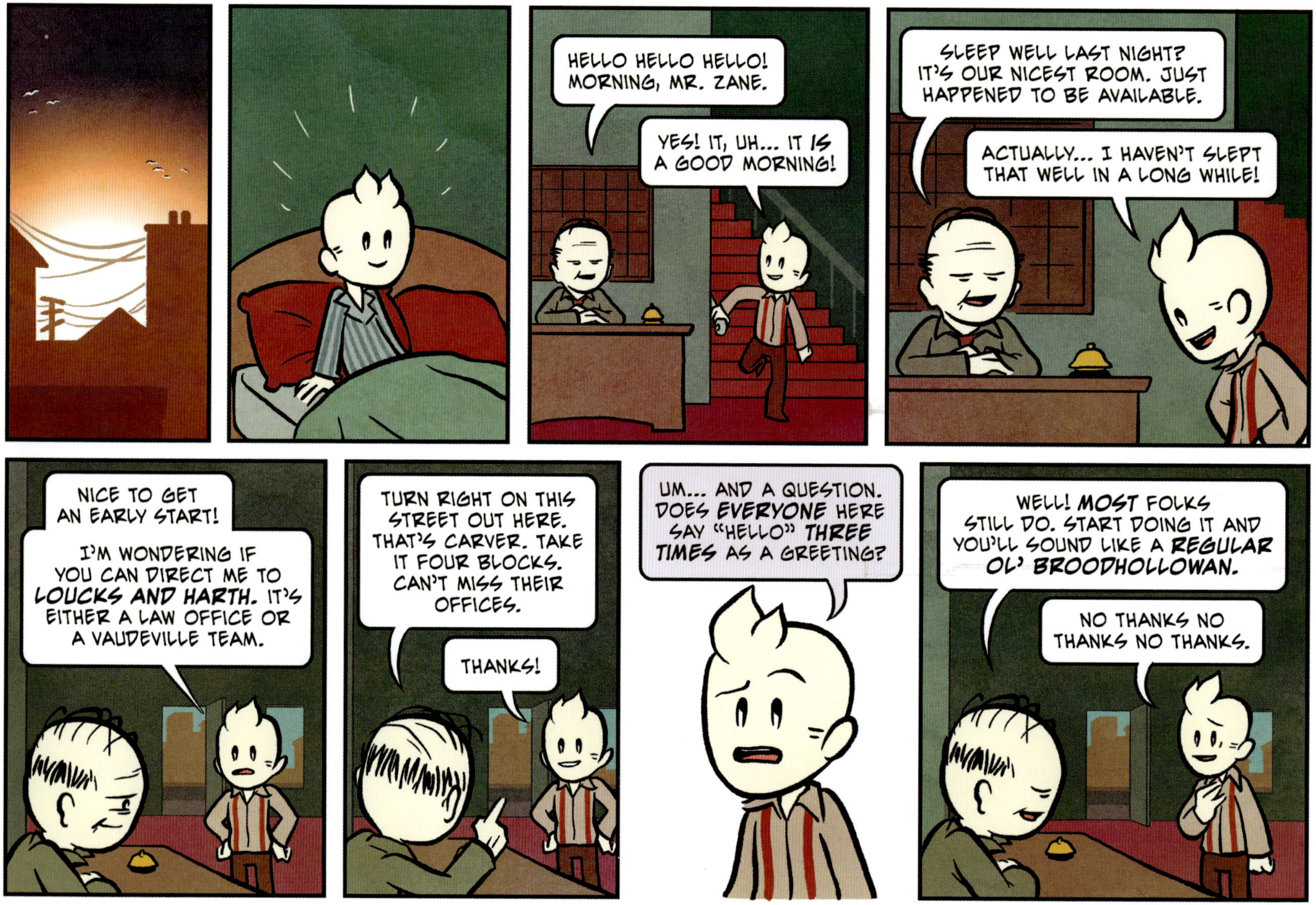
HELLO HELLO HELLO! MORNING, MR. ZANE.
YES! IT, UH... IT IS A GOOD MORNING!
SLEEP WELL LAST NIGHT? IT'S OUR NICEST ROOM. JUST HAPPENED TO BE AVAILABLE.
ACTUALLY... I HAVEN'T SLEPT THAT WELL IN A LONG WHILE!
NICE TO GET AN EARLY START!
I'M WONDERING IF YOU CAN DIRECT ME TO LOUCKS AND HARTH. IT'S EITHER A LAW OFFICE OR A VAUDEVILLE TEAM.
TURN RIGHT ON THIS STREET OUT HERE. THAT'S CARVER. TAKE IT FOUR BLOCKS. CAN'T MISS THEIR OFFICES.
THANKS!
UM... AND A QUESTION. DOES EVERYONE HERE SAY "HELLO" THREE TIMES AS A GREETING?
WELL! MOST FOLKS STILL DO. START DOING IT AND YOU'LL SOUND LIKE A REGULAR OL' BROODHOLLOWAN.
NO THANKS NO THANKS NO THANKS.

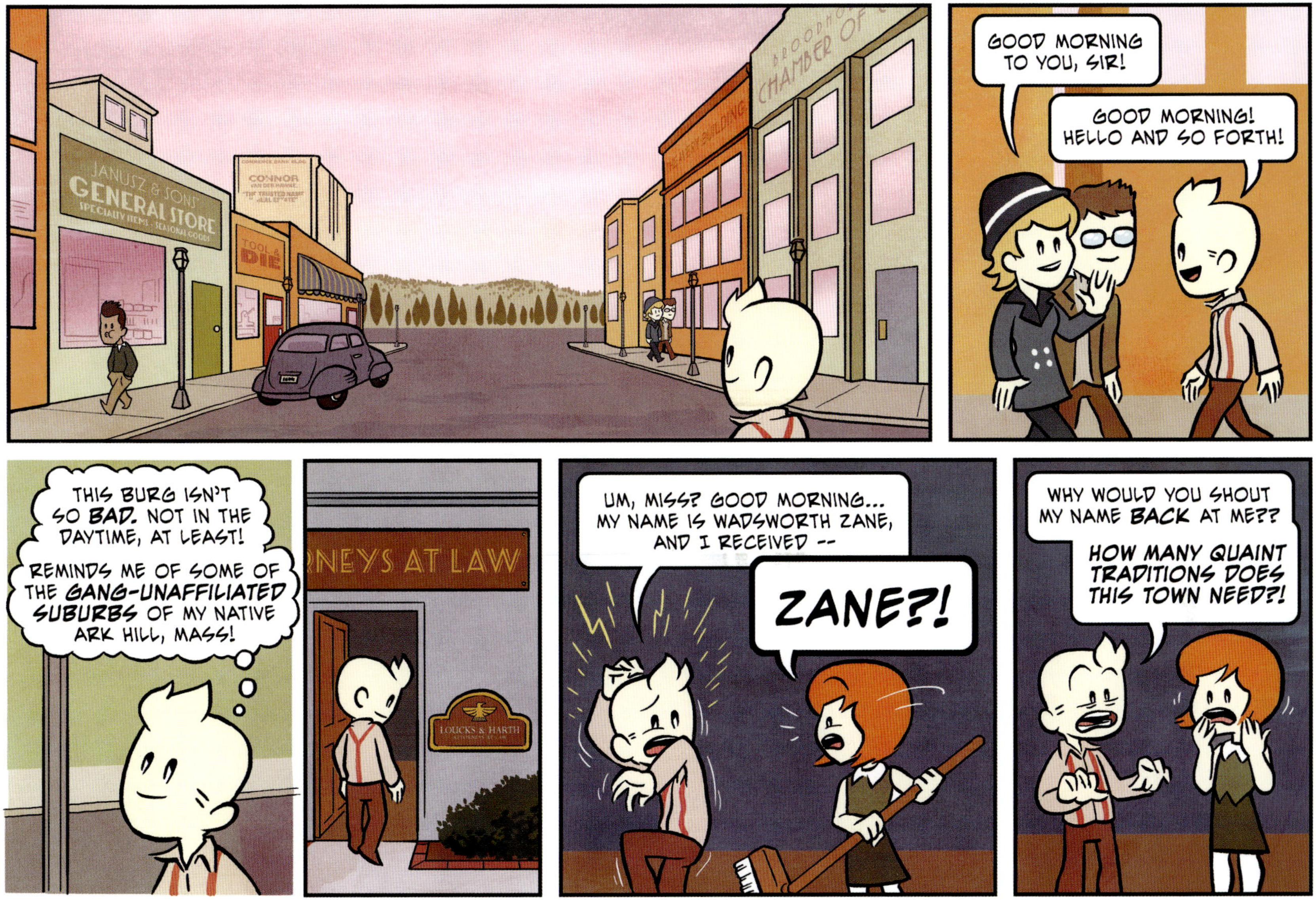
JANUSZ & SONS' GENERAL STORE
SPECIALTY ITEMS · SEASONAL GOODS
TOOL & DIE
GOOD MORNING TO YOU, SIR!
GOOD MORNING! HELLO AND SO FORTH!
THIS BURG ISN'T SO **BAD.** NOT IN THE DAYTIME, AT LEAST!
REMINDS ME OF SOME OF THE ***GANG-UNAFFILIATED SUBURBS*** OF MY NATIVE ARK HILL, MASS!
LOUCKS & HARTH
UM, MISS? GOOD MORNING... MY NAME IS WADSWORTH ZANE, AND I RECEIVED --
ZANE?!
WHY WOULD YOU SHOUT MY NAME **BACK** AT ME??
HOW MANY QUAINT TRADITIONS DOES THIS TOWN NEED?!

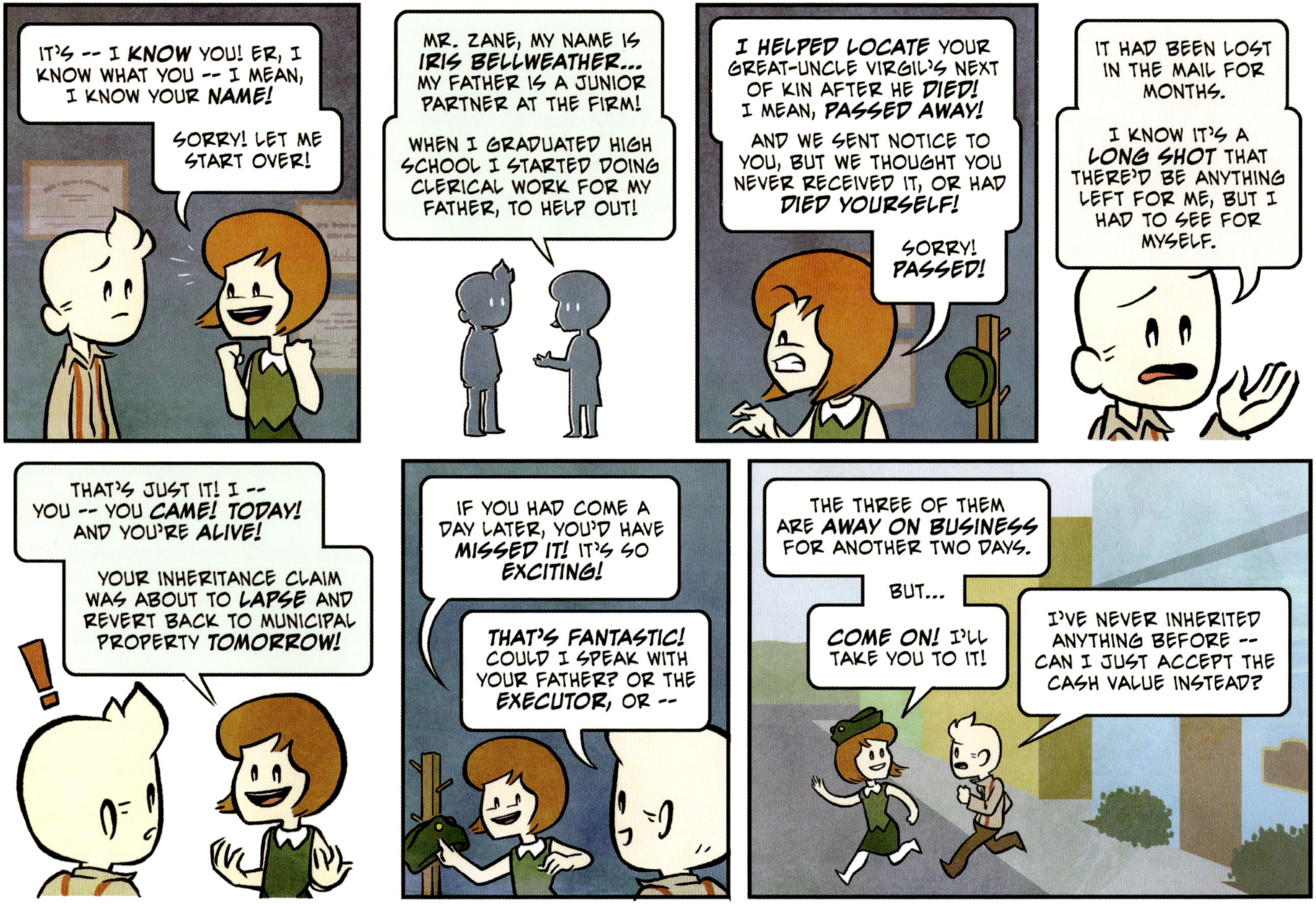
IT'S -- I KNOW YOU! ER, I KNOW WHAT YOU -- I MEAN, I KNOW YOUR NAME!
SORRY! LET ME START OVER!
MR. ZANE, MY NAME IS IRIS BELLWEATHER... MY FATHER IS A JUNIOR PARTNER AT THE FIRM!
WHEN I GRADUATED HIGH SCHOOL I STARTED DOING CLERICAL WORK FOR MY FATHER, TO HELP OUT!
I HELPED LOCATE YOUR GREAT-UNCLE VIRGIL'S NEXT OF KIN AFTER HE DIED! I MEAN, PASSED AWAY!
AND WE SENT NOTICE TO YOU, BUT WE THOUGHT YOU NEVER RECEIVED IT, OR HAD DIED YOURSELF!
SORRY! PASSED!
IT HAD BEEN LOST IN THE MAIL FOR MONTHS.
I KNOW IT'S A LONG SHOT THAT THERE'D BE ANYTHING LEFT FOR ME, BUT I HAD TO SEE FOR MYSELF.
THAT'S JUST IT! I -- YOU -- YOU CAME! TODAY! AND YOU'RE ALIVE!
YOUR INHERITANCE CLAIM WAS ABOUT TO LAPSE AND REVERT BACK TO MUNICIPAL PROPERTY TOMORROW!
!
IF YOU HAD COME A DAY LATER, YOU'D HAVE MISSED IT! IT'S SO EXCITING!
THAT'S FANTASTIC! COULD I SPEAK WITH YOUR FATHER? OR THE EXECUTOR, OR --
THE THREE OF THEM ARE AWAY ON BUSINESS FOR ANOTHER TWO DAYS.
BUT...
COME ON! I'LL TAKE YOU TO IT!
I'VE NEVER INHERITED ANYTHING BEFORE -- CAN I JUST ACCEPT THE CASH VALUE INSTEAD?

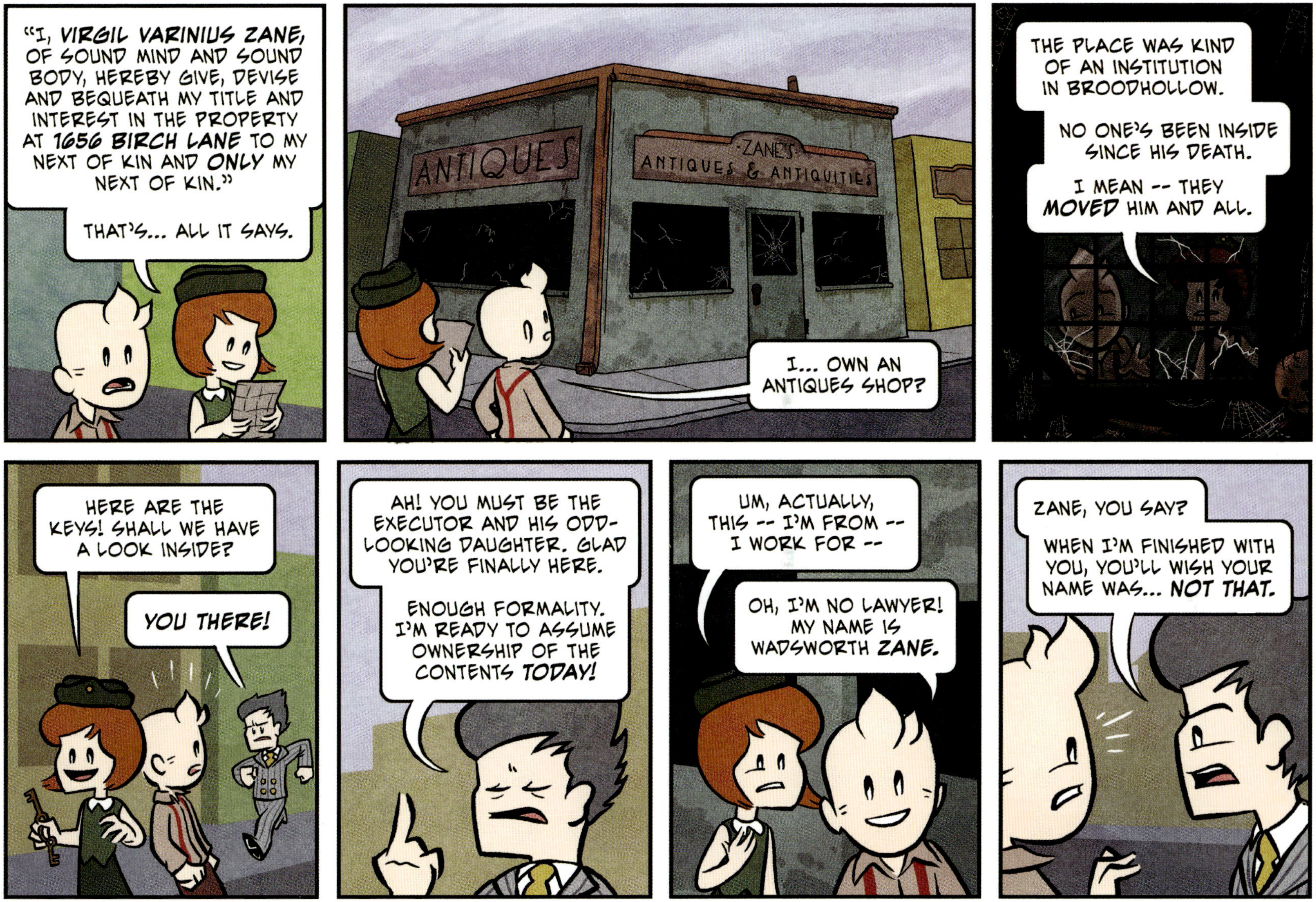

"I, **VIRGIL VARINIUS ZANE**, OF SOUND MIND AND SOUND BODY, HEREBY GIVE, DEVISE AND BEQUEATH MY TITLE AND INTEREST IN THE PROPERTY AT **1656 BIRCH LANE** TO MY NEXT OF KIN AND **ONLY** MY NEXT OF KIN."
THAT'S... ALL IT SAYS.
ANTIQUES
ZANE'S ANTIQUES & ANTIQUITIES
I... OWN AN ANTIQUES SHOP?
THE PLACE WAS KIND OF AN INSTITUTION IN BROODHOLLOW.
NO ONE'S BEEN INSIDE SINCE HIS DEATH.
I MEAN -- THEY **MOVED** HIM AND ALL.
HERE ARE THE KEYS! SHALL WE HAVE A LOOK INSIDE?
YOU THERE!
AH! YOU MUST BE THE EXECUTOR AND HIS ODD-LOOKING DAUGHTER. GLAD YOU'RE FINALLY HERE.
ENOUGH FORMALITY. I'M READY TO ASSUME OWNERSHIP OF THE CONTENTS *TODAY!*
UM, ACTUALLY, THIS -- I'M FROM -- I WORK FOR --
OH, I'M NO LAWYER! MY NAME IS WADSWORTH **ZANE**.
ZANE, YOU SAY?
WHEN I'M FINISHED WITH YOU, YOU'LL WISH YOUR NAME WAS... **NOT THAT.**

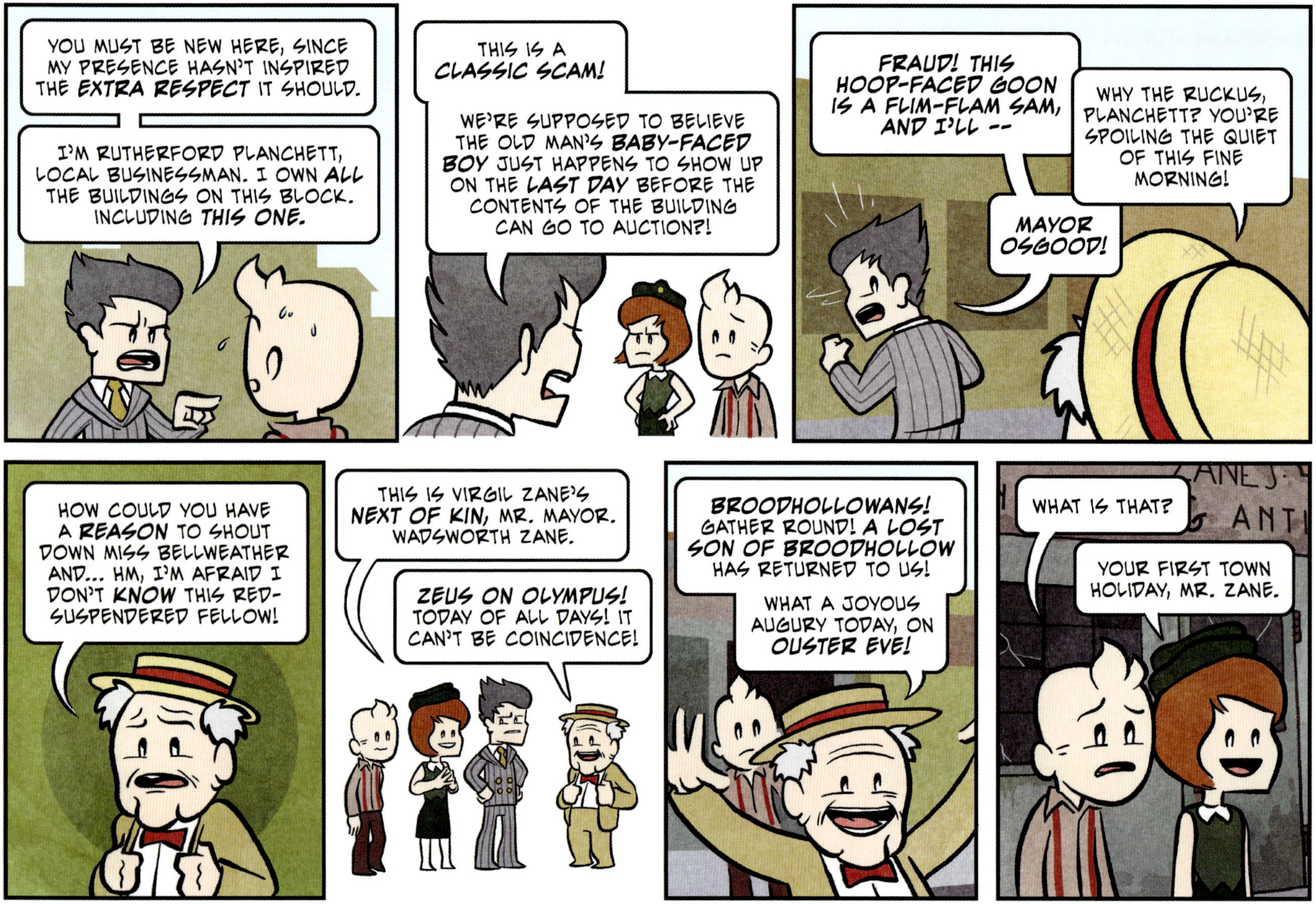

YOU MUST BE NEW HERE, SINCE MY PRESENCE HASN'T INSPIRED THE **EXTRA RESPECT** IT SHOULD.
I'M RUTHERFORD PLANCHETT, LOCAL BUSINESSMAN. I OWN **ALL** THE BUILDINGS ON THIS BLOCK. INCLUDING **THIS ONE.**
THIS IS A ***CLASSIC SCAM!***
WE'RE SUPPOSED TO BELIEVE THE OLD MAN'S ***BABY-FACED BOY*** JUST HAPPENS TO SHOW UP ON THE ***LAST DAY*** BEFORE THE CONTENTS OF THE BUILDING CAN GO TO AUCTION?!
FRAUD! THIS HOOP-FACED GOON IS A FLIM-FLAM SAM, AND I'LL --
MAYOR OSGOOD!
WHY THE RUCKUS, PLANCHETT? YOU'RE SPOILING THE QUIET OF THIS FINE MORNING!
HOW COULD YOU HAVE A ***REASON*** TO SHOUT DOWN MISS BELLWEATHER AND... HM, I'M AFRAID I DON'T ***KNOW*** THIS RED-SUSPENDERED FELLOW!
THIS IS VIRGIL ZANE'S ***NEXT OF KIN***, MR. MAYOR. WADSWORTH ZANE.
ZEUS ON OLYMPUS! TODAY OF ALL DAYS! IT CAN'T BE COINCIDENCE!
BROODHOLLOWANS! GATHER ROUND! ***A LOST SON OF BROODHOLLOW*** HAS RETURNED TO US!
WHAT A JOYOUS AUGURY TODAY, ON ***OUSTER EVE!***
WHAT IS THAT?
YOUR FIRST TOWN HOLIDAY, MR. ZANE.

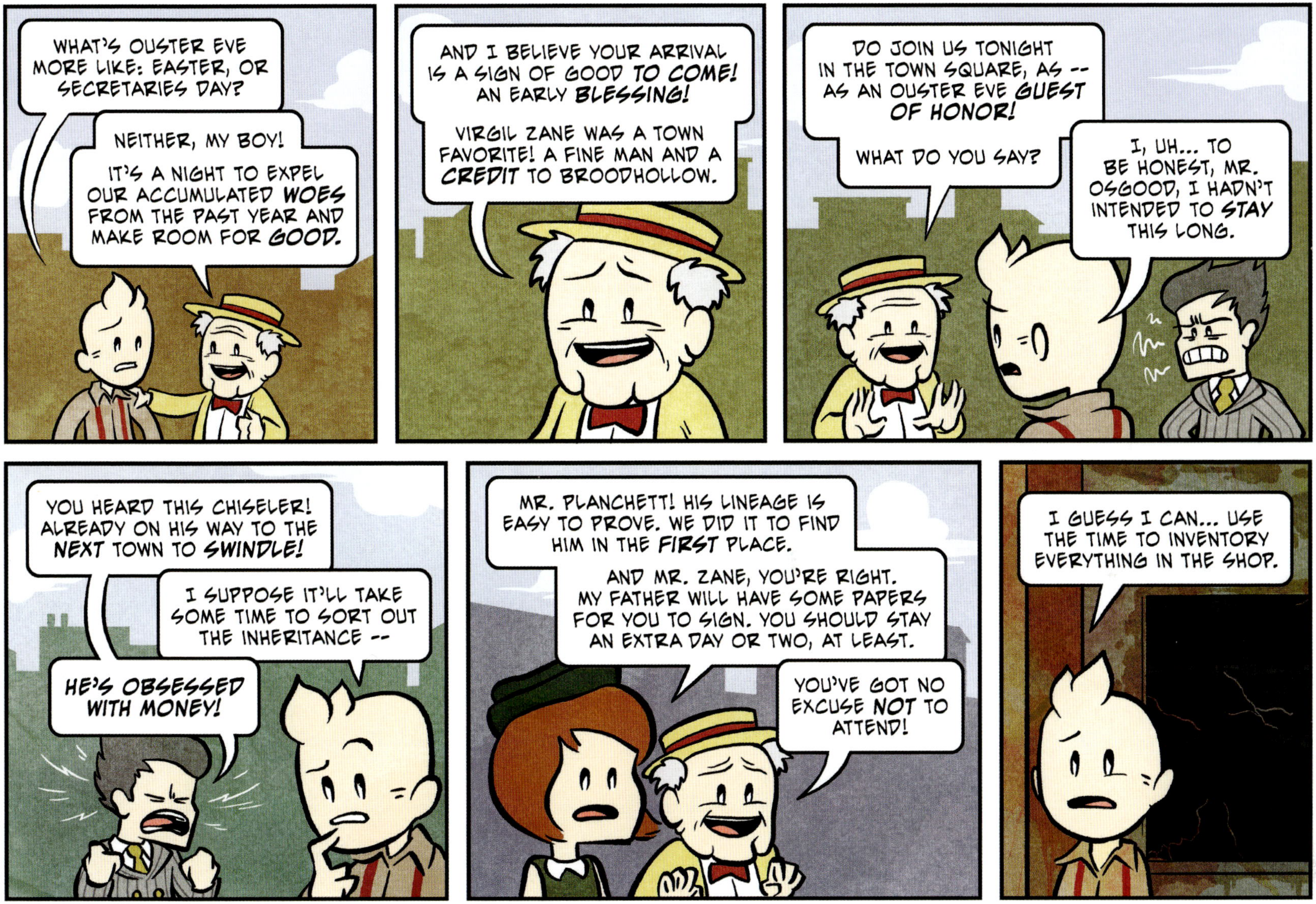

WHAT'S OUSTER EVE MORE LIKE: EASTER, OR SECRETARIES DAY?
NEITHER, MY BOY!
IT'S A NIGHT TO EXPEL OUR ACCUMULATED WOES FROM THE PAST YEAR AND MAKE ROOM FOR GOOD.
AND I BELIEVE YOUR ARRIVAL IS A SIGN OF GOOD TO COME! AN EARLY BLESSING!
VIRGIL ZANE WAS A TOWN FAVORITE! A FINE MAN AND A CREDIT TO BROODHOLLOW.
DO JOIN US TONIGHT IN THE TOWN SQUARE, AS -- AS AN OUSTER EVE GUEST OF HONOR!
WHAT DO YOU SAY?
I, UH... TO BE HONEST, MR. OSGOOD, I HADN'T INTENDED TO STAY THIS LONG.
YOU HEARD THIS CHISELER! ALREADY ON HIS WAY TO THE NEXT TOWN TO SWINDLE!
I SUPPOSE IT'LL TAKE SOME TIME TO SORT OUT THE INHERITANCE --
HE'S OBSESSED WITH MONEY!
MR. PLANCHETT! HIS LINEAGE IS EASY TO PROVE. WE DID IT TO FIND HIM IN THE FIRST PLACE.
AND MR. ZANE, YOU'RE RIGHT. MY FATHER WILL HAVE SOME PAPERS FOR YOU TO SIGN. YOU SHOULD STAY AN EXTRA DAY OR TWO, AT LEAST.
YOU'VE GOT NO EXCUSE NOT TO ATTEND!
I GUESS I CAN... USE THE TIME TO INVENTORY EVERYTHING IN THE SHOP.

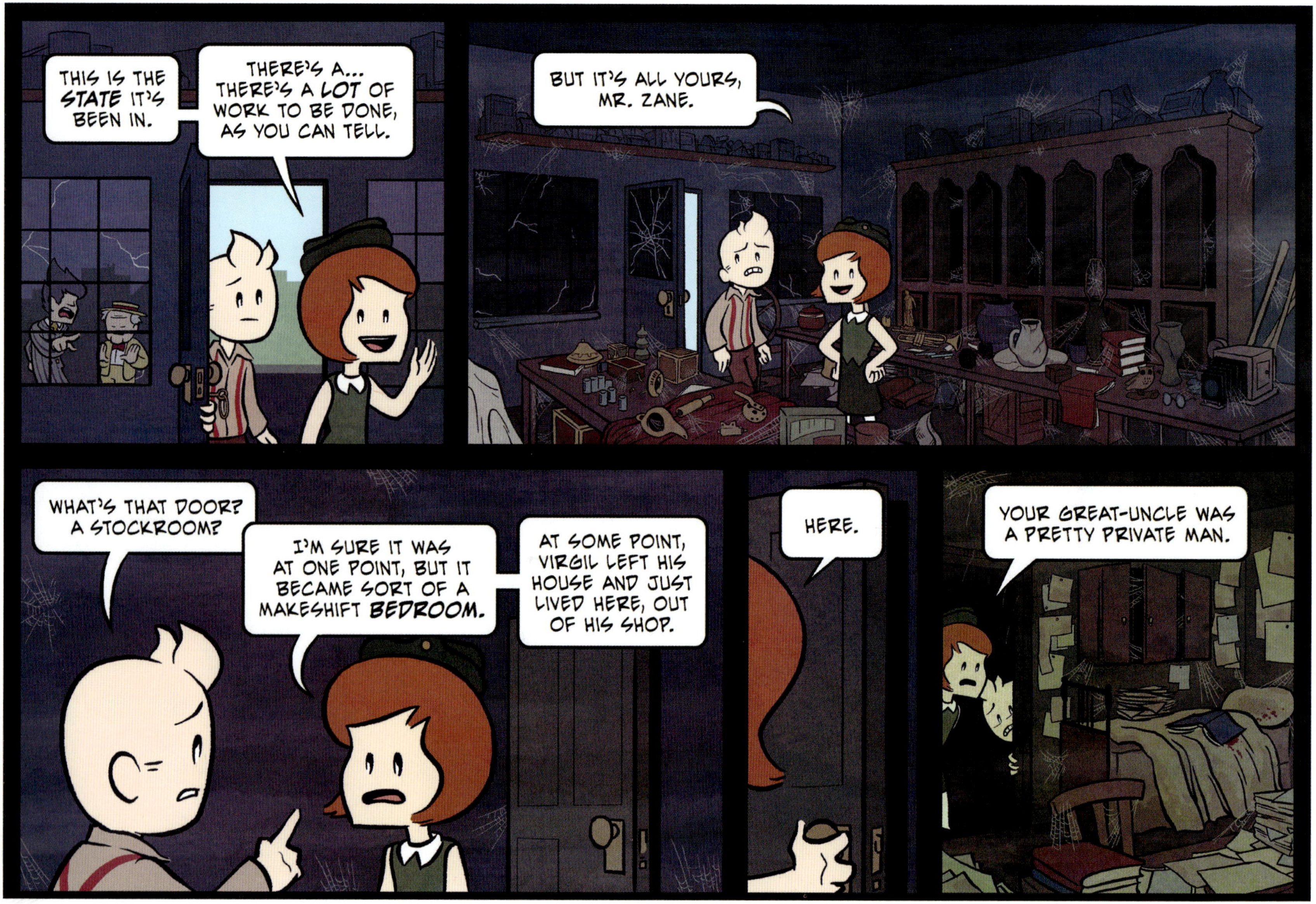
THIS IS THE STATE IT'S BEEN IN.
THERE'S A... THERE'S A LOT OF WORK TO BE DONE, AS YOU CAN TELL.
BUT IT'S ALL YOURS, MR. ZANE.
WHAT'S THAT DOOR? A STOCKROOM?
I'M SURE IT WAS AT ONE POINT, BUT IT BECAME SORT OF A MAKESHIFT BEDROOM.
AT SOME POINT, VIRGIL LEFT HIS HOUSE AND JUST LIVED HERE, OUT OF HIS SHOP.
HERE.
YOUR GREAT-UNCLE WAS A PRETTY PRIVATE MAN.

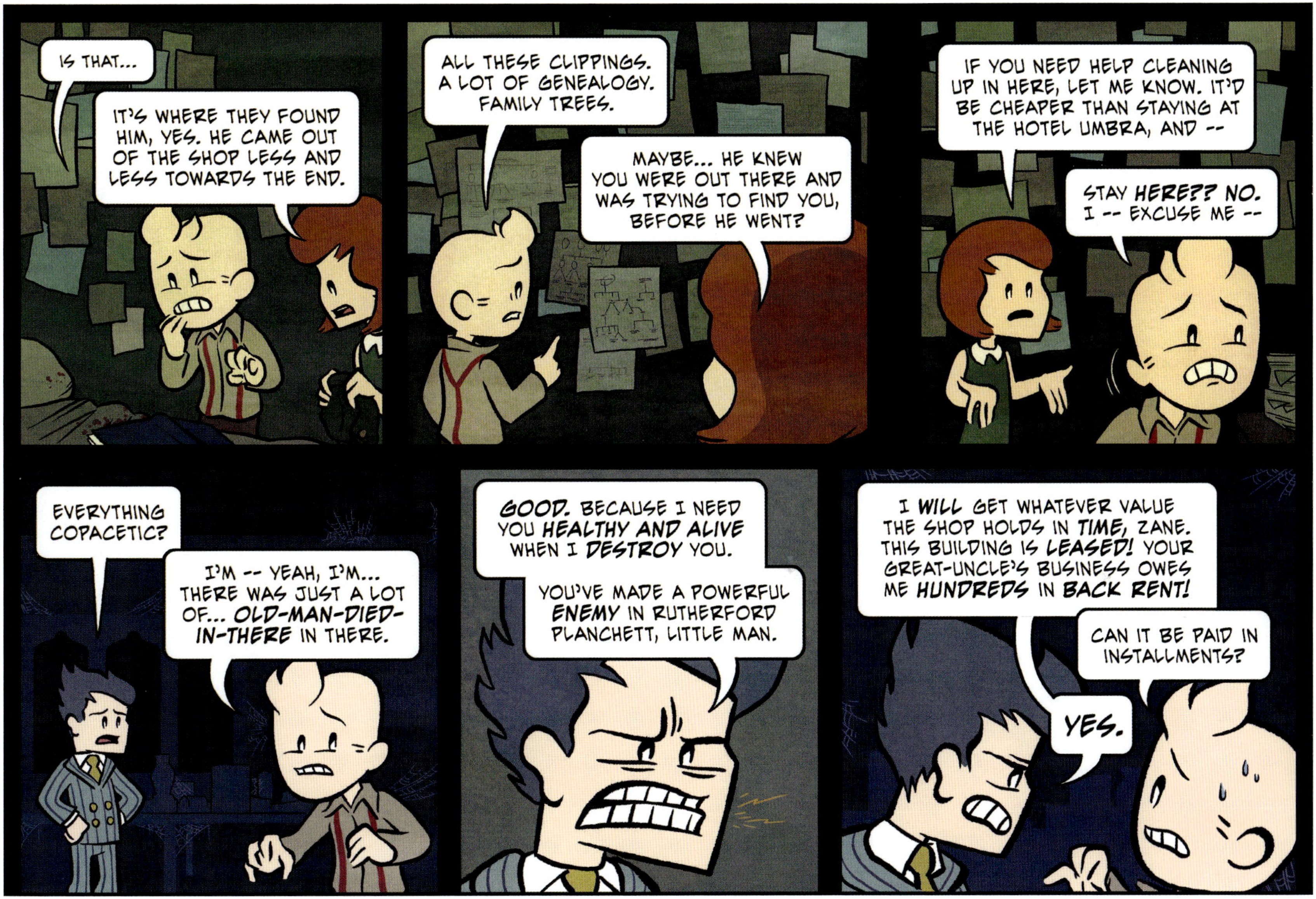
IS THAT...
IT'S WHERE THEY FOUND HIM, YES. HE CAME OUT OF THE SHOP LESS AND LESS TOWARDS THE END.
ALL THESE CLIPPINGS. A LOT OF GENEALOGY. FAMILY TREES.
MAYBE... HE KNEW YOU WERE OUT THERE AND WAS TRYING TO FIND YOU, BEFORE HE WENT?
IF YOU NEED HELP CLEANING UP IN HERE, LET ME KNOW. IT'D BE CHEAPER THAN STAYING AT THE HOTEL UMBRA, AND --
STAY HERE?? NO. I -- EXCUSE ME --
EVERYTHING COPACETIC?
I'M -- YEAH, I'M... THERE WAS JUST A LOT OF... OLD-MAN-DIED-IN-THERE IN THERE.
GOOD. BECAUSE I NEED YOU HEALTHY AND ALIVE WHEN I DESTROY YOU.
YOU'VE MADE A POWERFUL ENEMY IN RUTHERFORD PLANCHETT, LITTLE MAN.
I WILL GET WHATEVER VALUE THE SHOP HOLDS IN TIME, ZANE. THIS BUILDING IS LEASED! YOUR GREAT-UNCLE'S BUSINESS OWES ME HUNDREDS IN BACK RENT!
CAN IT BE PAID IN INSTALLMENTS?
YES.

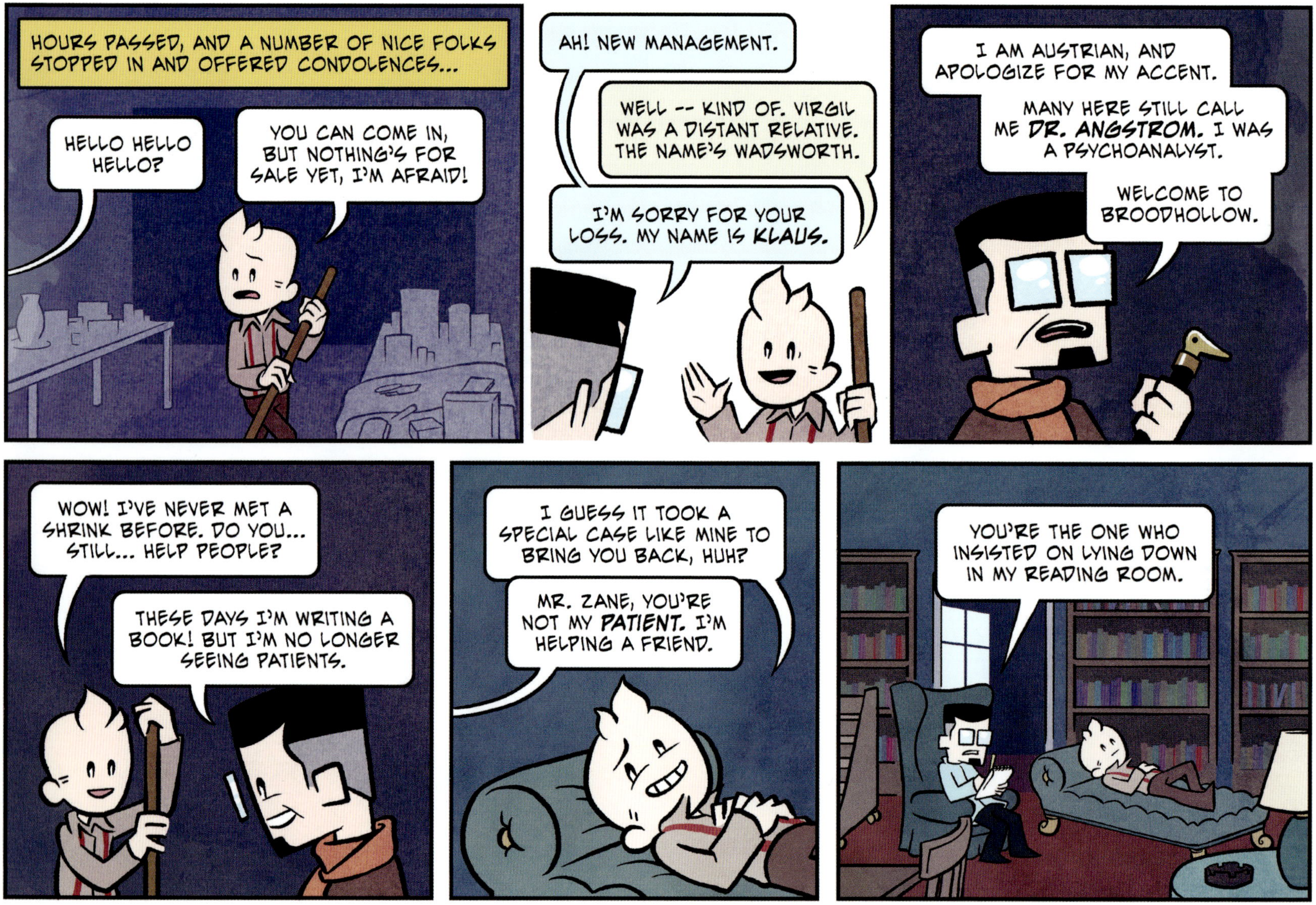
HOURS PASSED, AND A NUMBER OF NICE FOLKS STOPPED IN AND OFFERED CONDOLENCES...
HELLO HELLO HELLO?
YOU CAN COME IN, BUT NOTHING'S FOR SALE YET, I'M AFRAID!
AH! NEW MANAGEMENT.
WELL -- KIND OF. VIRGIL WAS A DISTANT RELATIVE. THE NAME'S WADSWORTH.
I'M SORRY FOR YOUR LOSS. MY NAME IS KLAUS.
I AM AUSTRIAN, AND APOLOGIZE FOR MY ACCENT.
MANY HERE STILL CALL ME DR. ANGSTROM. I WAS A PSYCHOANALYST.
WELCOME TO BROODHOLLOW.
WOW! I'VE NEVER MET A SHRINK BEFORE. DO YOU... STILL... HELP PEOPLE?
THESE DAYS I'M WRITING A BOOK! BUT I'M NO LONGER SEEING PATIENTS.
I GUESS IT TOOK A SPECIAL CASE LIKE MINE TO BRING YOU BACK, HUH?
MR. ZANE, YOU'RE NOT MY PATIENT. I'M HELPING A FRIEND.
YOU'RE THE ONE WHO INSISTED ON LYING DOWN IN MY READING ROOM.

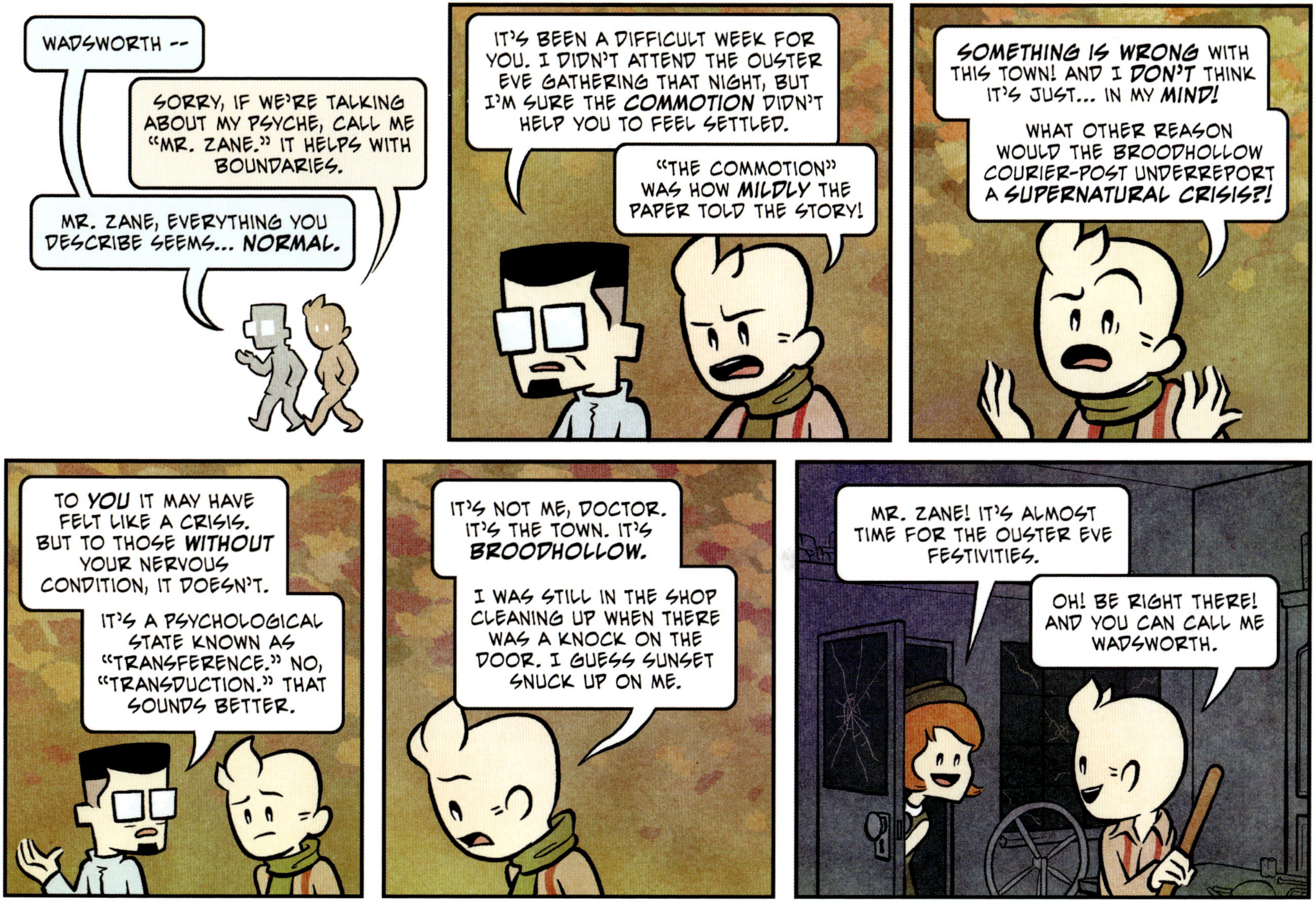
WADSWORTH --
SORRY, IF WE'RE TALKING ABOUT MY PSYCHE, CALL ME "MR. ZANE." IT HELPS WITH BOUNDARIES.
MR. ZANE, EVERYTHING YOU DESCRIBE SEEMS... NORMAL.
IT'S BEEN A DIFFICULT WEEK FOR YOU. I DIDN'T ATTEND THE OUSTER EVE GATHERING THAT NIGHT, BUT I'M SURE THE COMMOTION DIDN'T HELP YOU TO FEEL SETTLED.
"THE COMMOTION" WAS HOW MILDLY THE PAPER TOLD THE STORY!
SOMETHING IS WRONG WITH THIS TOWN! AND I DON'T THINK IT'S JUST... IN MY MIND!
WHAT OTHER REASON WOULD THE BROODHOLLOW COURIER-POST UNDERREPORT A SUPERNATURAL CRISIS?!
TO YOU IT MAY HAVE FELT LIKE A CRISIS. BUT TO THOSE WITHOUT YOUR NERVOUS CONDITION, IT DOESN'T.
IT'S A PSYCHOLOGICAL STATE KNOWN AS "TRANSFERENCE." NO, "TRANSDUCTION." THAT SOUNDS BETTER.
IT'S NOT ME, DOCTOR. IT'S THE TOWN. IT'S BROODHOLLOW.
I WAS STILL IN THE SHOP CLEANING UP WHEN THERE WAS A KNOCK ON THE DOOR. I GUESS SUNSET SNUCK UP ON ME.
MR. ZANE! IT'S ALMOST TIME FOR THE OUSTER EVE FESTIVITIES.
OH! BE RIGHT THERE! AND YOU CAN CALL ME WADSWORTH.

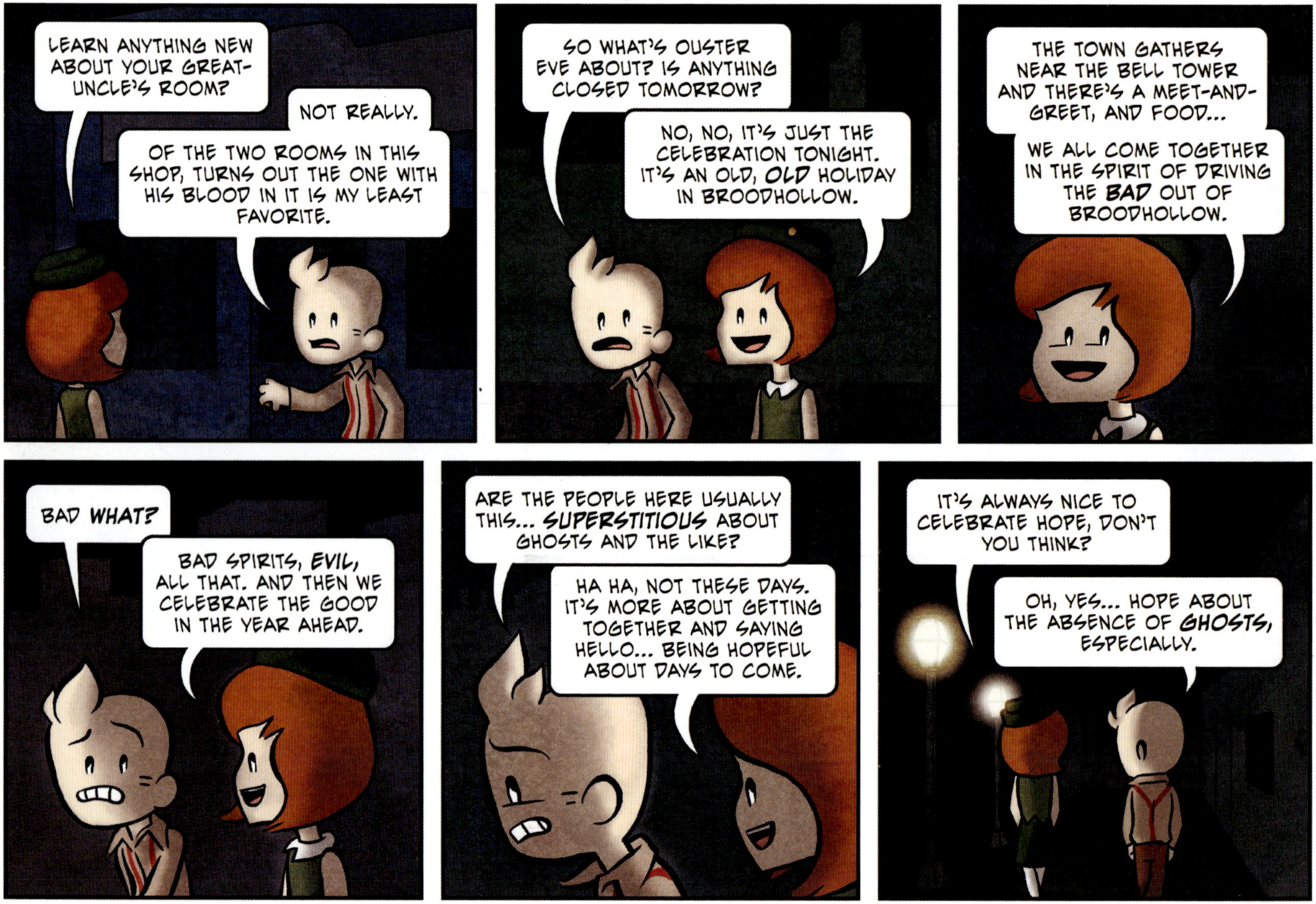
LEARN ANYTHING NEW ABOUT YOUR GREAT-UNCLE'S ROOM?
NOT REALLY.
OF THE TWO ROOMS IN THIS SHOP, TURNS OUT THE ONE WITH HIS BLOOD IN IT IS MY LEAST FAVORITE.
SO WHAT'S OUSTER EVE ABOUT? IS ANYTHING CLOSED TOMORROW?
NO, NO, IT'S JUST THE CELEBRATION TONIGHT. IT'S AN OLD, *OLD* HOLIDAY IN BROODHOLLOW.
THE TOWN GATHERS NEAR THE BELL TOWER AND THERE'S A MEET-AND-GREET, AND FOOD...
WE ALL COME TOGETHER IN THE SPIRIT OF DRIVING THE **BAD** OUT OF BROODHOLLOW.
BAD **WHAT?**
BAD SPIRITS, ***EVIL,*** ALL THAT. AND THEN WE CELEBRATE THE GOOD IN THE YEAR AHEAD.
ARE THE PEOPLE HERE USUALLY THIS... ***SUPERSTITIOUS*** ABOUT GHOSTS AND THE LIKE?
HA HA, NOT THESE DAYS. IT'S MORE ABOUT GETTING TOGETHER AND SAYING HELLO... BEING HOPEFUL ABOUT DAYS TO COME.
IT'S ALWAYS NICE TO CELEBRATE HOPE, DON'T YOU THINK?
OH, YES... HOPE ABOUT THE ABSENCE OF ***GHOSTS,*** ESPECIALLY.

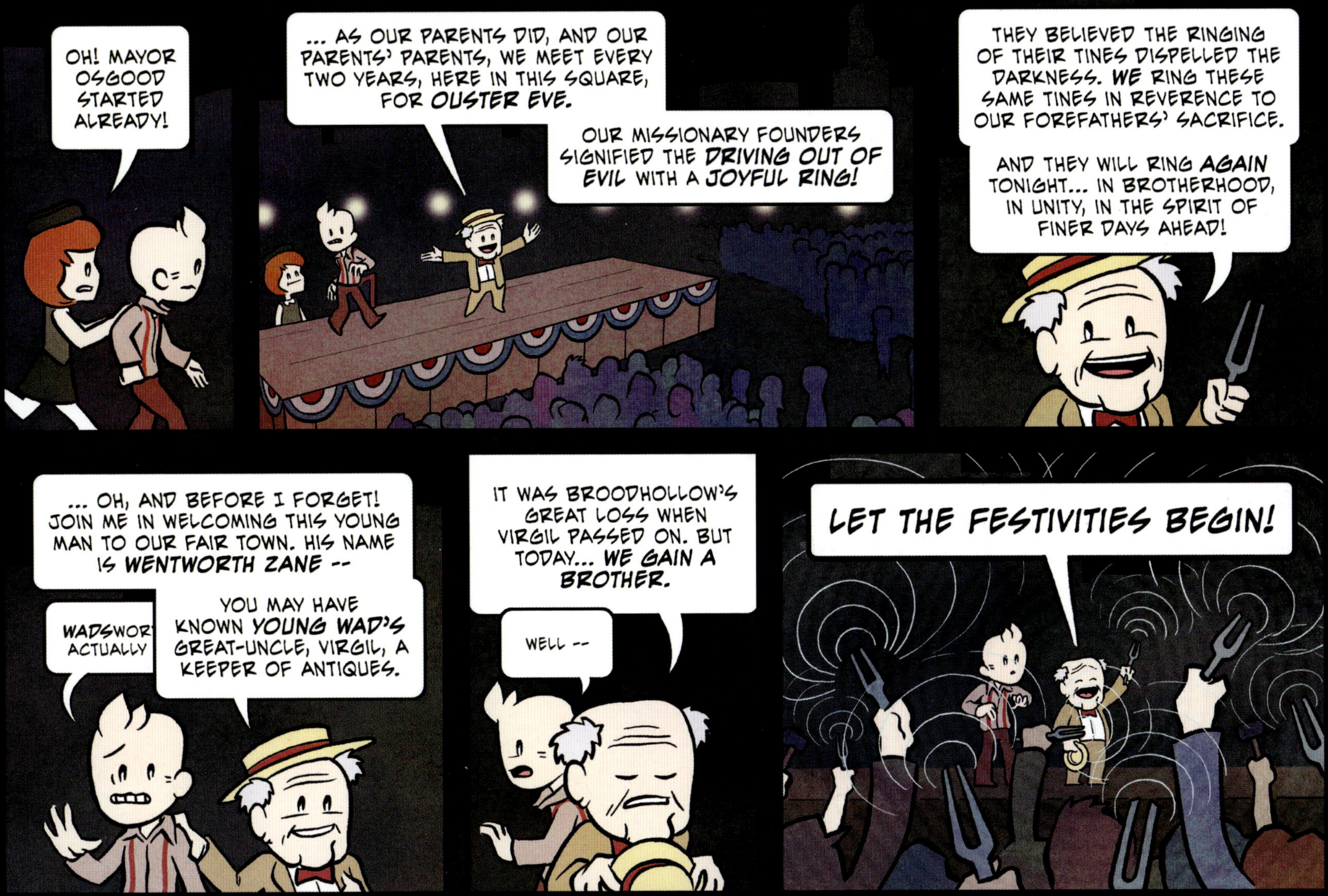
OH! MAYOR OSGOOD STARTED ALREADY!
... AS OUR PARENTS DID, AND OUR PARENTS' PARENTS, WE MEET EVERY TWO YEARS, HERE IN THIS SQUARE, FOR OUSTER EVE.
OUR MISSIONARY FOUNDERS SIGNIFIED THE DRIVING OUT OF EVIL WITH A JOYFUL RING!
THEY BELIEVED THE RINGING OF THEIR TINES DISPELLED THE DARKNESS. WE RING THESE SAME TINES IN REVERENCE TO OUR FOREFATHERS' SACRIFICE.
AND THEY WILL RING AGAIN TONIGHT... IN BROTHERHOOD, IN UNITY, IN THE SPIRIT OF FINER DAYS AHEAD!
... OH, AND BEFORE I FORGET! JOIN ME IN WELCOMING THIS YOUNG MAN TO OUR FAIR TOWN. HIS NAME IS WENTWORTH ZANE --
WADSWOR ACTUALLY
YOU MAY HAVE KNOWN YOUNG WAD'S GREAT-UNCLE, VIRGIL, A KEEPER OF ANTIQUES.
IT WAS BROODHOLLOW'S GREAT LOSS WHEN VIRGIL PASSED ON. BUT TODAY... WE GAIN A BROTHER.
WELL --
LET THE FESTIVITIES BEGIN!

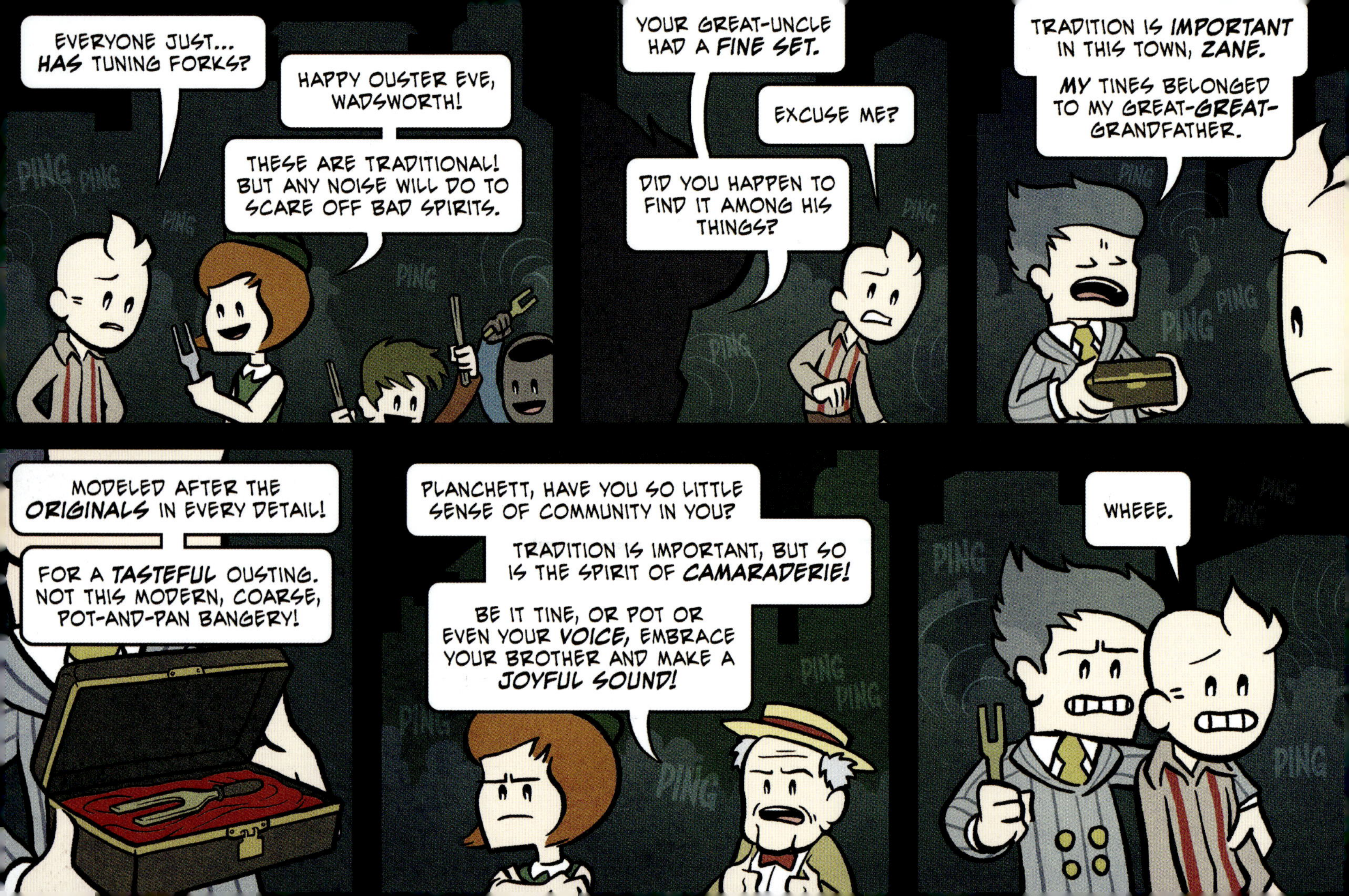
EVERYONE JUST... HAS TUNING FORKS?
HAPPY OUSTER EVE, WADSWORTH!
THESE ARE TRADITIONAL! BUT ANY NOISE WILL DO TO SCARE OFF BAD SPIRITS.
PING PING
PING
PING
YOUR GREAT-UNCLE HAD A **FINE SET.**
EXCUSE ME?
DID YOU HAPPEN TO FIND IT AMONG HIS THINGS?
PING
PING
TRADITION IS ***IMPORTANT*** IN THIS TOWN, ***ZANE.***
MY TINES BELONGED TO MY GREAT-***GREAT***-GRANDFATHER.
PING
PING PING
MODELED AFTER THE ***ORIGINALS*** IN EVERY DETAIL!
FOR A ***TASTEFUL*** OUSTING. NOT THIS MODERN, COARSE, POT-AND-PAN BANGERY!
PLANCHETT, HAVE YOU SO LITTLE SENSE OF COMMUNITY IN YOU?
TRADITION IS IMPORTANT, BUT SO IS THE SPIRIT OF ***CAMARADERIE!***
BE IT TINE, OR POT OR EVEN YOUR ***VOICE,*** EMBRACE YOUR BROTHER AND MAKE A ***JOYFUL SOUND!***
PING PING
PING
WHEEE.
PING
PING
PING

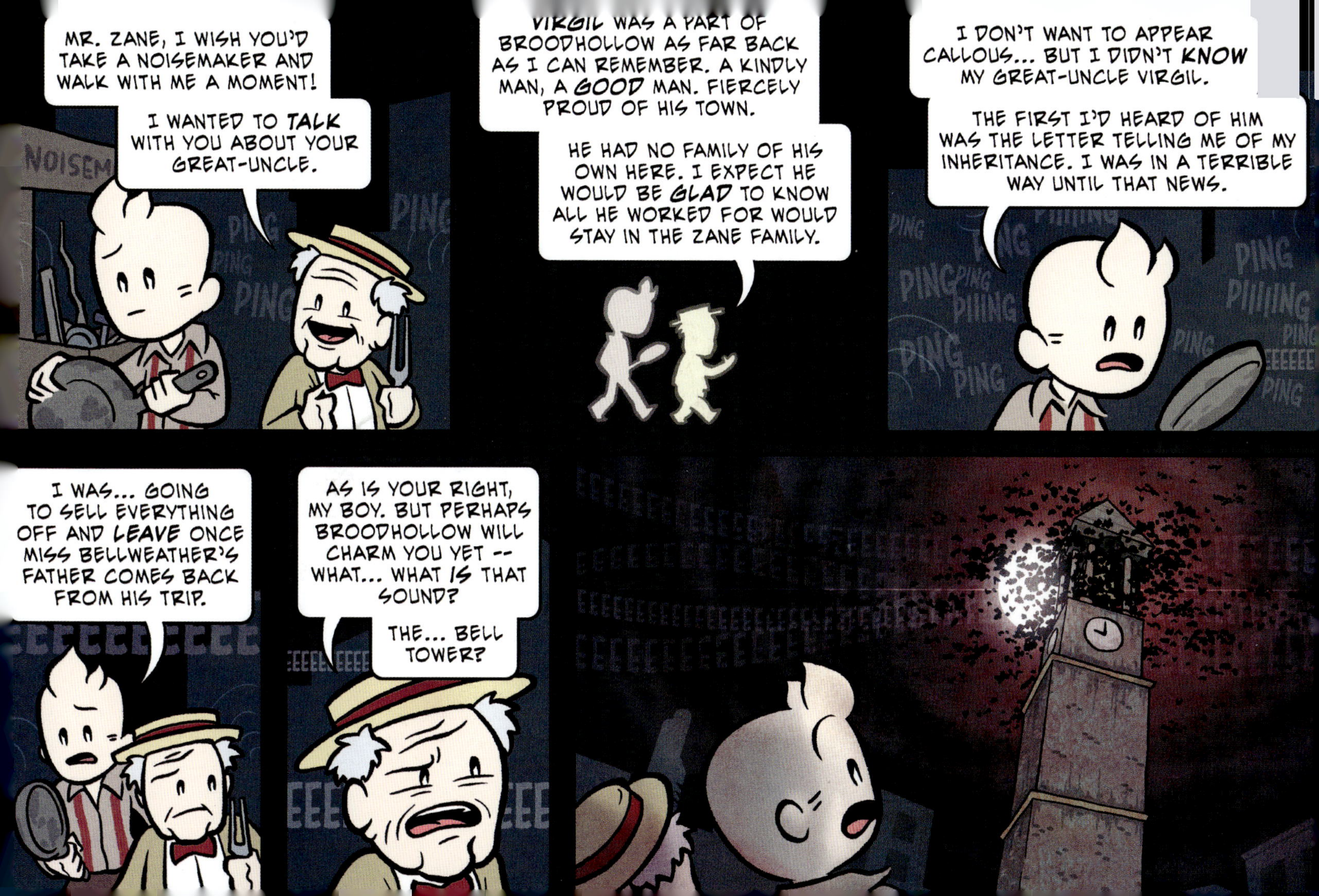
MR. ZANE, I WISH YOU'D TAKE A NOISEMAKER AND WALK WITH ME A MOMENT!
I WANTED TO TALK WITH YOU ABOUT YOUR GREAT-UNCLE.
NOISEM
PING
PING
PING
PING
VIRGIL WAS A PART OF BROODHOLLOW AS FAR BACK AS I CAN REMEMBER. A KINDLY MAN, A GOOD MAN. FIERCELY PROUD OF HIS TOWN.
HE HAD NO FAMILY OF HIS OWN HERE. I EXPECT HE WOULD BE GLAD TO KNOW ALL HE WORKED FOR WOULD STAY IN THE ZANE FAMILY.
I DON'T WANT TO APPEAR CALLOUS... BUT I DIDN'T KNOW MY GREAT-UNCLE VIRGIL.
THE FIRST I'D HEARD OF HIM WAS THE LETTER TELLING ME OF MY INHERITANCE. I WAS IN A TERRIBLE WAY UNTIL THAT NEWS.
PING
PING PING
PIIING
PING
PING
PIIIING
PING
PING
I WAS... GOING TO SELL EVERYTHING OFF AND LEAVE ONCE MISS BELLWEATHER'S FATHER COMES BACK FROM HIS TRIP.
AS IS YOUR RIGHT, MY BOY. BUT PERHAPS BROODHOLLOW WILL CHARM YOU YET -- WHAT... WHAT IS THAT SOUND?
THE... BELL TOWER?

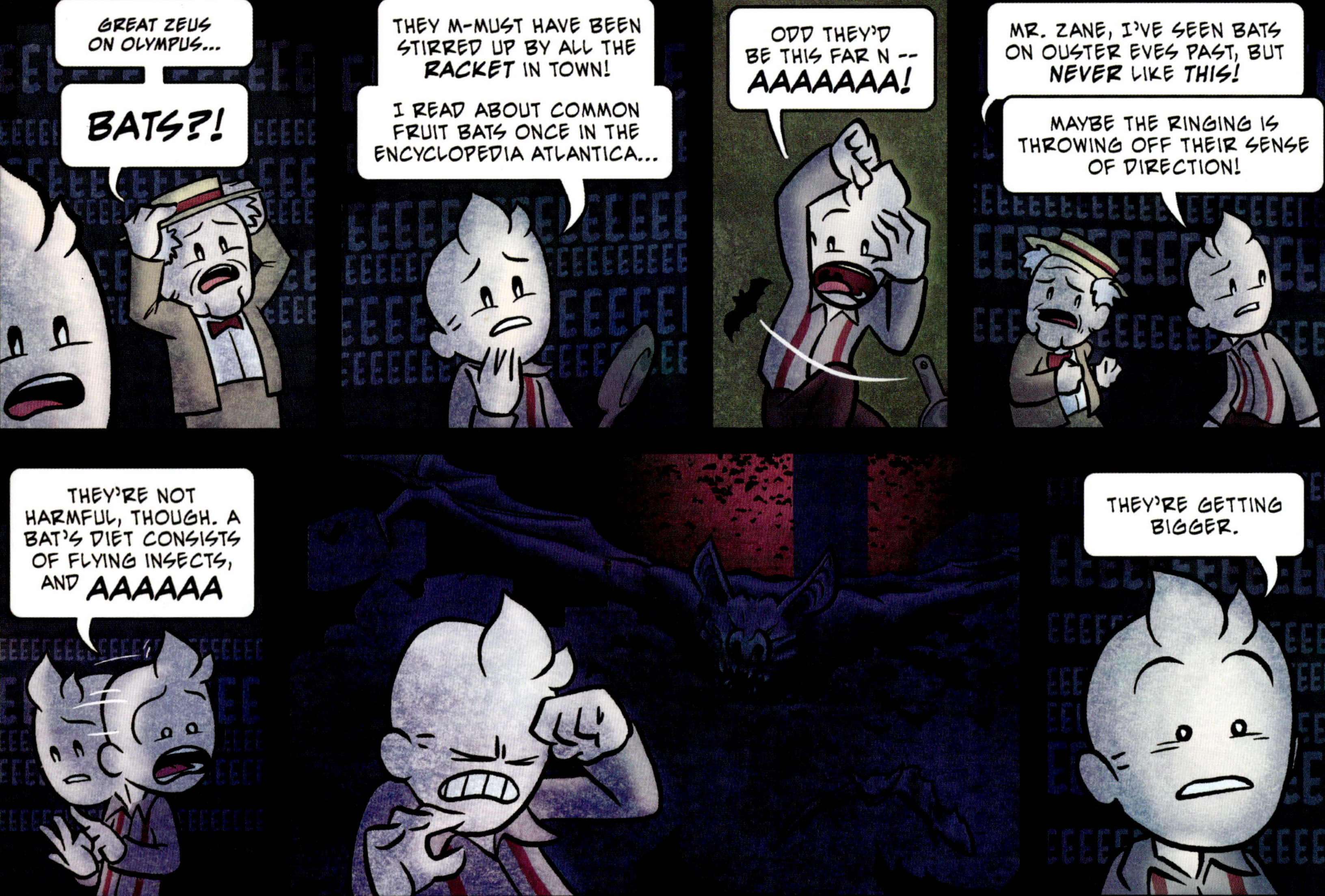
GREAT ZEUS ON OLYMPUS...
BATS?!
THEY M-MUST HAVE BEEN STIRRED UP BY ALL THE RACKET IN TOWN!
I READ ABOUT COMMON FRUIT BATS ONCE IN THE ENCYCLOPEDIA ATLANTICA...
ODD THEY'D BE THIS FAR N -- AAAAAAA!
MR. ZANE, I'VE SEEN BATS ON OUSTER EVES PAST, BUT NEVER LIKE THIS!
MAYBE THE RINGING IS THROWING OFF THEIR SENSE OF DIRECTION!
THEY'RE NOT HARMFUL, THOUGH. A BAT'S DIET CONSISTS OF FLYING INSECTS, AND AAAAAA
THEY'RE GETTING BIGGER.

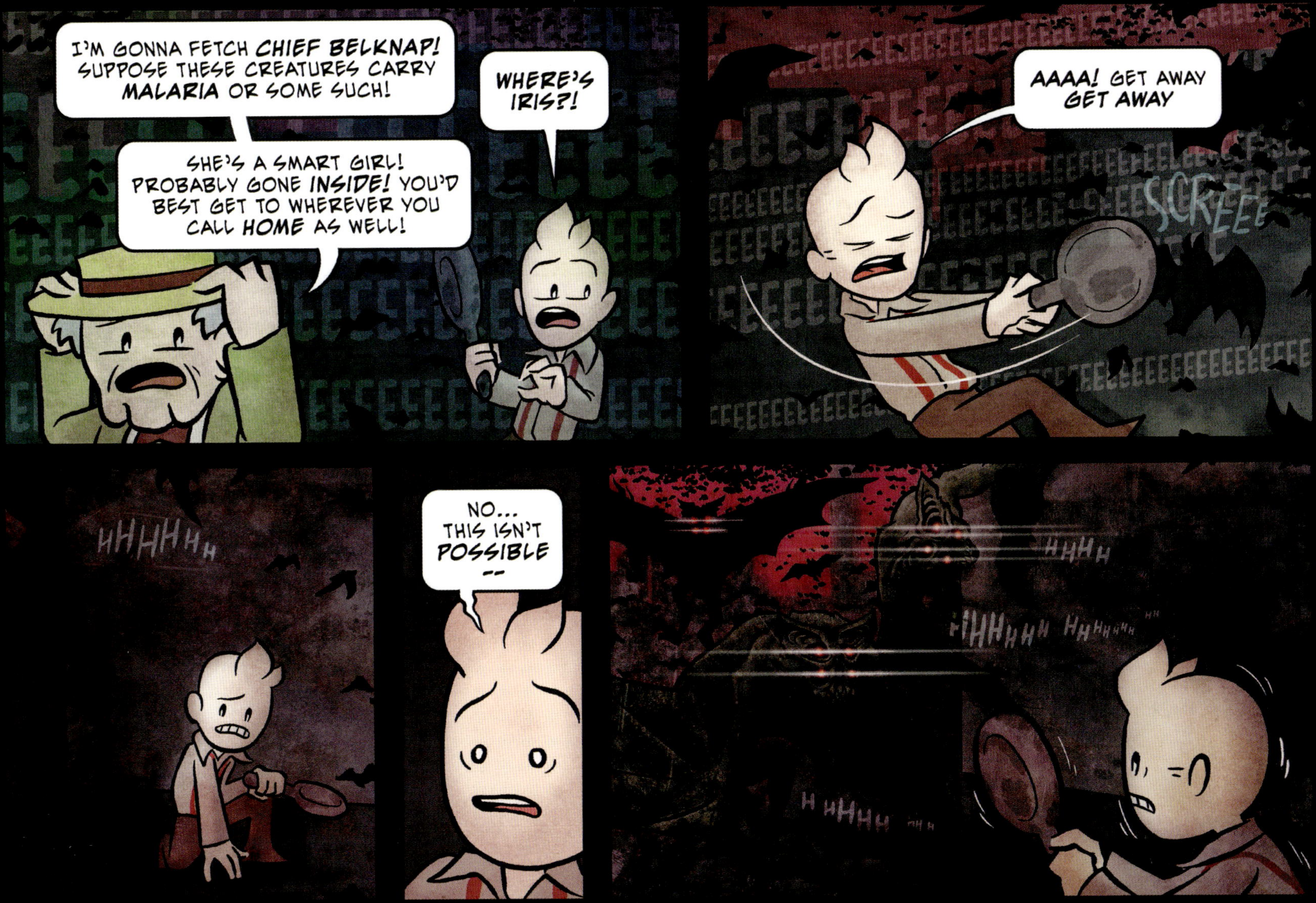
I'M GONNA FETCH CHIEF BELKNAP! SUPPOSE THESE CREATURES CARRY MALARIA OR SOME SUCH!
WHERE'S IRIS?!
SHE'S A SMART GIRL! PROBABLY GONE INSIDE! YOU'D BEST GET TO WHEREVER YOU CALL HOME AS WELL!
AAAA! GET AWAY GET AWAY
SCREEEE
HHHHHH
NO... THIS ISN'T POSSIBLE --
HHHH
HHHHHH HHHHHH
HHHHH

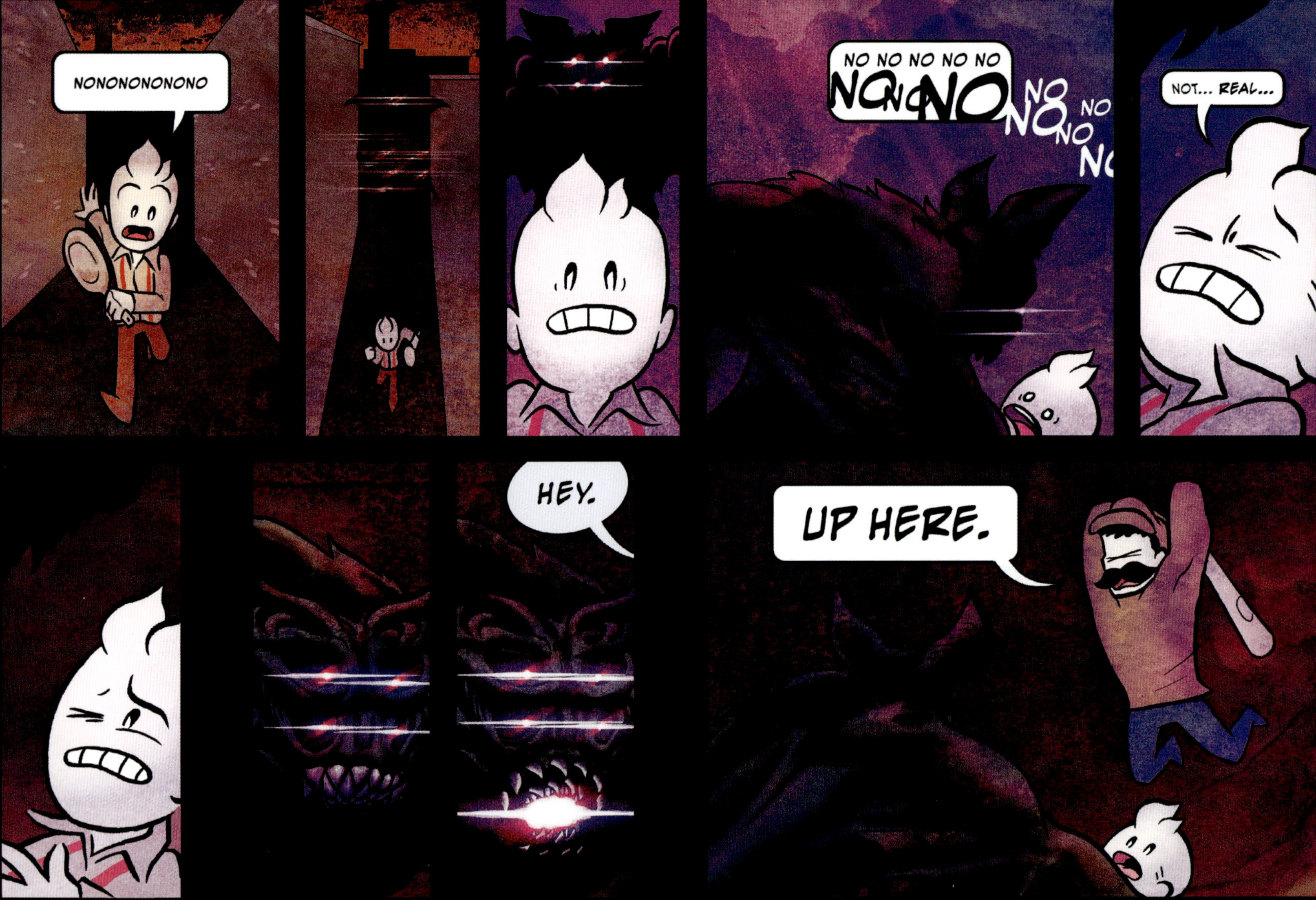

NONONONONONO
NO NO NO NO NO
NONONONO
NO NO
NO NO
NO
NOT... REAL...
HEY.
UP HERE.

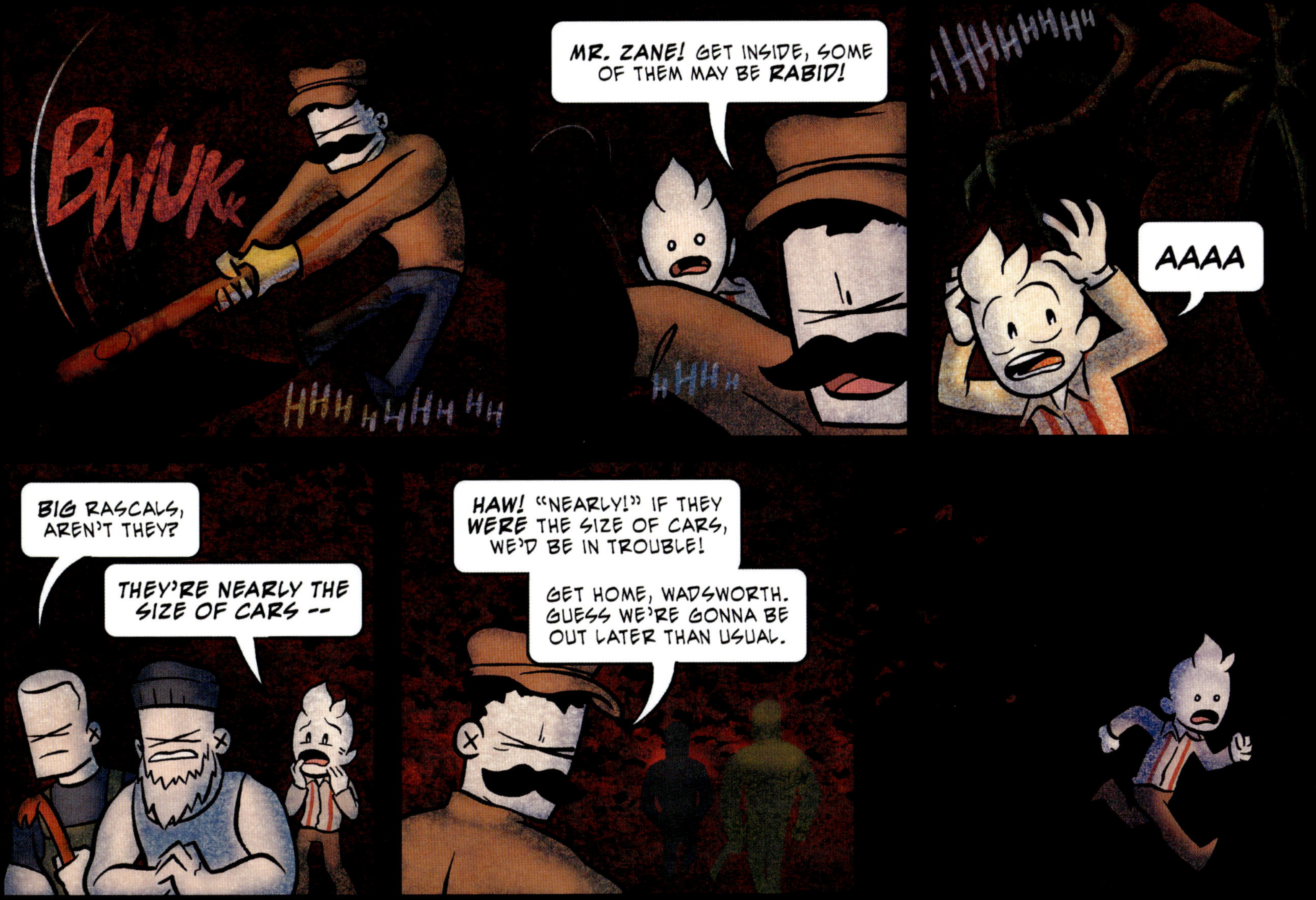

BWUKK
HHHHHHHHHH
MR. ZANE! GET INSIDE, SOME OF THEM MAY BE RABID!
HHHH
HHHHHHHHH
AAAA
BIG RASCALS, AREN'T THEY?
THEY'RE NEARLY THE SIZE OF CARS --
HAW! "NEARLY!" IF THEY WERE THE SIZE OF CARS, WE'D BE IN TROUBLE!
GET HOME, WADSWORTH. GUESS WE'RE GONNA BE OUT LATER THAN USUAL.

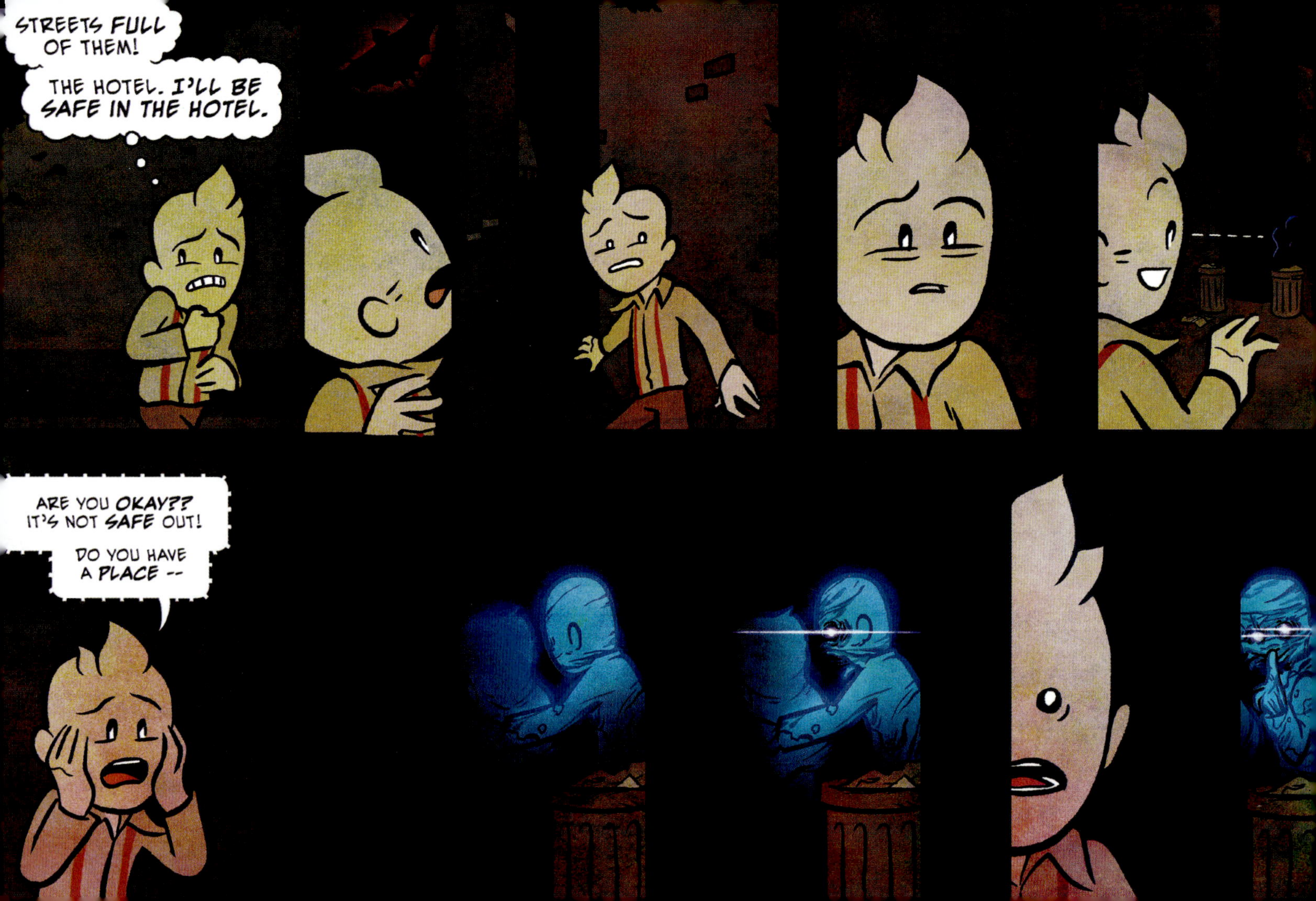
STREETS FULL OF THEM!
THE HOTEL. I'LL BE SAFE IN THE HOTEL.
ARE YOU OKAY?? IT'S NOT SAFE OUT!
DO YOU HAVE A PLACE --

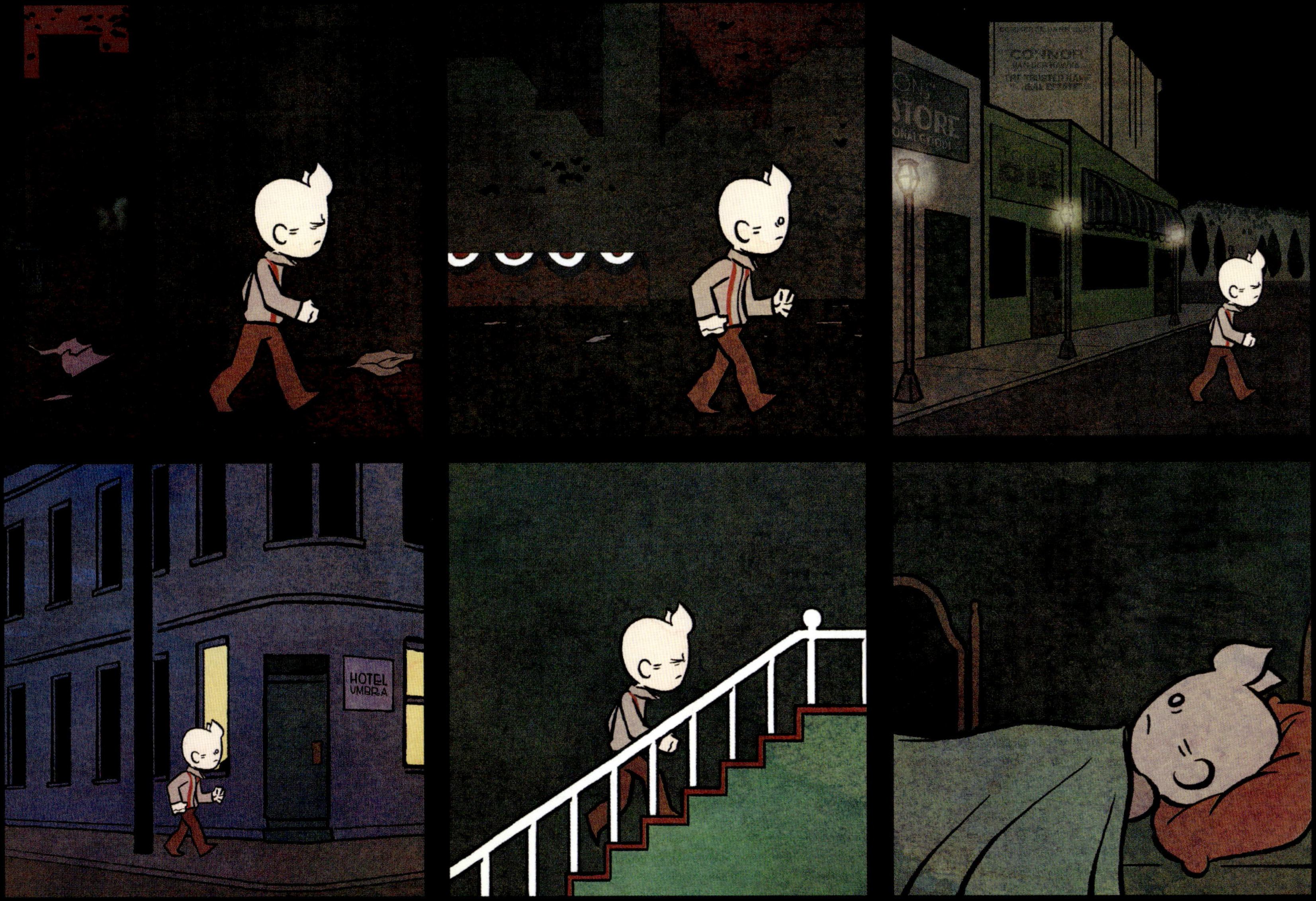
CONNOR
STORE
HOTEL UMBRA

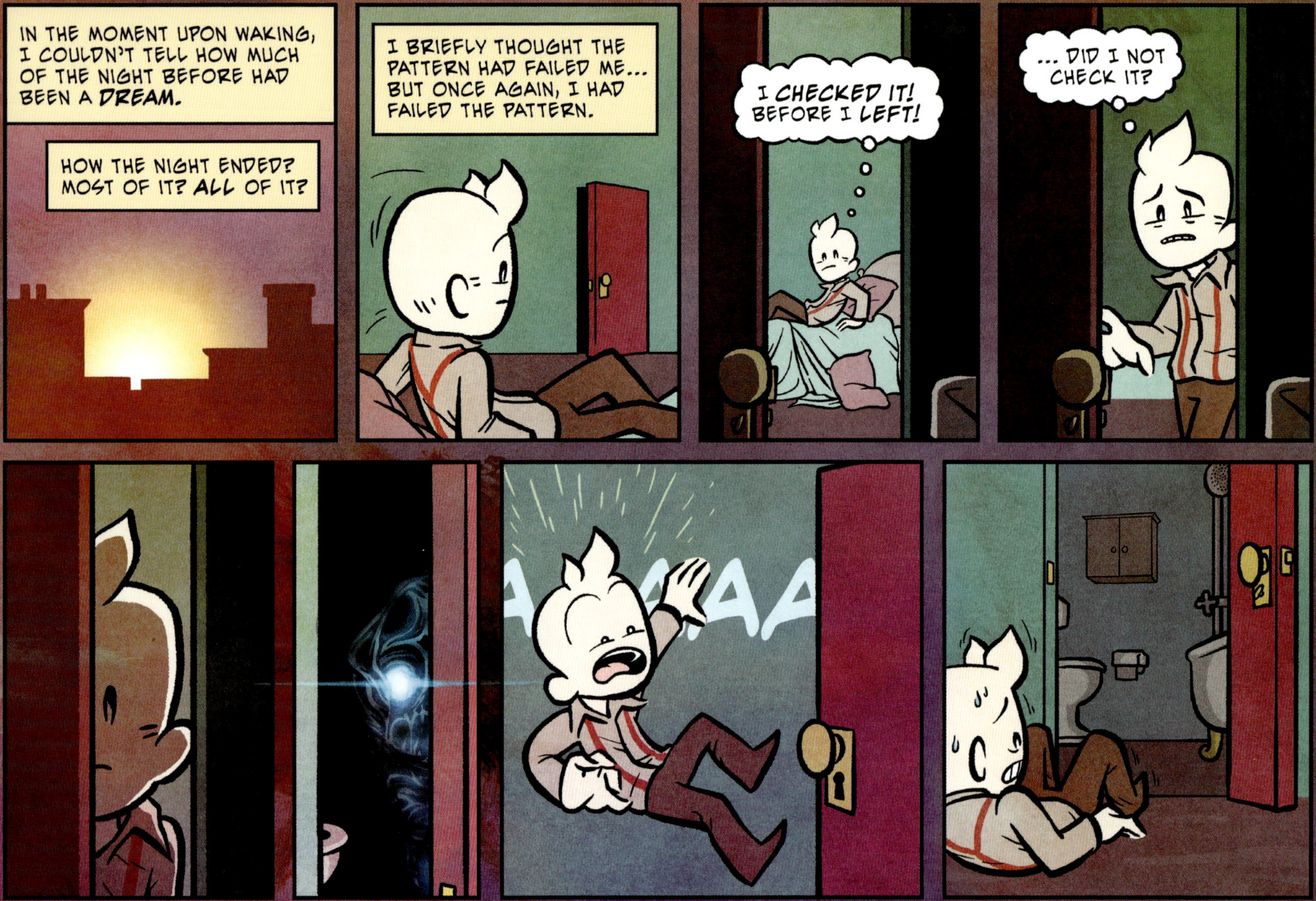
IN THE MOMENT UPON WAKING, I COULDN'T TELL HOW MUCH OF THE NIGHT BEFORE HAD BEEN A DREAM.
HOW THE NIGHT ENDED? MOST OF IT? ALL OF IT?
I BRIEFLY THOUGHT THE PATTERN HAD FAILED ME... BUT ONCE AGAIN, I HAD FAILED THE PATTERN.
I CHECKED IT! BEFORE I LEFT!
... DID I NOT CHECK IT?

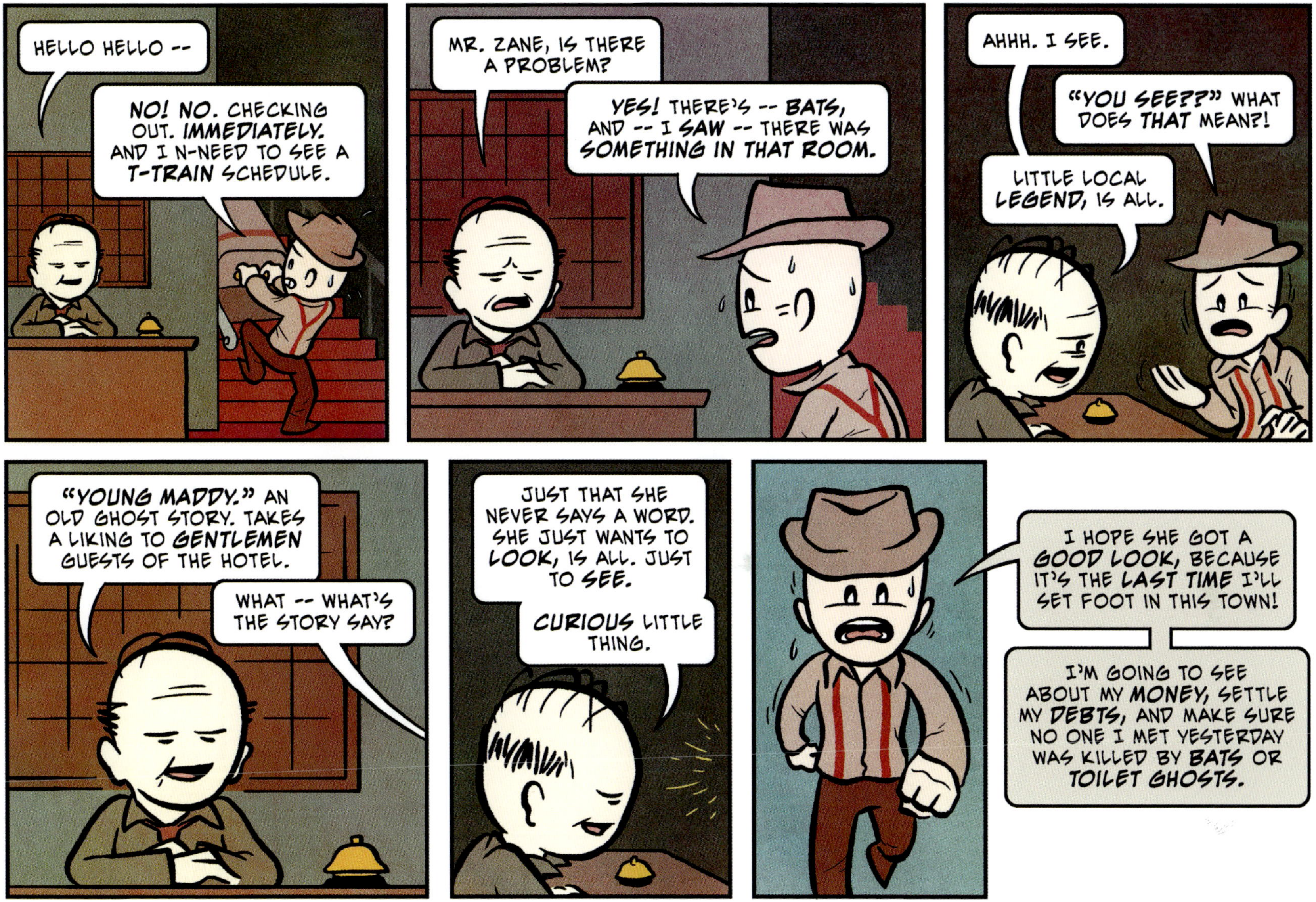
HELLO HELLO --
NO! NO. CHECKING OUT. IMMEDIATELY. AND I N-NEED TO SEE A T-TRAIN SCHEDULE.
MR. ZANE, IS THERE A PROBLEM?
YES! THERE'S -- BATS, AND -- I SAW -- THERE WAS SOMETHING IN THAT ROOM.
AHHH. I SEE.
"YOU SEE??" WHAT DOES THAT MEAN?!
LITTLE LOCAL LEGEND, IS ALL.
"YOUNG MADDY." AN OLD GHOST STORY. TAKES A LIKING TO GENTLEMEN GUESTS OF THE HOTEL.
WHAT -- WHAT'S THE STORY SAY?
JUST THAT SHE NEVER SAYS A WORD. SHE JUST WANTS TO LOOK, IS ALL. JUST TO SEE.
CURIOUS LITTLE THING.
I HOPE SHE GOT A GOOD LOOK, BECAUSE IT'S THE LAST TIME I'LL SET FOOT IN THIS TOWN!
I'M GOING TO SEE ABOUT MY MONEY, SETTLE MY DEBTS, AND MAKE SURE NO ONE I MET YESTERDAY WAS KILLED BY BATS OR TOILET GHOSTS.

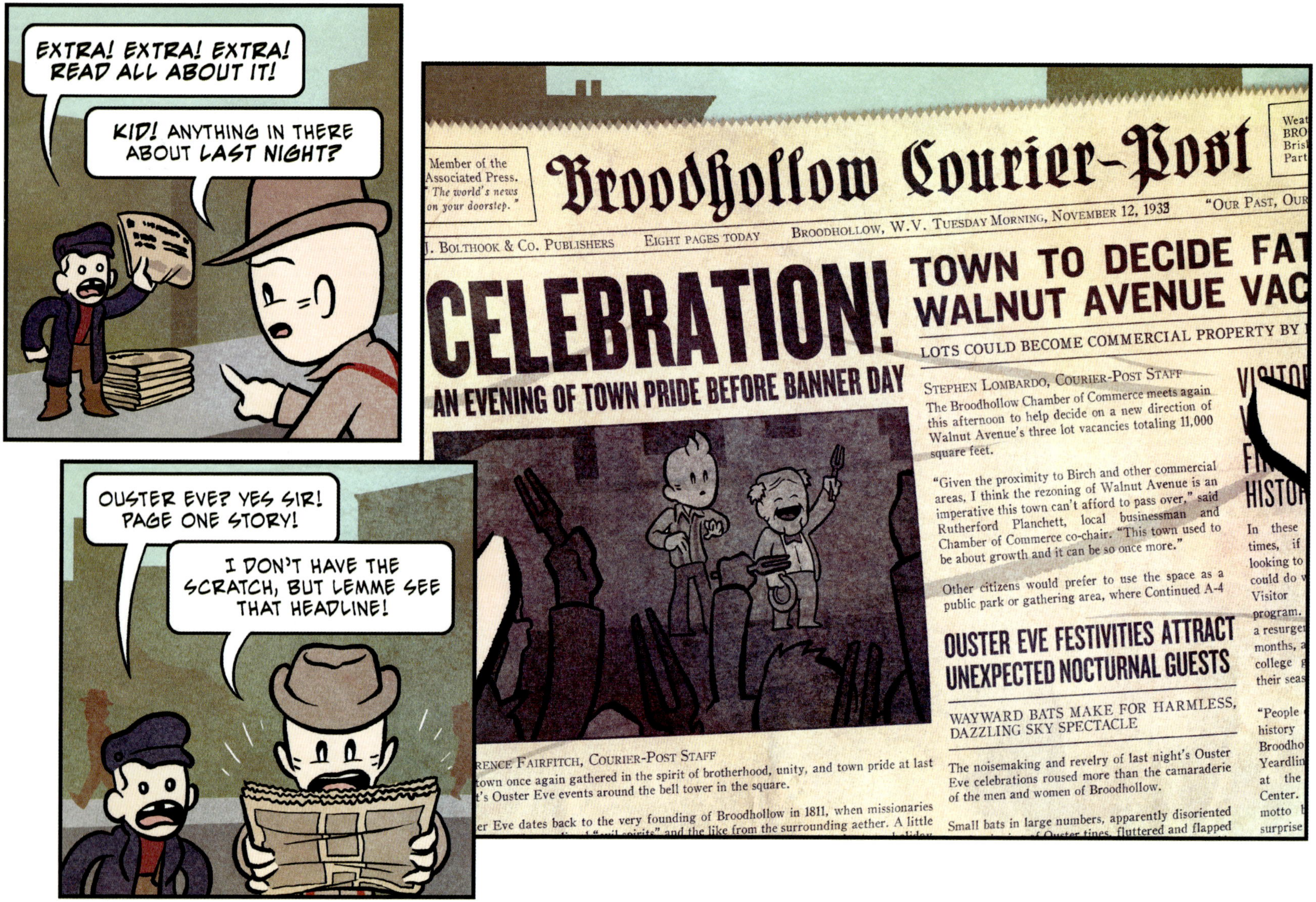

EXTRA! EXTRA! EXTRA! READ ALL ABOUT IT!
KID! ANYTHING IN THERE ABOUT LAST NIGHT?
OUSTER EVE? YES SIR! PAGE ONE STORY!
I DON'T HAVE THE SCRATCH, BUT LEMME SEE THAT HEADLINE!
Member of the Associated Press. "The world's news on your doorstep."
BroodHollow Courier-Post
J. Bolthook & Co. Publishers
Eight pages today
Broodhollow, W.V. Tuesday Morning, November 12, 1933
"Our Past, Our
CELEBRATION!
AN EVENING OF TOWN PRIDE BEFORE BANNER DAY
rence Fairfitch, Courier-Post Staff
town once again gathered in the spirit of brotherhood, unity, and town pride at last
t's Ouster Eve events around the bell tower in the square.
er Eve dates back to the very founding of Broodhollow in 1811, when missionaries
the surrounding aether. A little
TOWN TO DECIDE FAT
WALNUT AVENUE VAC
LOTS COULD BECOME COMMERCIAL PROPERTY BY
Stephen Lombardo, Courier-Post Staff
The Broodhollow Chamber of Commerce meets again this afternoon to help decide on a new direction of Walnut Avenue's three lot vacancies totaling 11,000 square feet.
"Given the proximity to Birch and other commercial areas, I think the rezoning of Walnut Avenue is an imperative this town can't afford to pass over," said Rutherford Planchett, local businessman and Chamber of Commerce co-chair. "This town used to be about growth and it can be so once more."
Other citizens would prefer to use the space as a public park or gathering area, where Continued A-4
OUSTER EVE FESTIVITIES ATTRACT UNEXPECTED NOCTURNAL GUESTS
WAYWARD BATS MAKE FOR HARMLESS, DAZZLING SKY SPECTACLE
The noisemaking and revelry of last night's Ouster Eve celebrations roused more than the camaraderie of the men and women of Broodhollow.
Small bats in large numbers, apparently disoriented
HISTOR
In these times, if looking to could do Visitor program. a resurge months, college their seas
"People history Broodho Yeardlin at the Center. motto surprise

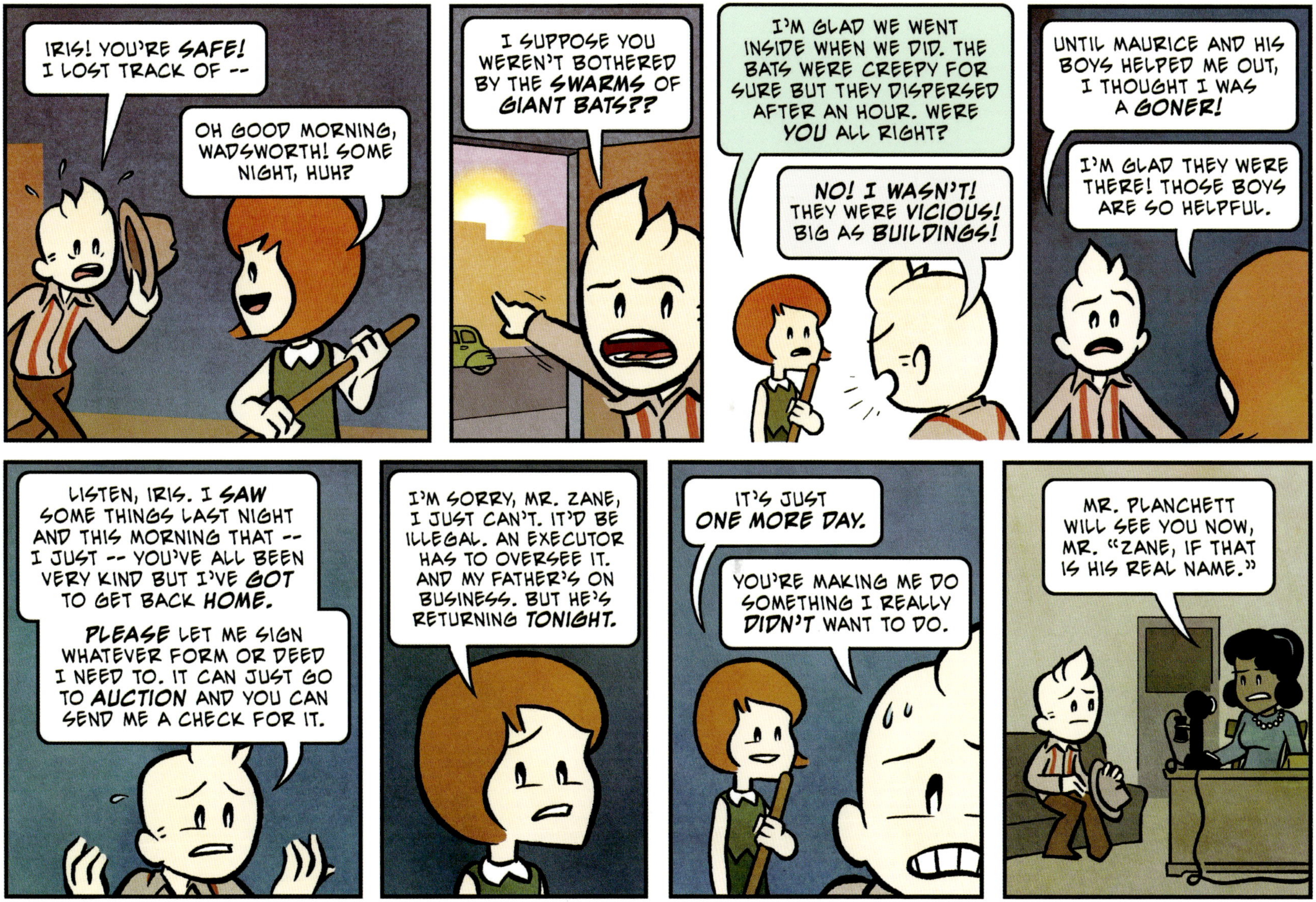
IRIS! YOU'RE SAFE! I LOST TRACK OF --
OH GOOD MORNING, WADSWORTH! SOME NIGHT, HUH?
I SUPPOSE YOU WEREN'T BOTHERED BY THE SWARMS OF GIANT BATS??
I'M GLAD WE WENT INSIDE WHEN WE DID. THE BATS WERE CREEPY FOR SURE BUT THEY DISPERSED AFTER AN HOUR. WERE YOU ALL RIGHT?
NO! I WASN'T! THEY WERE VICIOUS! BIG AS BUILDINGS!
UNTIL MAURICE AND HIS BOYS HELPED ME OUT, I THOUGHT I WAS A GONER!
I'M GLAD THEY WERE THERE! THOSE BOYS ARE SO HELPFUL.
LISTEN, IRIS. I SAW SOME THINGS LAST NIGHT AND THIS MORNING THAT -- I JUST -- YOU'VE ALL BEEN VERY KIND BUT I'VE GOT TO GET BACK HOME.
PLEASE LET ME SIGN WHATEVER FORM OR DEED I NEED TO. IT CAN JUST GO TO AUCTION AND YOU CAN SEND ME A CHECK FOR IT.
I'M SORRY, MR. ZANE, I JUST CAN'T. IT'D BE ILLEGAL. AN EXECUTOR HAS TO OVERSEE IT. AND MY FATHER'S ON BUSINESS. BUT HE'S RETURNING TONIGHT.
IT'S JUST ONE MORE DAY.
YOU'RE MAKING ME DO SOMETHING I REALLY DIDN'T WANT TO DO.
MR. PLANCHETT WILL SEE YOU NOW, MR. "ZANE, IF THAT IS HIS REAL NAME."

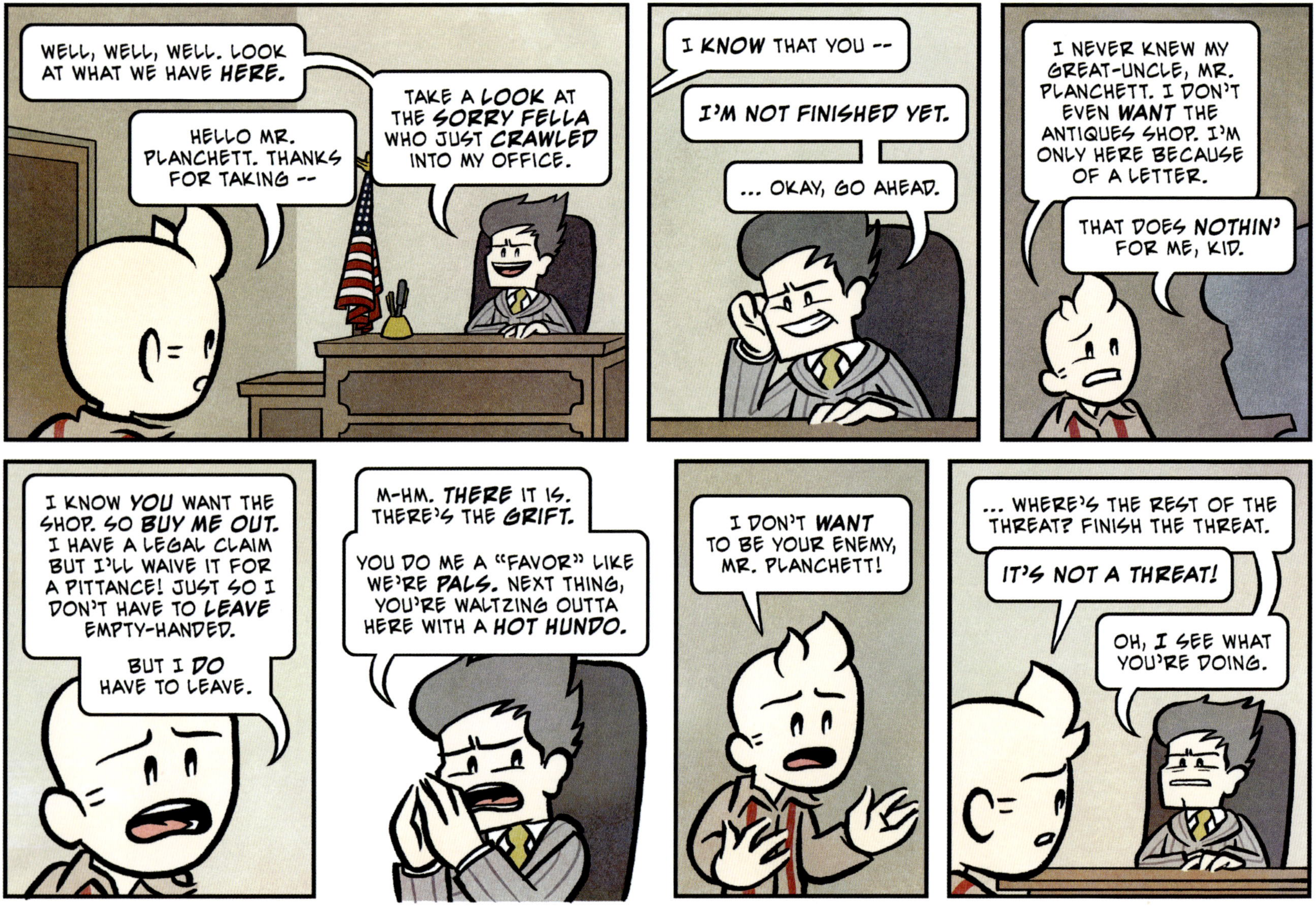
WELL, WELL, WELL. LOOK AT WHAT WE HAVE HERE.
HELLO MR. PLANCHETT. THANKS FOR TAKING --
TAKE A LOOK AT THE SORRY FELLA WHO JUST CRAWLED INTO MY OFFICE.
I KNOW THAT YOU --
I'M NOT FINISHED YET.
... OKAY, GO AHEAD.
I NEVER KNEW MY GREAT-UNCLE, MR. PLANCHETT. I DON'T EVEN WANT THE ANTIQUES SHOP. I'M ONLY HERE BECAUSE OF A LETTER.
THAT DOES NOTHIN' FOR ME, KID.
I KNOW YOU WANT THE SHOP. SO BUY ME OUT. I HAVE A LEGAL CLAIM BUT I'LL WAIVE IT FOR A PITTANCE! JUST SO I DON'T HAVE TO LEAVE EMPTY-HANDED.
BUT I DO HAVE TO LEAVE.
M-HM. THERE IT IS. THERE'S THE GRIFT.
YOU DO ME A "FAVOR" LIKE WE'RE PALS. NEXT THING, YOU'RE WALTZING OUTTA HERE WITH A HOT HUNDO.
I DON'T WANT TO BE YOUR ENEMY, MR. PLANCHETT!
... WHERE'S THE REST OF THE THREAT? FINISH THE THREAT.
IT'S NOT A THREAT!
OH, I SEE WHAT YOU'RE DOING.

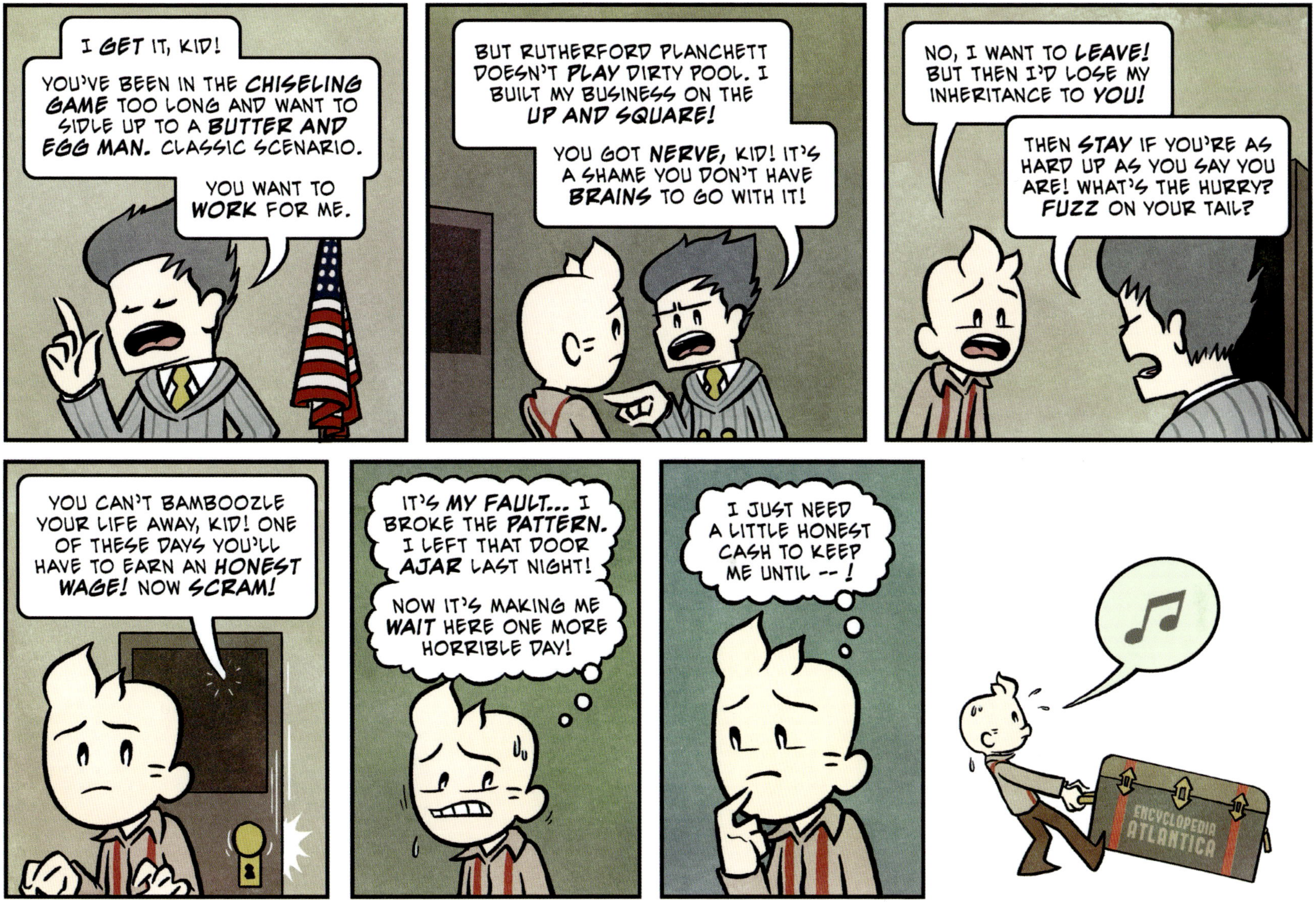
I GET IT, KID!
YOU'VE BEEN IN THE CHISELING GAME TOO LONG AND WANT TO SIDLE UP TO A BUTTER AND EGG MAN. CLASSIC SCENARIO.
YOU WANT TO WORK FOR ME.
BUT RUTHERFORD PLANCHETT DOESN'T PLAY DIRTY POOL. I BUILT MY BUSINESS ON THE UP AND SQUARE!
YOU GOT NERVE, KID! IT'S A SHAME YOU DON'T HAVE BRAINS TO GO WITH IT!
NO, I WANT TO LEAVE! BUT THEN I'D LOSE MY INHERITANCE TO YOU!
THEN STAY IF YOU'RE AS HARD UP AS YOU SAY YOU ARE! WHAT'S THE HURRY? FUZZ ON YOUR TAIL?
YOU CAN'T BAMBOOZLE YOUR LIFE AWAY, KID! ONE OF THESE DAYS YOU'LL HAVE TO EARN AN HONEST WAGE! NOW SCRAM!
IT'S MY FAULT... I BROKE THE PATTERN. I LEFT THAT DOOR AJAR LAST NIGHT!
NOW IT'S MAKING ME WAIT HERE ONE MORE HORRIBLE DAY!
I JUST NEED A LITTLE HONEST CASH TO KEEP ME UNTIL -- !
ENCYCLOPEDIA ATLANTICA

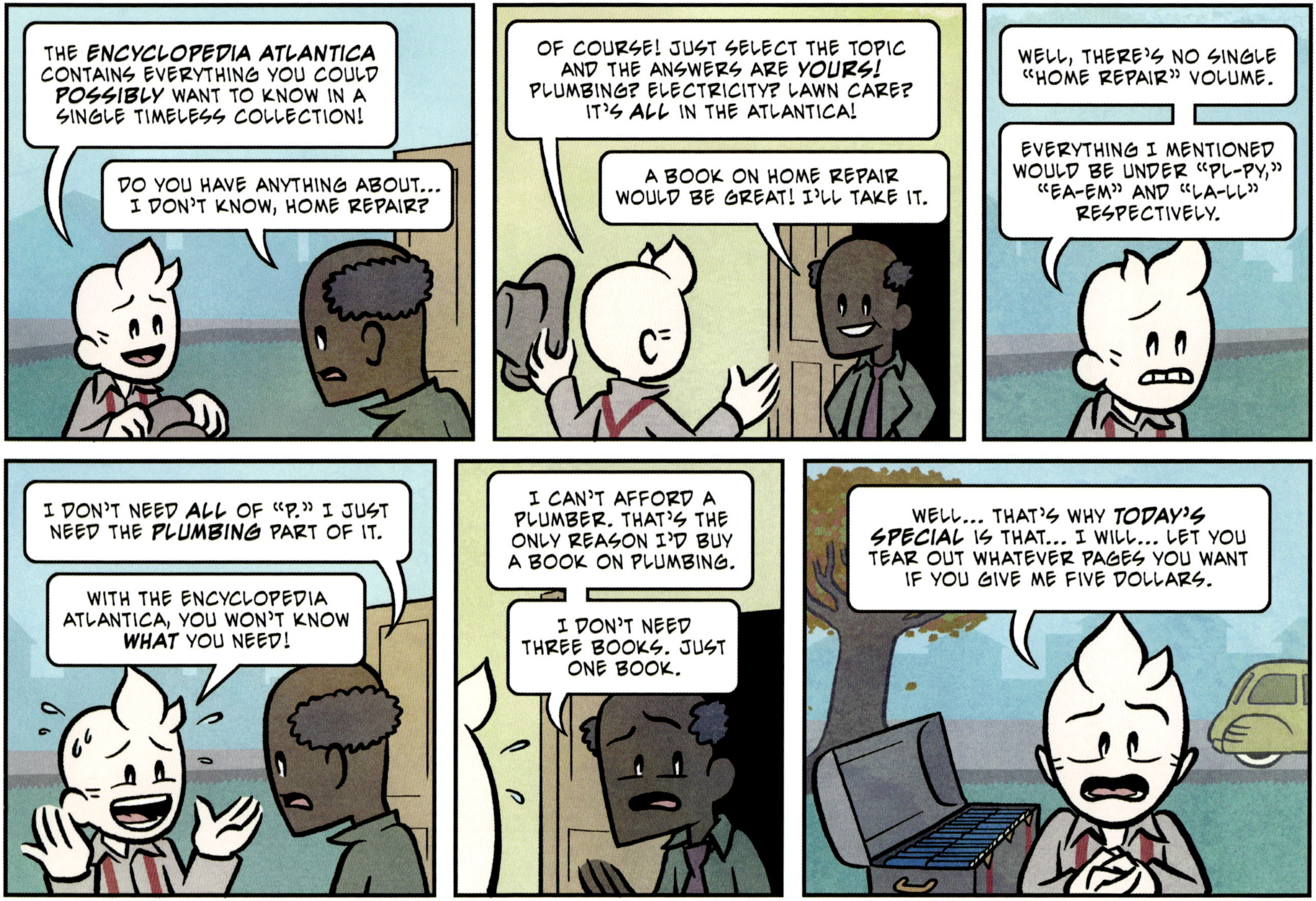
THE ENCYCLOPEDIA ATLANTICA CONTAINS EVERYTHING YOU COULD POSSIBLY WANT TO KNOW IN A SINGLE TIMELESS COLLECTION!
DO YOU HAVE ANYTHING ABOUT... I DON'T KNOW, HOME REPAIR?
OF COURSE! JUST SELECT THE TOPIC AND THE ANSWERS ARE YOURS! PLUMBING? ELECTRICITY? LAWN CARE? IT'S ALL IN THE ATLANTICA!
A BOOK ON HOME REPAIR WOULD BE GREAT! I'LL TAKE IT.
WELL, THERE'S NO SINGLE "HOME REPAIR" VOLUME.
EVERYTHING I MENTIONED WOULD BE UNDER "PL-PY," "EA-EM" AND "LA-LL" RESPECTIVELY.
I DON'T NEED ALL OF "P." I JUST NEED THE PLUMBING PART OF IT.
WITH THE ENCYCLOPEDIA ATLANTICA, YOU WON'T KNOW WHAT YOU NEED!
I CAN'T AFFORD A PLUMBER. THAT'S THE ONLY REASON I'D BUY A BOOK ON PLUMBING.
I DON'T NEED THREE BOOKS. JUST ONE BOOK.
WELL... THAT'S WHY TODAY'S SPECIAL IS THAT... I WILL... LET YOU TEAR OUT WHATEVER PAGES YOU WANT IF YOU GIVE ME FIVE DOLLARS.

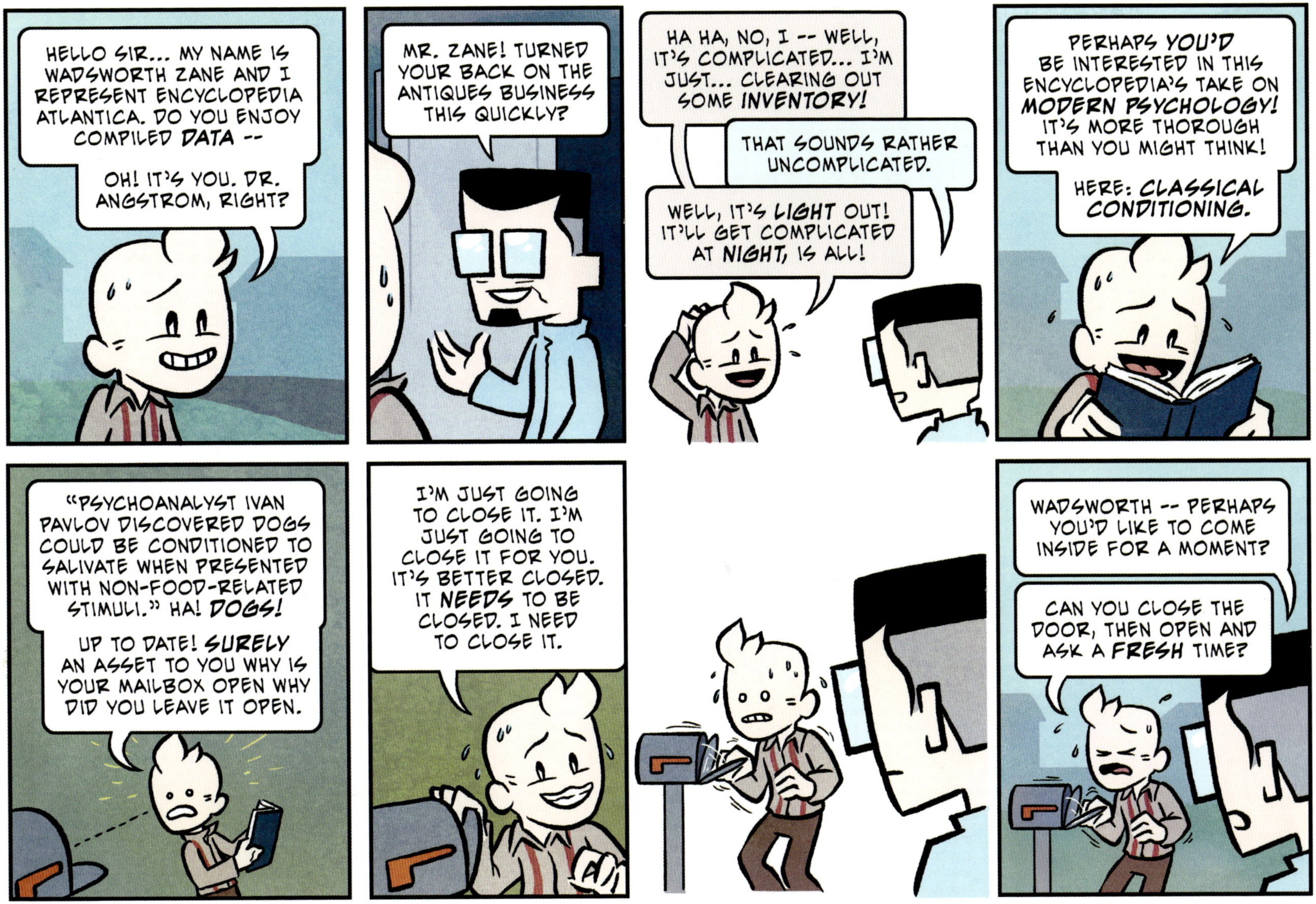
HELLO SIR... MY NAME IS WADSWORTH ZANE AND I REPRESENT ENCYCLOPEDIA ATLANTICA. DO YOU ENJOY COMPILED DATA --
OH! IT'S YOU. DR. ANGSTROM, RIGHT?
MR. ZANE! TURNED YOUR BACK ON THE ANTIQUES BUSINESS THIS QUICKLY?
HA HA, NO, I -- WELL, IT'S COMPLICATED... I'M JUST... CLEARING OUT SOME INVENTORY!
THAT SOUNDS RATHER UNCOMPLICATED.
WELL, IT'S LIGHT OUT! IT'LL GET COMPLICATED AT NIGHT, IS ALL!
PERHAPS YOU'D BE INTERESTED IN THIS ENCYCLOPEDIA'S TAKE ON MODERN PSYCHOLOGY! IT'S MORE THOROUGH THAN YOU MIGHT THINK!
HERE: CLASSICAL CONDITIONING.
"PSYCHOANALYST IVAN PAVLOV DISCOVERED DOGS COULD BE CONDITIONED TO SALIVATE WHEN PRESENTED WITH NON-FOOD-RELATED STIMULI." HA! DOGS!
UP TO DATE! SURELY AN ASSET TO YOU WHY IS YOUR MAILBOX OPEN WHY DID YOU LEAVE IT OPEN.
I'M JUST GOING TO CLOSE IT. I'M JUST GOING TO CLOSE IT FOR YOU. IT'S BETTER CLOSED. IT NEEDS TO BE CLOSED. I NEED TO CLOSE IT.
WADSWORTH -- PERHAPS YOU'D LIKE TO COME INSIDE FOR A MOMENT?
CAN YOU CLOSE THE DOOR, THEN OPEN AND ASK A FRESH TIME?

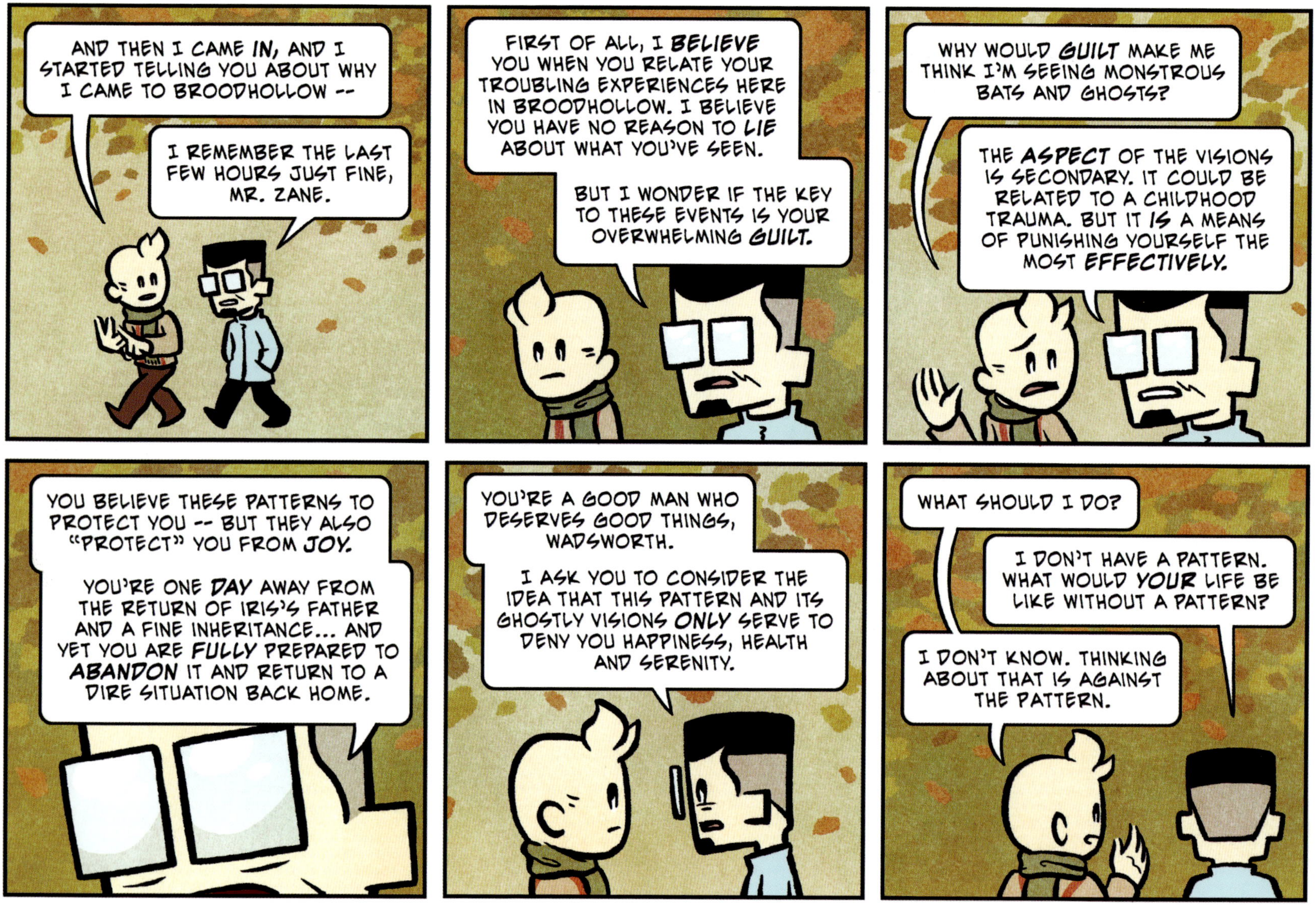
AND THEN I CAME IN, AND I STARTED TELLING YOU ABOUT WHY I CAME TO BROODHOLLOW --
I REMEMBER THE LAST FEW HOURS JUST FINE, MR. ZANE.
FIRST OF ALL, I BELIEVE YOU WHEN YOU RELATE YOUR TROUBLING EXPERIENCES HERE IN BROODHOLLOW. I BELIEVE YOU HAVE NO REASON TO LIE ABOUT WHAT YOU'VE SEEN.
BUT I WONDER IF THE KEY TO THESE EVENTS IS YOUR OVERWHELMING GUILT.
WHY WOULD GUILT MAKE ME THINK I'M SEEING MONSTROUS BATS AND GHOSTS?
THE ASPECT OF THE VISIONS IS SECONDARY. IT COULD BE RELATED TO A CHILDHOOD TRAUMA. BUT IT IS A MEANS OF PUNISHING YOURSELF THE MOST EFFECTIVELY.
YOU BELIEVE THESE PATTERNS TO PROTECT YOU -- BUT THEY ALSO "PROTECT" YOU FROM JOY.
YOU'RE ONE DAY AWAY FROM THE RETURN OF IRIS'S FATHER AND A FINE INHERITANCE... AND YET YOU ARE FULLY PREPARED TO ABANDON IT AND RETURN TO A DIRE SITUATION BACK HOME.
YOU'RE A GOOD MAN WHO DESERVES GOOD THINGS, WADSWORTH.
I ASK YOU TO CONSIDER THE IDEA THAT THIS PATTERN AND ITS GHOSTLY VISIONS ONLY SERVE TO DENY YOU HAPPINESS, HEALTH AND SERENITY.
WHAT SHOULD I DO?
I DON'T HAVE A PATTERN. WHAT WOULD YOUR LIFE BE LIKE WITHOUT A PATTERN?
I DON'T KNOW. THINKING ABOUT THAT IS AGAINST THE PATTERN.

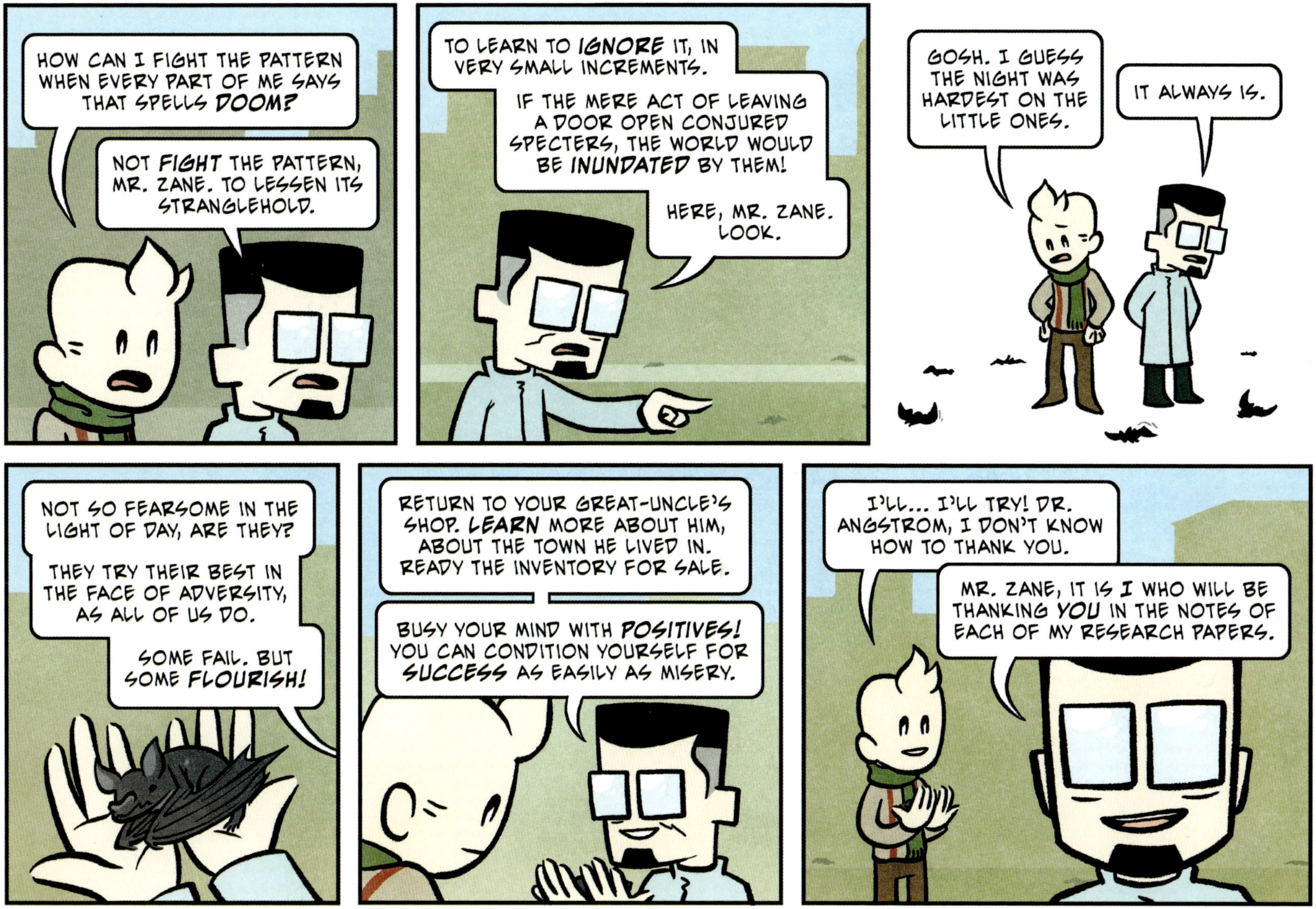
HOW CAN I FIGHT THE PATTERN WHEN EVERY PART OF ME SAYS THAT SPELLS DOOM?
NOT FIGHT THE PATTERN, MR. ZANE. TO LESSEN ITS STRANGLEHOLD.
TO LEARN TO IGNORE IT, IN VERY SMALL INCREMENTS.
IF THE MERE ACT OF LEAVING A DOOR OPEN CONJURED SPECTERS, THE WORLD WOULD BE INUNDATED BY THEM!
HERE, MR. ZANE. LOOK.
GOSH. I GUESS THE NIGHT WAS HARDEST ON THE LITTLE ONES.
IT ALWAYS IS.
NOT SO FEARSOME IN THE LIGHT OF DAY, ARE THEY?
THEY TRY THEIR BEST IN THE FACE OF ADVERSITY, AS ALL OF US DO.
SOME FAIL. BUT SOME FLOURISH!
RETURN TO YOUR GREAT-UNCLE'S SHOP. LEARN MORE ABOUT HIM, ABOUT THE TOWN HE LIVED IN. READY THE INVENTORY FOR SALE.
BUSY YOUR MIND WITH POSITIVES! YOU CAN CONDITION YOURSELF FOR SUCCESS AS EASILY AS MISERY.
I'LL... I'LL TRY! DR. ANGSTROM, I DON'T KNOW HOW TO THANK YOU.
MR. ZANE, IT IS I WHO WILL BE THANKING YOU IN THE NOTES OF EACH OF MY RESEARCH PAPERS.

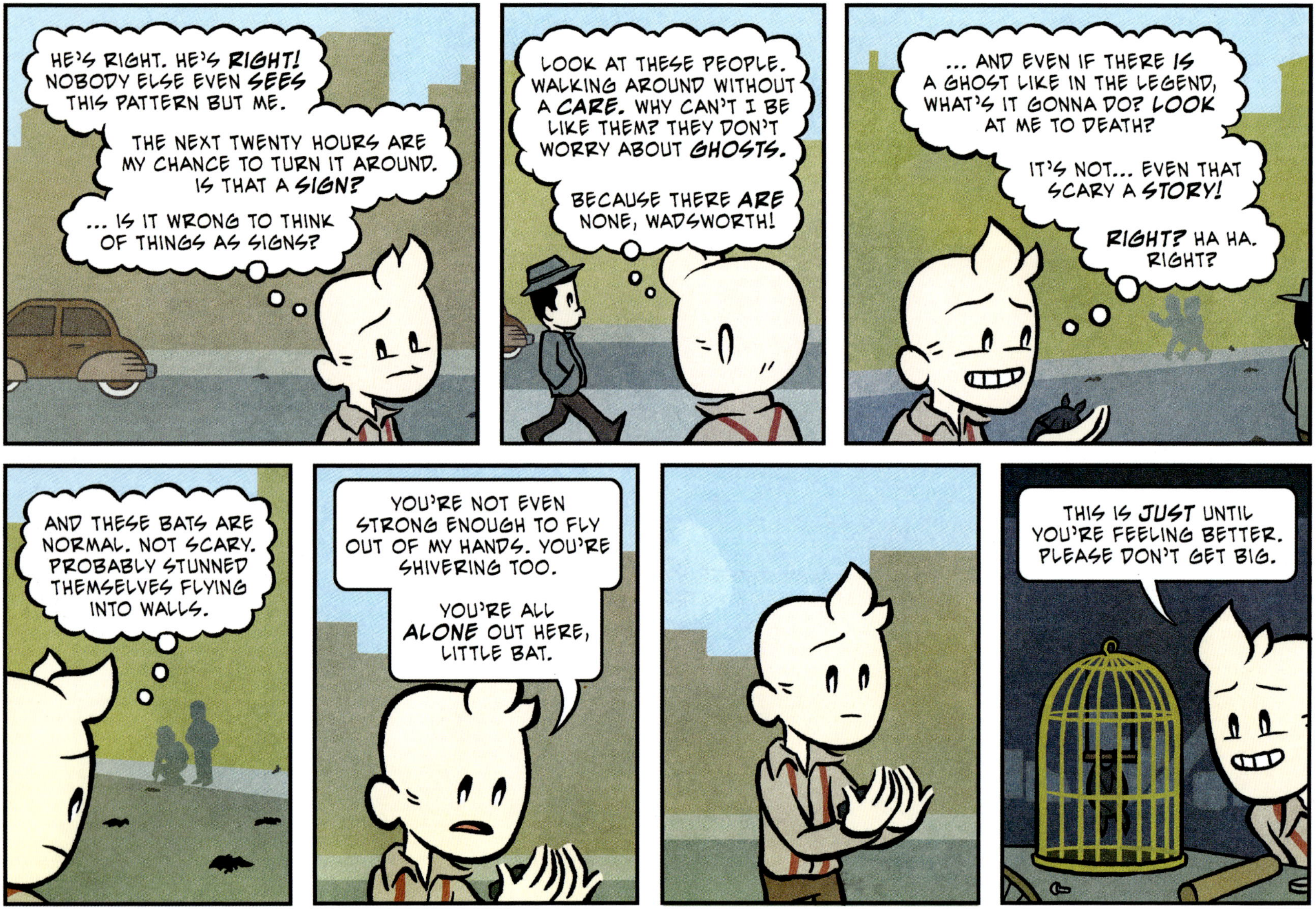
HE'S RIGHT. HE'S **RIGHT!** NOBODY ELSE EVEN **SEES** THIS PATTERN BUT ME.
THE NEXT TWENTY HOURS ARE MY CHANCE TO TURN IT AROUND. IS THAT A **SIGN?**
... IS IT WRONG TO THINK OF THINGS AS SIGNS?
LOOK AT THESE PEOPLE. WALKING AROUND WITHOUT A **CARE.** WHY CAN'T I BE LIKE THEM? THEY DON'T WORRY ABOUT **GHOSTS.**
BECAUSE THERE **ARE** NONE, WADSWORTH!
... AND EVEN IF THERE **IS** A GHOST LIKE IN THE LEGEND, WHAT'S IT GONNA DO? **LOOK** AT ME TO DEATH?
IT'S NOT... EVEN THAT SCARY A **STORY!**
RIGHT? HA HA. RIGHT?
AND THESE BATS ARE NORMAL. NOT SCARY. PROBABLY STUNNED THEMSELVES FLYING INTO WALLS.
YOU'RE NOT EVEN STRONG ENOUGH TO FLY OUT OF MY HANDS. YOU'RE SHIVERING TOO.
YOU'RE ALL **ALONE** OUT HERE, LITTLE BAT.
THIS IS **JUST** UNTIL YOU'RE FEELING BETTER. PLEASE DON'T GET BIG.

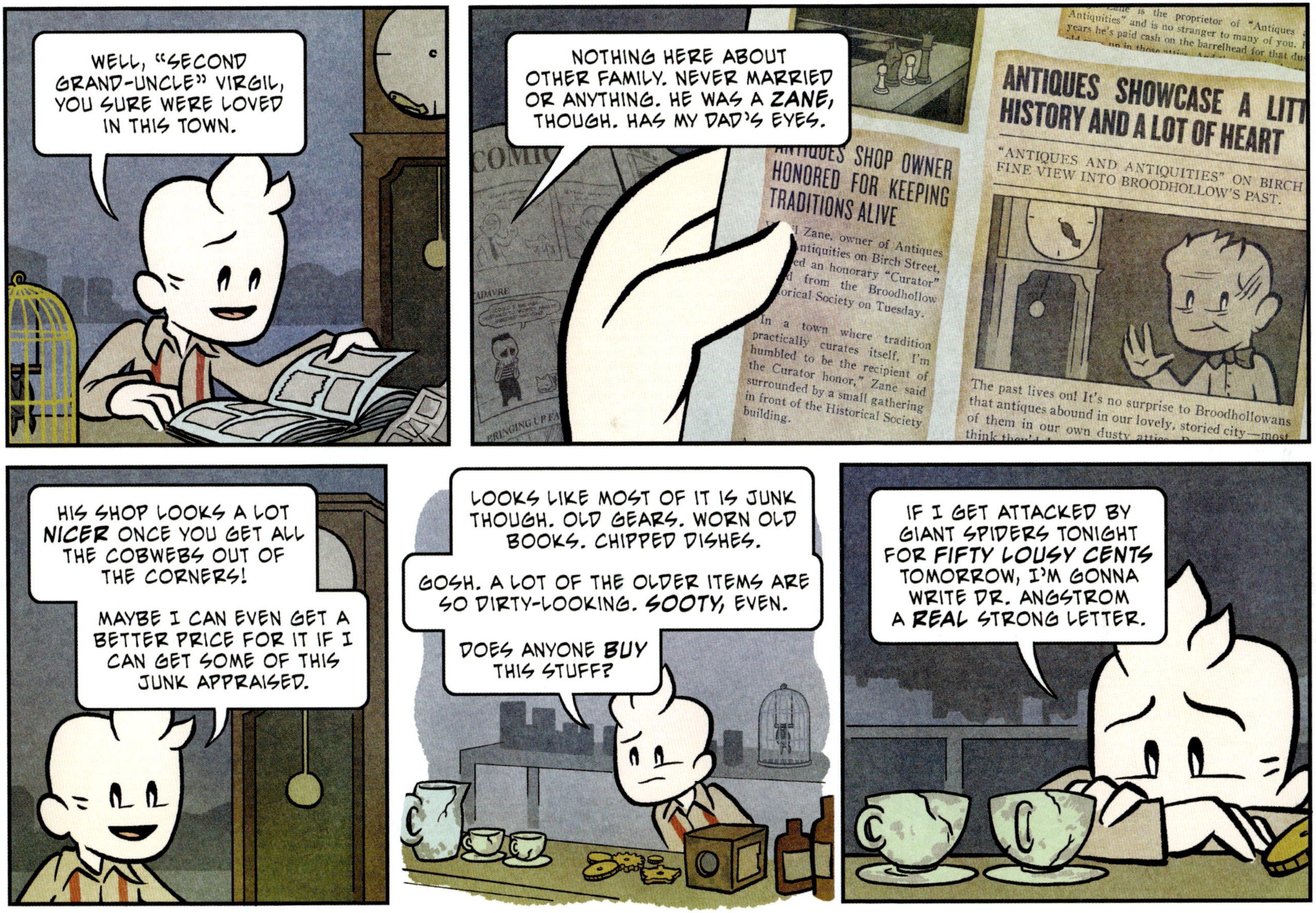
WELL, "SECOND GRAND-UNCLE" VIRGIL, YOU SURE WERE LOVED IN THIS TOWN.
NOTHING HERE ABOUT OTHER FAMILY. NEVER MARRIED OR ANYTHING. HE WAS A ZANE, THOUGH. HAS MY DAD'S EYES.
ANTIQUES SHOWCASE A LIT
HISTORY AND A LOT OF HEART
"ANTIQUES AND ANTIQUITIES" ON BIRCH
FINE VIEW INTO BROODHOLLOW'S PAST.
HONORED FOR KEEPING TRADITIONS ALIVE
In a town where tradition practically curates itself, I'm humbled to be the recipient of the Curator honor," Zane said surrounded by a small gathering in front of the Historical Society building.
The past lives on! It's no surprise to Broodhollowans that antiques abound in our lovely, storied city
HIS SHOP LOOKS A LOT NICER ONCE YOU GET ALL THE COBWEBS OUT OF THE CORNERS!
MAYBE I CAN EVEN GET A BETTER PRICE FOR IT IF I CAN GET SOME OF THIS JUNK APPRAISED.
LOOKS LIKE MOST OF IT IS JUNK THOUGH. OLD GEARS. WORN OLD BOOKS. CHIPPED DISHES.
GOSH. A LOT OF THE OLDER ITEMS ARE SO DIRTY-LOOKING. SOOTY, EVEN.
DOES ANYONE BUY THIS STUFF?
IF I GET ATTACKED BY GIANT SPIDERS TONIGHT FOR FIFTY LOUSY CENTS TOMORROW, I'M GONNA WRITE DR. ANGSTROM A REAL STRONG LETTER.

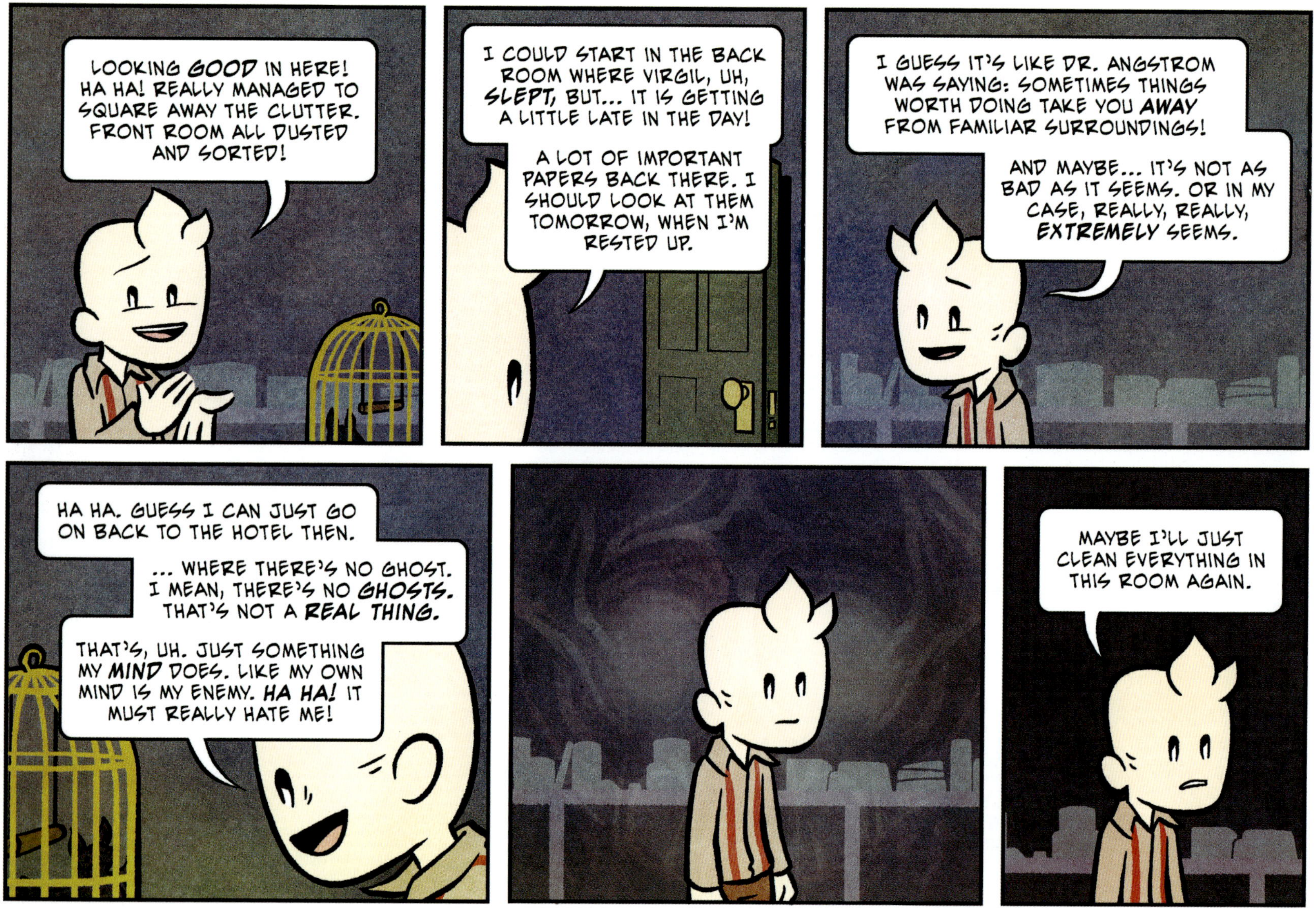
LOOKING GOOD IN HERE! HA HA! REALLY MANAGED TO SQUARE AWAY THE CLUTTER. FRONT ROOM ALL DUSTED AND SORTED!
I COULD START IN THE BACK ROOM WHERE VIRGIL, UH, SLEPT, BUT... IT IS GETTING A LITTLE LATE IN THE DAY!
A LOT OF IMPORTANT PAPERS BACK THERE. I SHOULD LOOK AT THEM TOMORROW, WHEN I'M RESTED UP.
I GUESS IT'S LIKE DR. ANGSTROM WAS SAYING: SOMETIMES THINGS WORTH DOING TAKE YOU AWAY FROM FAMILIAR SURROUNDINGS!
AND MAYBE... IT'S NOT AS BAD AS IT SEEMS. OR IN MY CASE, REALLY, REALLY, EXTREMELY SEEMS.
HA HA. GUESS I CAN JUST GO ON BACK TO THE HOTEL THEN.
... WHERE THERE'S NO GHOST. I MEAN, THERE'S NO GHOSTS. THAT'S NOT A REAL THING.
THAT'S, UH. JUST SOMETHING MY MIND DOES. LIKE MY OWN MIND IS MY ENEMY. HA HA! IT MUST REALLY HATE ME!
MAYBE I'LL JUST CLEAN EVERYTHING IN THIS ROOM AGAIN.

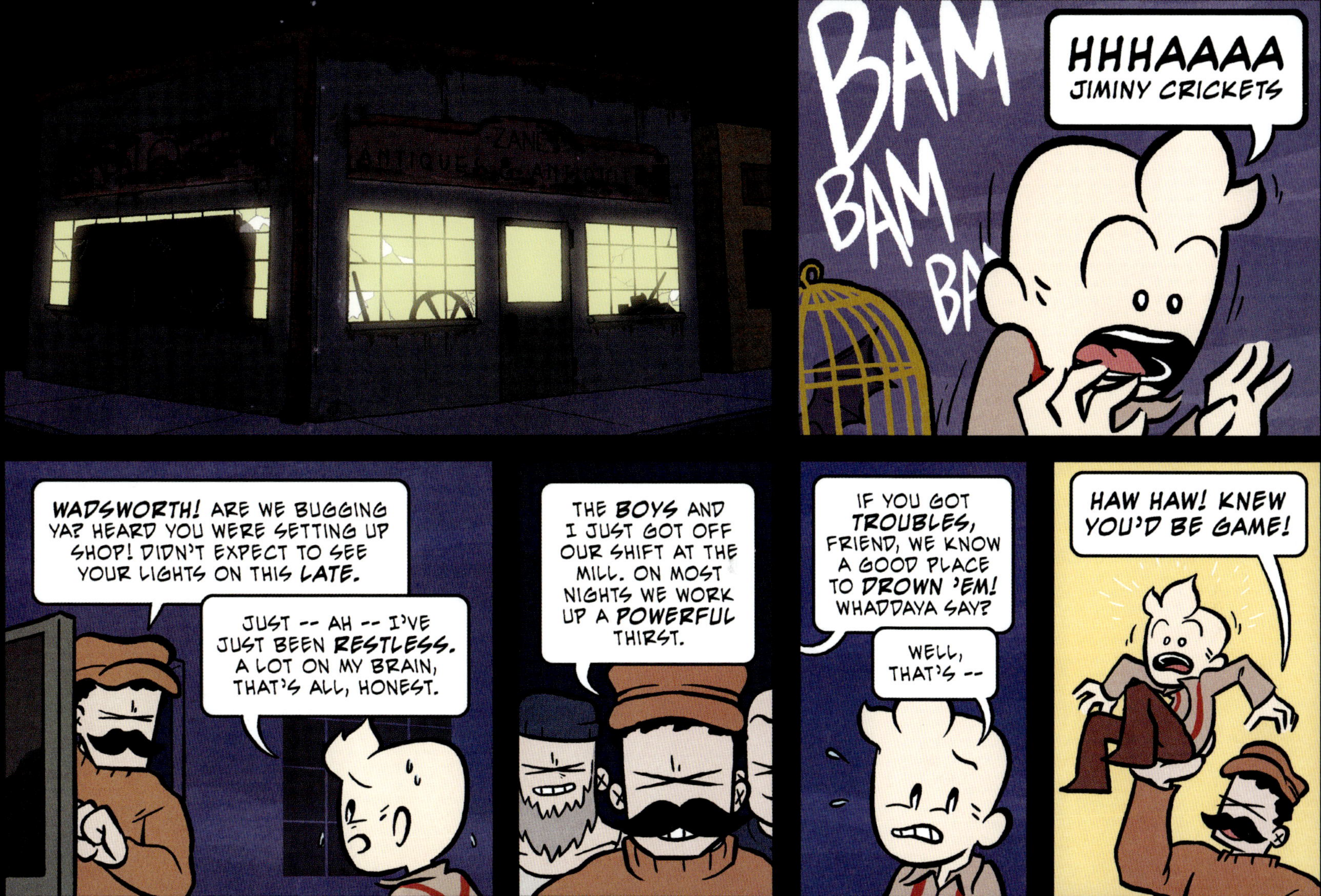
BAM
BAM
BA
HHHAAAA
JIMINY CRICKETS
WADSWORTH! ARE WE BUGGING YA? HEARD YOU WERE SETTING UP SHOP! DIDN'T EXPECT TO SEE YOUR LIGHTS ON THIS LATE.
JUST -- AH -- I'VE JUST BEEN RESTLESS. A LOT ON MY BRAIN, THAT'S ALL, HONEST.
THE BOYS AND I JUST GOT OFF OUR SHIFT AT THE MILL. ON MOST NIGHTS WE WORK UP A POWERFUL THIRST.
IF YOU GOT TROUBLES, FRIEND, WE KNOW A GOOD PLACE TO DROWN 'EM! WHADDAYA SAY?
WELL, THAT'S --
HAW HAW! KNEW YOU'D BE GAME!

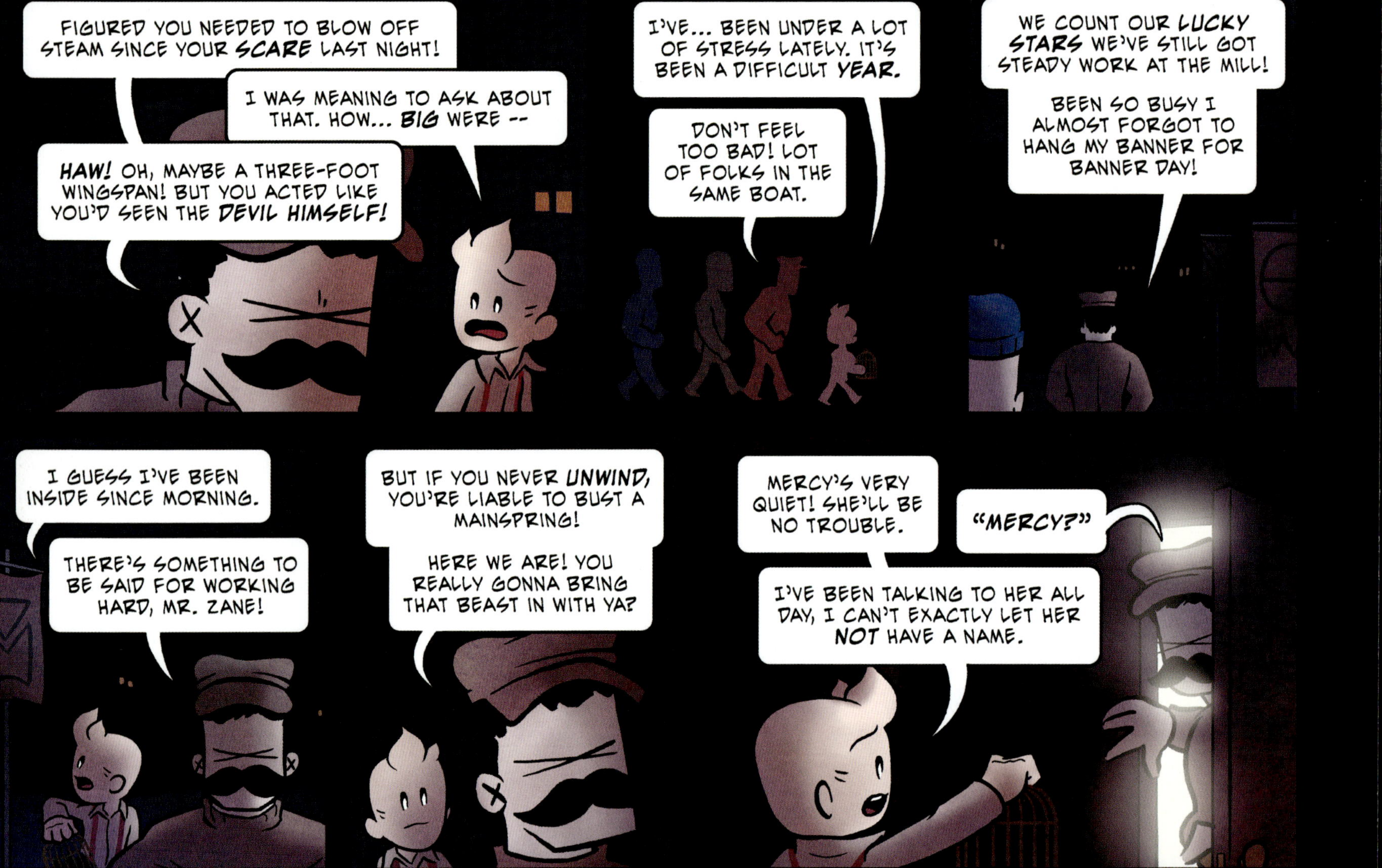
FIGURED YOU NEEDED TO BLOW OFF STEAM SINCE YOUR SCARE LAST NIGHT!
I WAS MEANING TO ASK ABOUT THAT. HOW... BIG WERE --
HAW! OH, MAYBE A THREE-FOOT WINGSPAN! BUT YOU ACTED LIKE YOU'D SEEN THE DEVIL HIMSELF!
I'VE... BEEN UNDER A LOT OF STRESS LATELY. IT'S BEEN A DIFFICULT YEAR.
DON'T FEEL TOO BAD! LOT OF FOLKS IN THE SAME BOAT.
WE COUNT OUR LUCKY STARS WE'VE STILL GOT STEADY WORK AT THE MILL!
BEEN SO BUSY I ALMOST FORGOT TO HANG MY BANNER FOR BANNER DAY!
I GUESS I'VE BEEN INSIDE SINCE MORNING.
THERE'S SOMETHING TO BE SAID FOR WORKING HARD, MR. ZANE!
BUT IF YOU NEVER UNWIND, YOU'RE LIABLE TO BUST A MAINSPRING!
HERE WE ARE! YOU REALLY GONNA BRING THAT BEAST IN WITH YA?
MERCY'S VERY QUIET! SHE'LL BE NO TROUBLE.
"MERCY?"
I'VE BEEN TALKING TO HER ALL DAY, I CAN'T EXACTLY LET HER NOT HAVE A NAME.

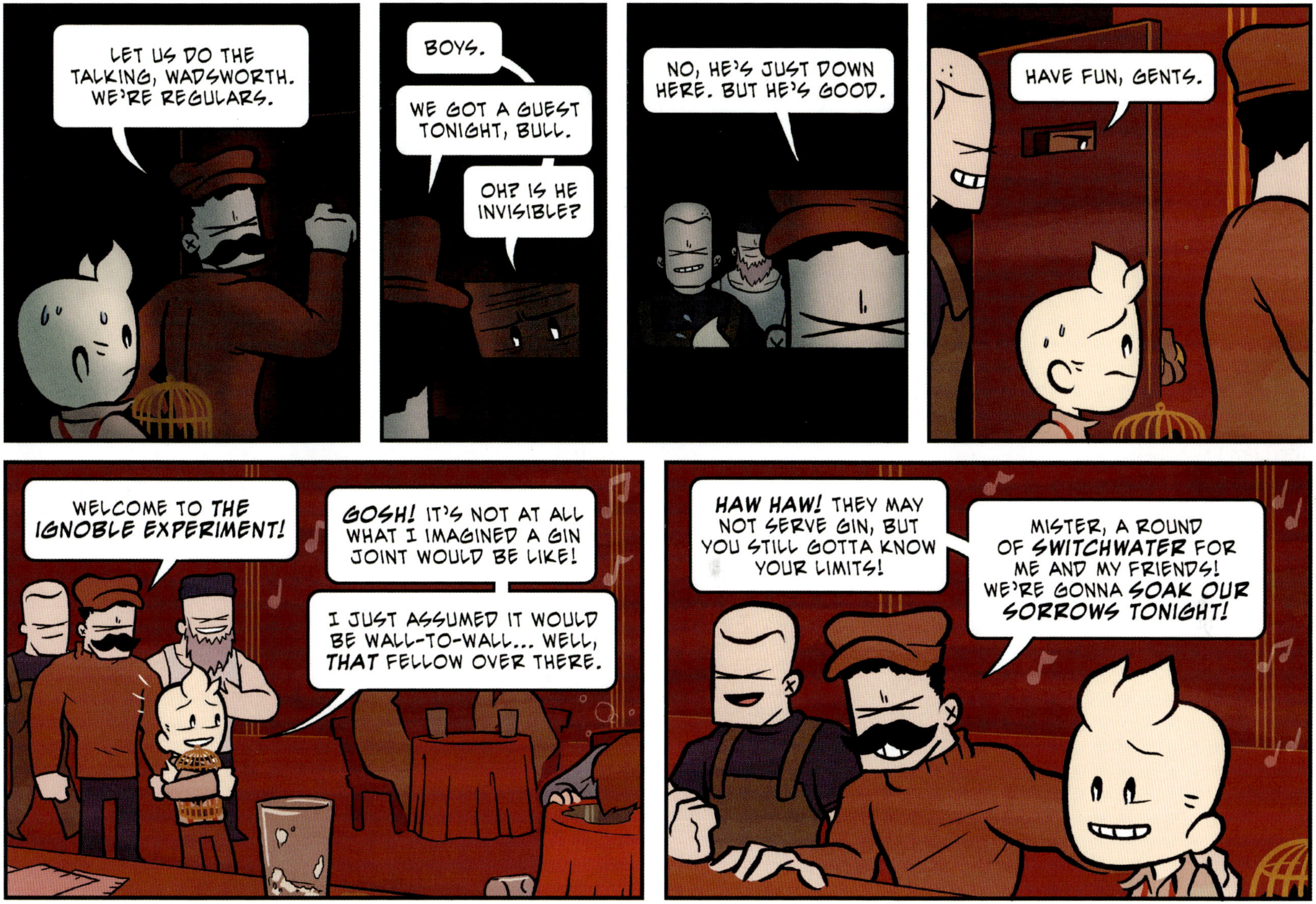
LET US DO THE TALKING, WADSWORTH. WE'RE REGULARS.
BOYS.
WE GOT A GUEST TONIGHT, BULL.
OH? IS HE INVISIBLE?
NO, HE'S JUST DOWN HERE. BUT HE'S GOOD.
HAVE FUN, GENTS.
WELCOME TO THE IGNOBLE EXPERIMENT!
GOSH! IT'S NOT AT ALL WHAT I IMAGINED A GIN JOINT WOULD BE LIKE!
I JUST ASSUMED IT WOULD BE WALL-TO-WALL... WELL, THAT FELLOW OVER THERE.
HAW HAW! THEY MAY NOT SERVE GIN, BUT YOU STILL GOTTA KNOW YOUR LIMITS!
MISTER, A ROUND OF SWITCHWATER FOR ME AND MY FRIENDS! WE'RE GONNA SOAK OUR SORROWS TONIGHT!

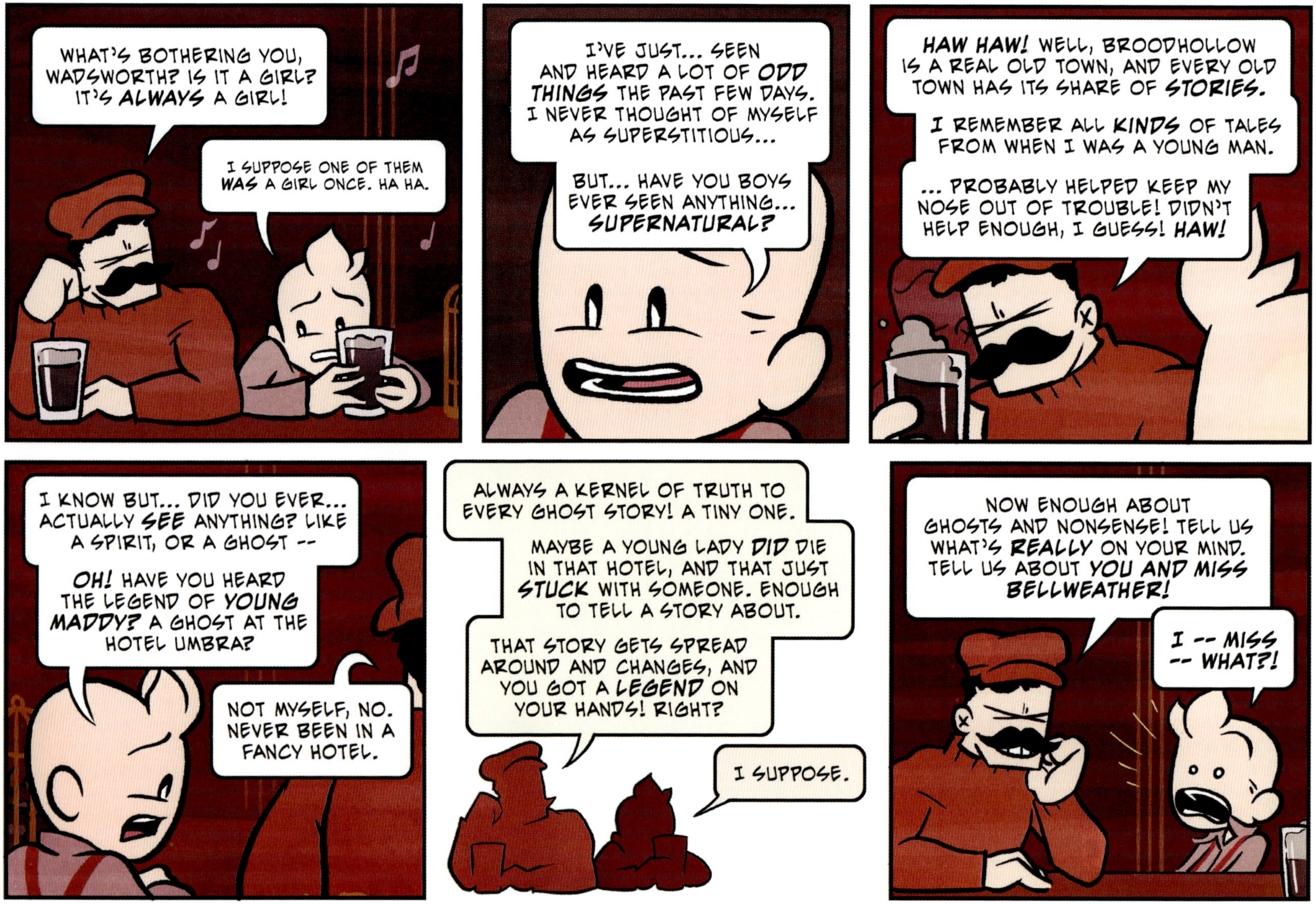

WHAT'S BOTHERING YOU, WADSWORTH? IS IT A GIRL? IT'S ALWAYS A GIRL!
I SUPPOSE ONE OF THEM WAS A GIRL ONCE. HA HA.
I'VE JUST... SEEN AND HEARD A LOT OF ODD THINGS THE PAST FEW DAYS. I NEVER THOUGHT OF MYSELF AS SUPERSTITIOUS...
BUT... HAVE YOU BOYS EVER SEEN ANYTHING... SUPERNATURAL?
HAW HAW! WELL, BROODHOLLOW IS A REAL OLD TOWN, AND EVERY OLD TOWN HAS ITS SHARE OF STORIES.
I REMEMBER ALL KINDS OF TALES FROM WHEN I WAS A YOUNG MAN.
... PROBABLY HELPED KEEP MY NOSE OUT OF TROUBLE! DIDN'T HELP ENOUGH, I GUESS! HAW!
I KNOW BUT... DID YOU EVER... ACTUALLY SEE ANYTHING? LIKE A SPIRIT, OR A GHOST --
OH! HAVE YOU HEARD THE LEGEND OF YOUNG MADDY? A GHOST AT THE HOTEL UMBRA?
NOT MYSELF, NO. NEVER BEEN IN A FANCY HOTEL.
ALWAYS A KERNEL OF TRUTH TO EVERY GHOST STORY! A TINY ONE.
MAYBE A YOUNG LADY DID DIE IN THAT HOTEL, AND THAT JUST STUCK WITH SOMEONE. ENOUGH TO TELL A STORY ABOUT.
THAT STORY GETS SPREAD AROUND AND CHANGES, AND YOU GOT A LEGEND ON YOUR HANDS! RIGHT?
I SUPPOSE.
NOW ENOUGH ABOUT GHOSTS AND NONSENSE! TELL US WHAT'S REALLY ON YOUR MIND. TELL US ABOUT YOU AND MISS BELLWEATHER!
I -- MISS -- WHAT?!

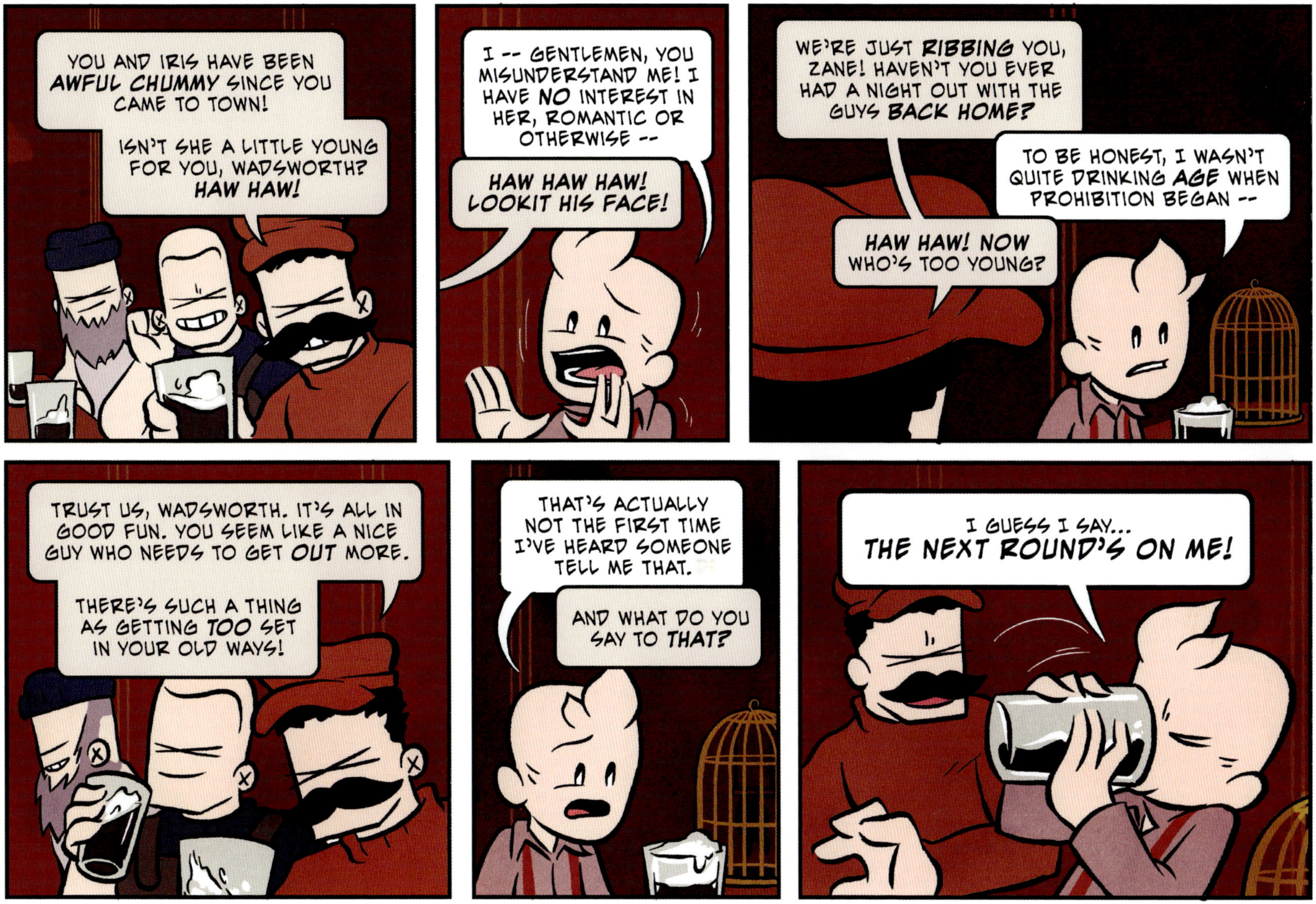
YOU AND IRIS HAVE BEEN AWFUL CHUMMY SINCE YOU CAME TO TOWN!
ISN'T SHE A LITTLE YOUNG FOR YOU, WADSWORTH? HAW HAW!
I -- GENTLEMEN, YOU MISUNDERSTAND ME! I HAVE NO INTEREST IN HER, ROMANTIC OR OTHERWISE --
HAW HAW HAW! LOOKIT HIS FACE!
WE'RE JUST RIBBING YOU, ZANE! HAVEN'T YOU EVER HAD A NIGHT OUT WITH THE GUYS BACK HOME?
TO BE HONEST, I WASN'T QUITE DRINKING AGE WHEN PROHIBITION BEGAN --
HAW HAW! NOW WHO'S TOO YOUNG?
TRUST US, WADSWORTH. IT'S ALL IN GOOD FUN. YOU SEEM LIKE A NICE GUY WHO NEEDS TO GET OUT MORE.
THERE'S SUCH A THING AS GETTING TOO SET IN YOUR OLD WAYS!
THAT'S ACTUALLY NOT THE FIRST TIME I'VE HEARD SOMEONE TELL ME THAT.
AND WHAT DO YOU SAY TO THAT?
I GUESS I SAY... THE NEXT ROUND'S ON ME!

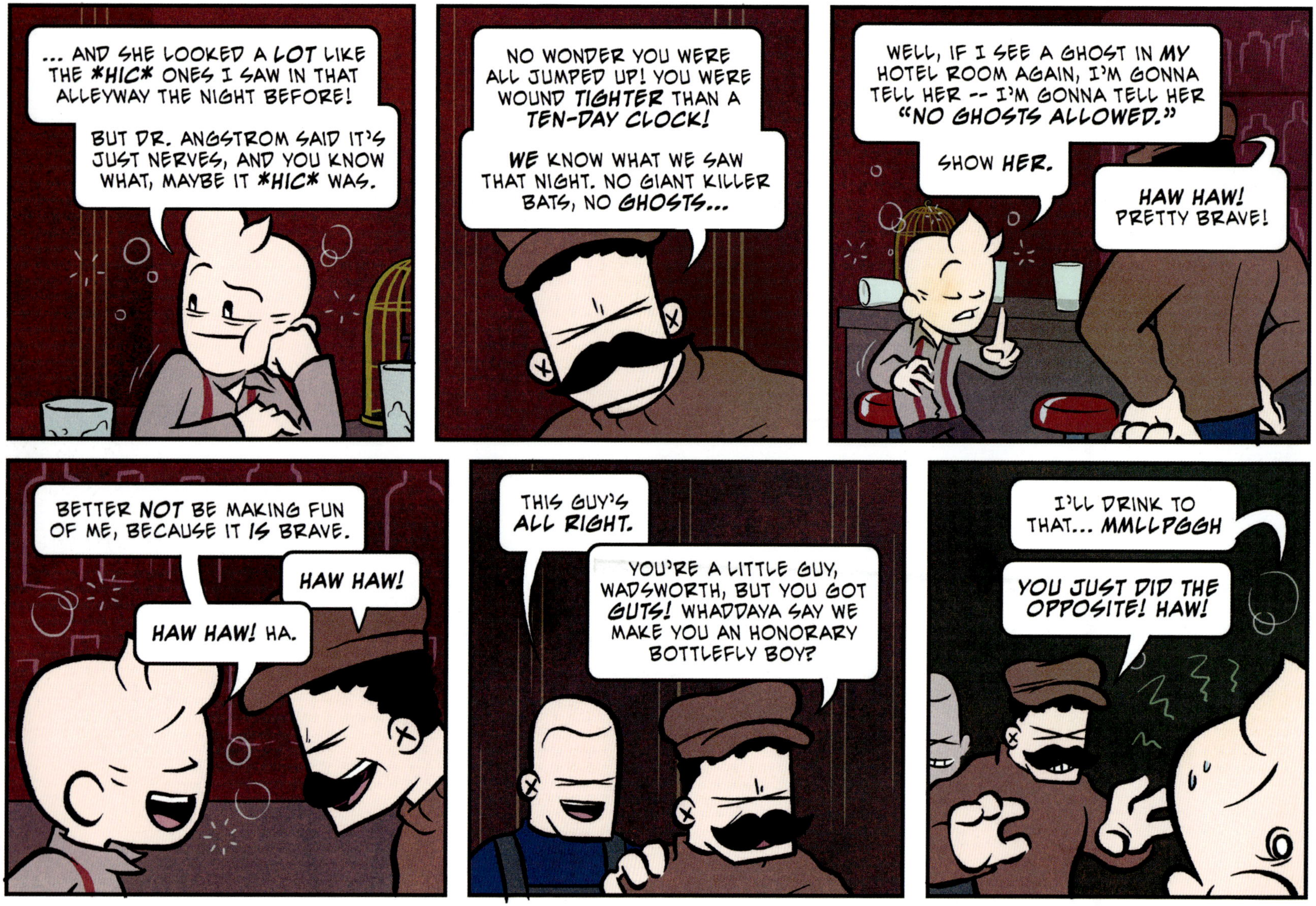
... AND SHE LOOKED A LOT LIKE THE *HIC* ONES I SAW IN THAT ALLEYWAY THE NIGHT BEFORE!
BUT DR. ANGSTROM SAID IT'S JUST NERVES, AND YOU KNOW WHAT, MAYBE IT *HIC* WAS.
NO WONDER YOU WERE ALL JUMPED UP! YOU WERE WOUND TIGHTER THAN A TEN-DAY CLOCK!
WE KNOW WHAT WE SAW THAT NIGHT. NO GIANT KILLER BATS, NO GHOSTS...
WELL, IF I SEE A GHOST IN MY HOTEL ROOM AGAIN, I'M GONNA TELL HER -- I'M GONNA TELL HER "NO GHOSTS ALLOWED."
SHOW HER.
HAW HAW! PRETTY BRAVE!
BETTER NOT BE MAKING FUN OF ME, BECAUSE IT IS BRAVE.
HAW HAW!
HAW HAW! HA.
THIS GUY'S ALL RIGHT.
YOU'RE A LITTLE GUY, WADSWORTH, BUT YOU GOT GUTS! WHADDAYA SAY WE MAKE YOU AN HONORARY BOTTLEFLY BOY?
I'LL DRINK TO THAT... MMLLPGGH
YOU JUST DID THE OPPOSITE! HAW!

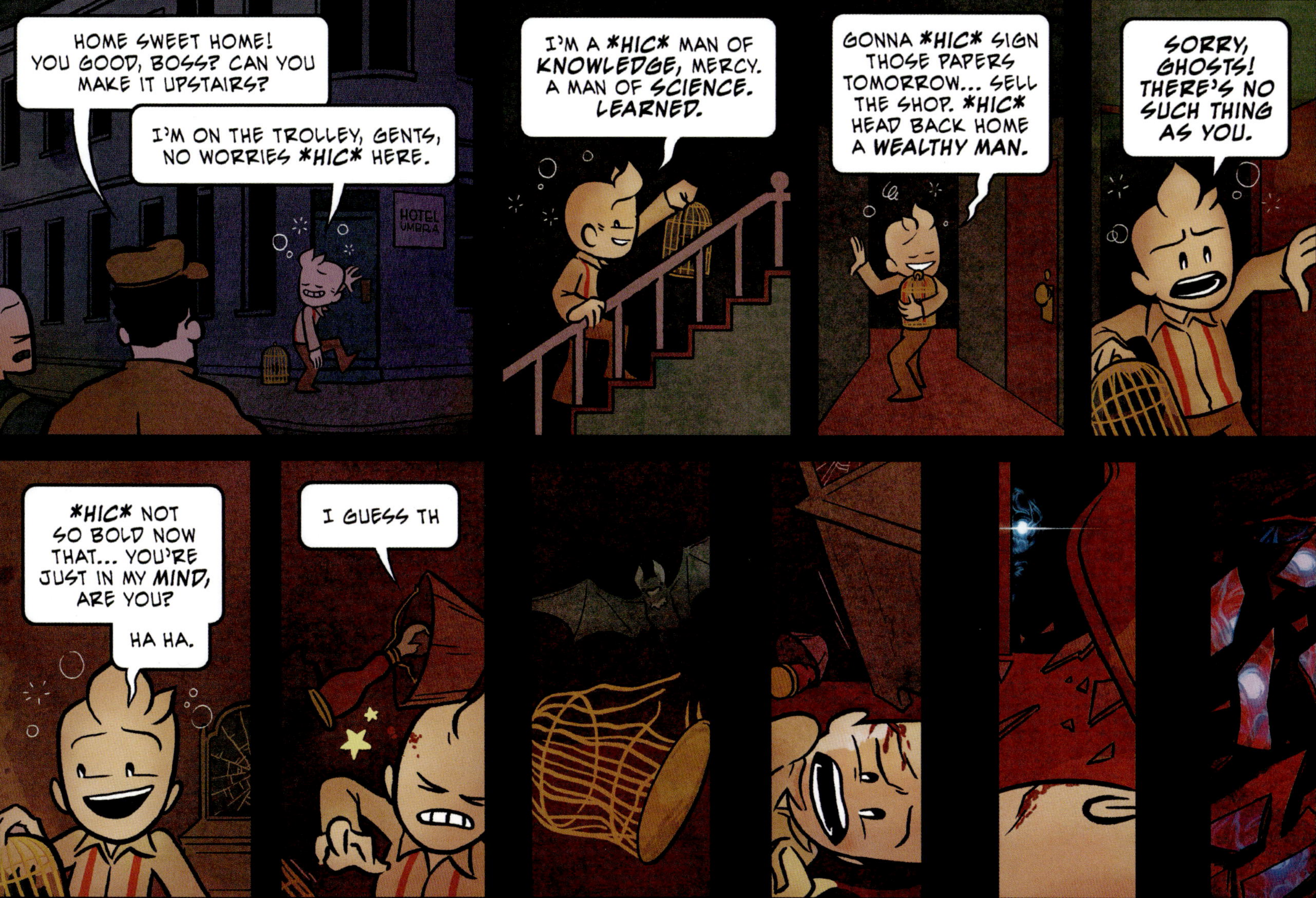
HOME SWEET HOME! YOU GOOD, BOSS? CAN YOU MAKE IT UPSTAIRS?
I'M ON THE TROLLEY, GENTS, NO WORRIES *HIC* HERE.
HOTEL UMBRA
I'M A *HIC* MAN OF KNOWLEDGE, MERCY. A MAN OF SCIENCE. LEARNED.
GONNA *HIC* SIGN THOSE PAPERS TOMORROW... SELL THE SHOP. *HIC* HEAD BACK HOME A WEALTHY MAN.
SORRY, GHOSTS! THERE'S NO SUCH THING AS YOU.
HIC NOT SO BOLD NOW THAT... YOU'RE JUST IN MY MIND, ARE YOU?
HA HA.
I GUESS TH

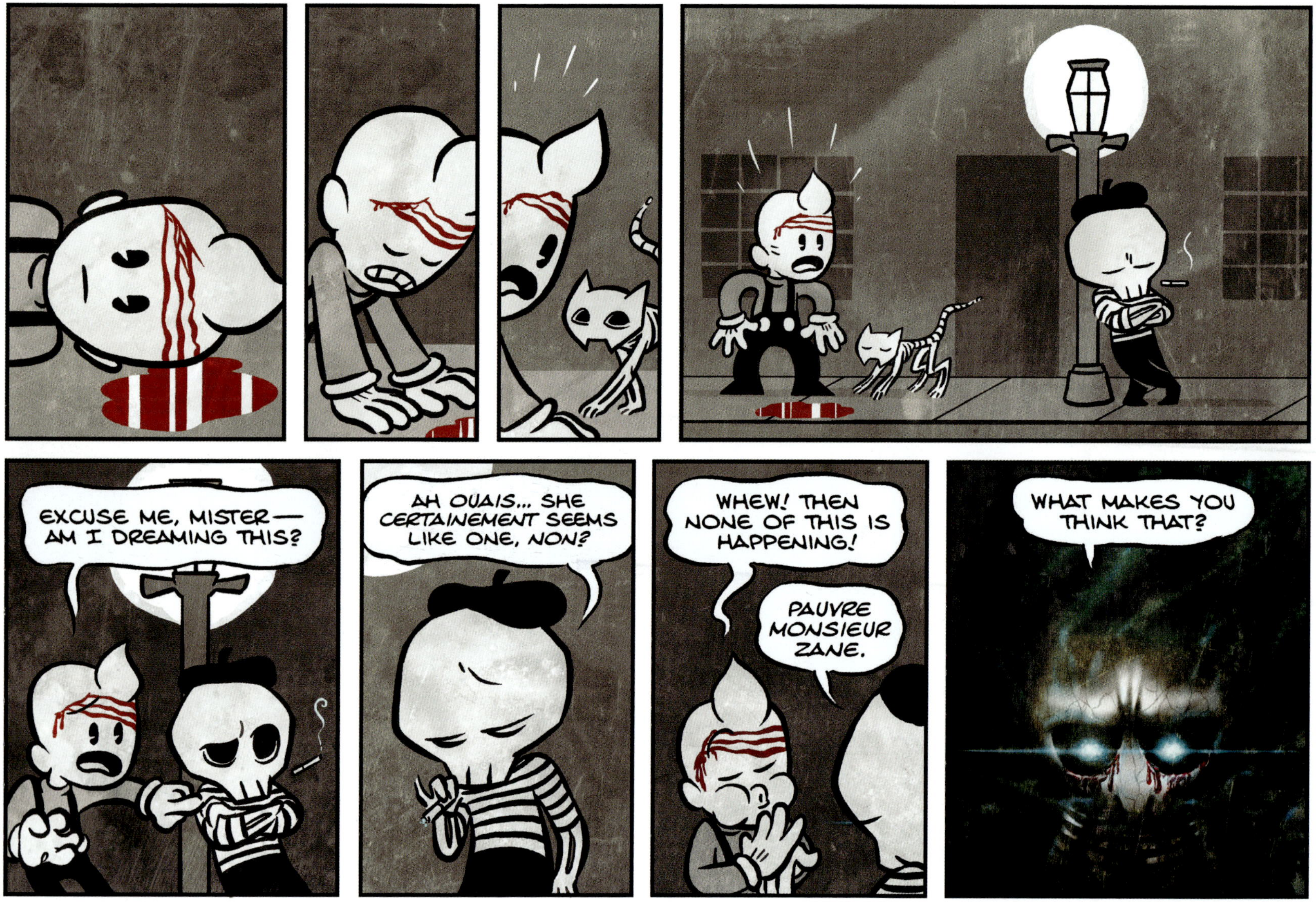
EXCUSE ME, MISTER— AM I DREAMING THIS?
AH OUAIS... SHE CERTAINEMENT SEEMS LIKE ONE, NON?
WHEW! THEN NONE OF THIS IS HAPPENING!
PAUVRE MONSIEUR ZANE.
WHAT MAKES YOU THINK THAT?

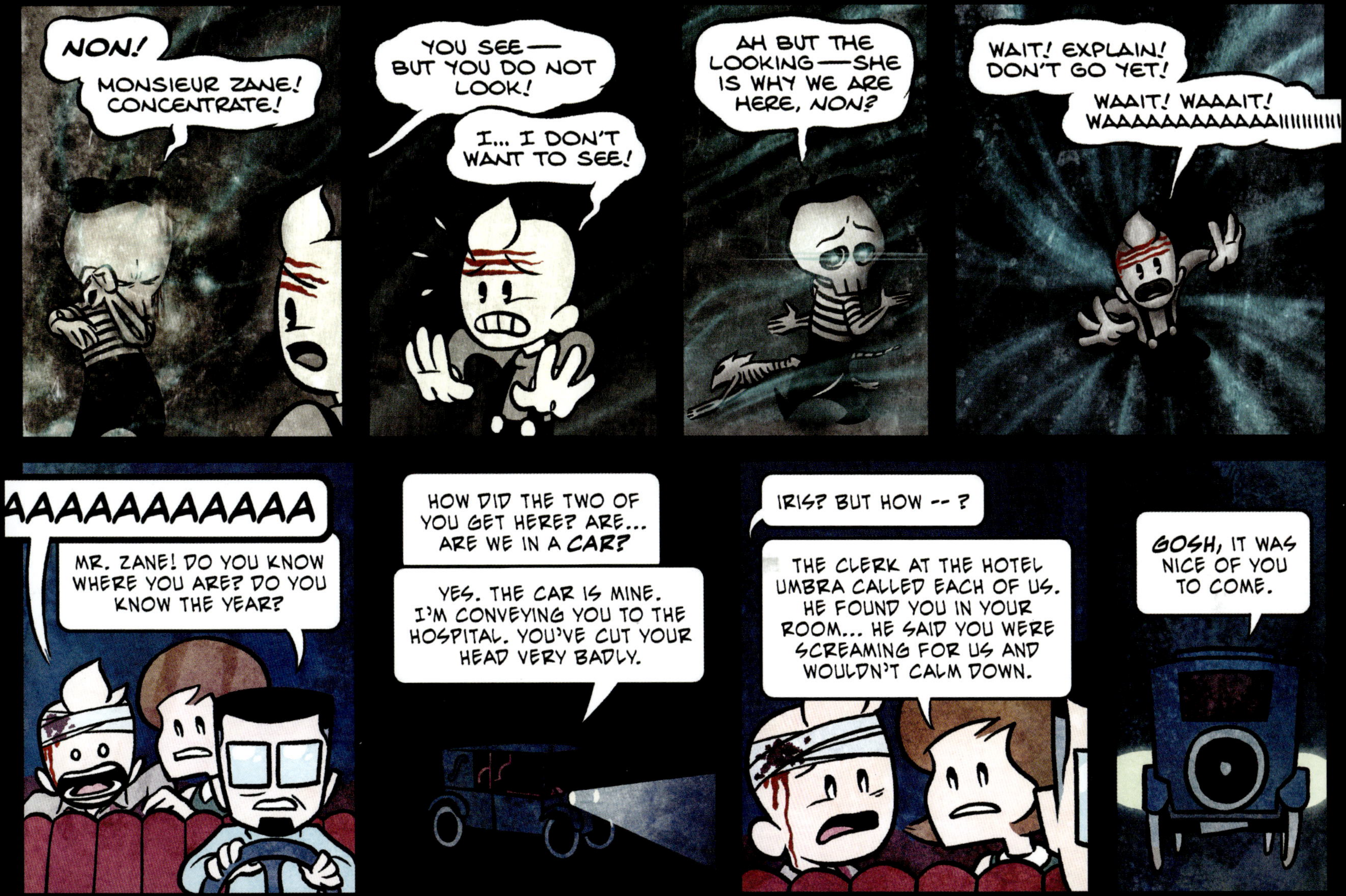
NON!
MONSIEUR ZANE! CONCENTRATE!
YOU SEE— BUT YOU DO NOT LOOK!
I... I DON'T WANT TO SEE!
AH BUT THE LOOKING—SHE IS WHY WE ARE HERE, NON?
WAIT! EXPLAIN! DON'T GO YET!
WAAIT! WAAAIT! WAAAAAAAAAAAAAIIIIIIIIII
AAAAAAAAAAAA
MR. ZANE! DO YOU KNOW WHERE YOU ARE? DO YOU KNOW THE YEAR?
HOW DID THE TWO OF YOU GET HERE? ARE... ARE WE IN A CAR?
YES. THE CAR IS MINE. I'M CONVEYING YOU TO THE HOSPITAL. YOU'VE CUT YOUR HEAD VERY BADLY.
IRIS? BUT HOW -- ?
THE CLERK AT THE HOTEL UMBRA CALLED EACH OF US. HE FOUND YOU IN YOUR ROOM... HE SAID YOU WERE SCREAMING FOR US AND WOULDN'T CALM DOWN.
GOSH, IT WAS NICE OF YOU TO COME.

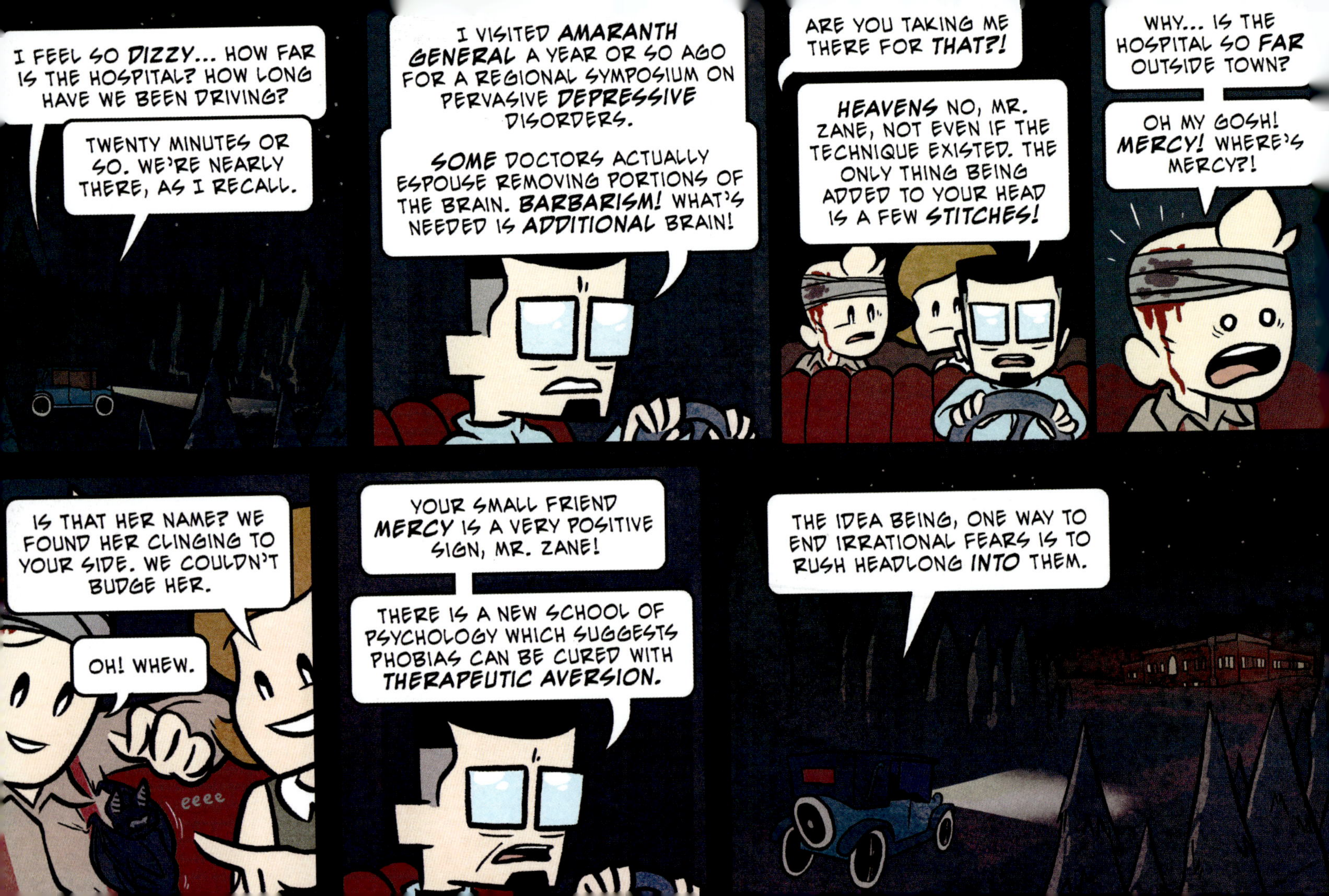
I FEEL SO DIZZY... HOW FAR IS THE HOSPITAL? HOW LONG HAVE WE BEEN DRIVING?
TWENTY MINUTES OR SO. WE'RE NEARLY THERE, AS I RECALL.
I VISITED AMARANTH GENERAL A YEAR OR SO AGO FOR A REGIONAL SYMPOSIUM ON PERVASIVE DEPRESSIVE DISORDERS.
SOME DOCTORS ACTUALLY ESPOUSE REMOVING PORTIONS OF THE BRAIN. BARBARISM! WHAT'S NEEDED IS ADDITIONAL BRAIN!
ARE YOU TAKING ME THERE FOR THAT?!
HEAVENS NO, MR. ZANE, NOT EVEN IF THE TECHNIQUE EXISTED. THE ONLY THING BEING ADDED TO YOUR HEAD IS A FEW STITCHES!
WHY... IS THE HOSPITAL SO FAR OUTSIDE TOWN?
OH MY GOSH! MERCY! WHERE'S MERCY?!
IS THAT HER NAME? WE FOUND HER CLINGING TO YOUR SIDE. WE COULDN'T BUDGE HER.
OH! WHEW.
eeee
YOUR SMALL FRIEND MERCY IS A VERY POSITIVE SIGN, MR. ZANE!
THERE IS A NEW SCHOOL OF PSYCHOLOGY WHICH SUGGESTS PHOBIAS CAN BE CURED WITH THERAPEUTIC AVERSION.
THE IDEA BEING, ONE WAY TO END IRRATIONAL FEARS IS TO RUSH HEADLONG INTO THEM.

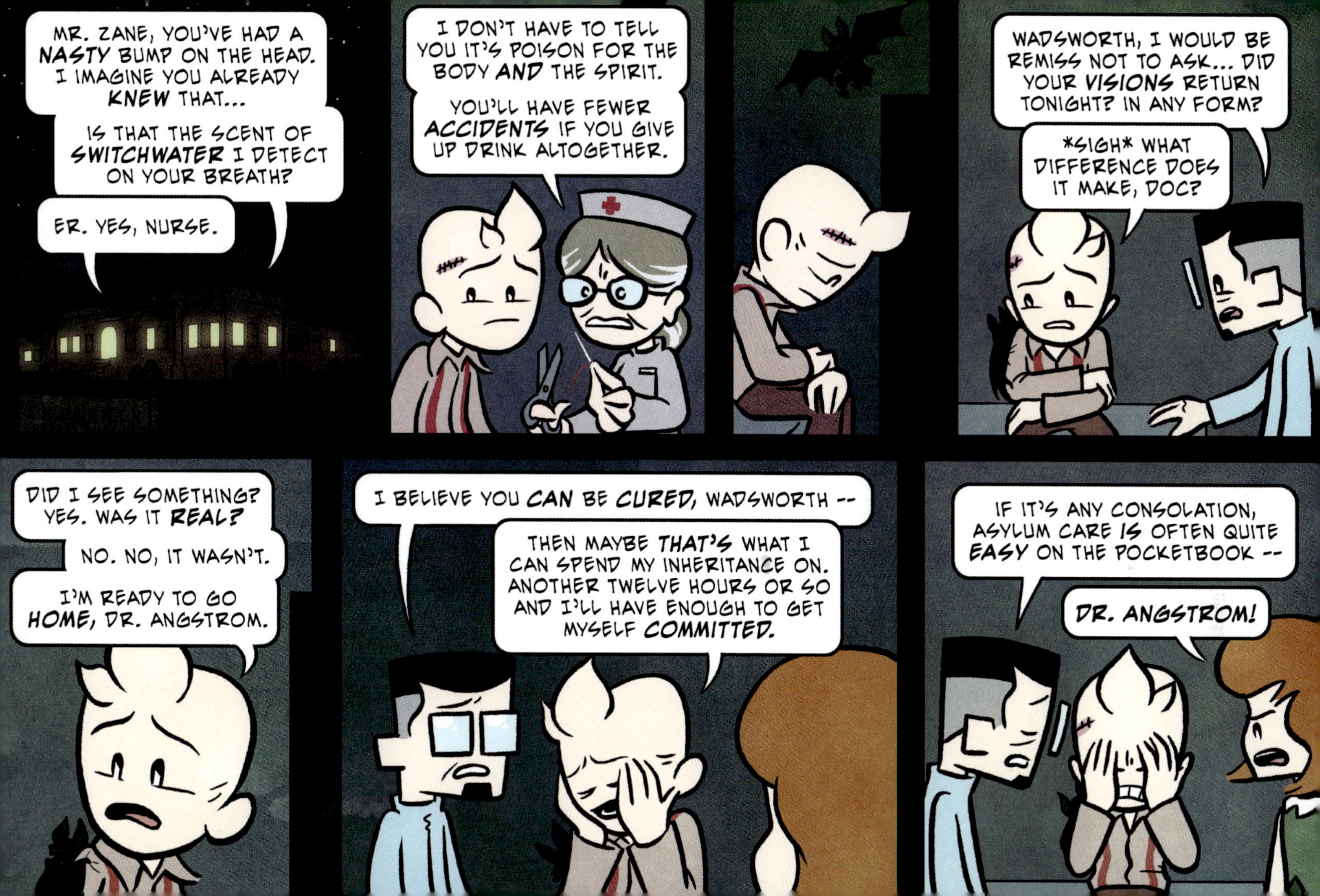

MR. ZANE, YOU'VE HAD A NASTY BUMP ON THE HEAD. I IMAGINE YOU ALREADY KNEW THAT...
IS THAT THE SCENT OF SWITCHWATER I DETECT ON YOUR BREATH?
ER. YES, NURSE.
I DON'T HAVE TO TELL YOU IT'S POISON FOR THE BODY AND THE SPIRIT.
YOU'LL HAVE FEWER ACCIDENTS IF YOU GIVE UP DRINK ALTOGETHER.
WADSWORTH, I WOULD BE REMISS NOT TO ASK... DID YOUR VISIONS RETURN TONIGHT? IN ANY FORM?
SIGH WHAT DIFFERENCE DOES IT MAKE, DOC?
DID I SEE SOMETHING? YES. WAS IT REAL?
NO. NO, IT WASN'T.
I'M READY TO GO HOME, DR. ANGSTROM.
I BELIEVE YOU CAN BE CURED, WADSWORTH --
THEN MAYBE THAT'S WHAT I CAN SPEND MY INHERITANCE ON. ANOTHER TWELVE HOURS OR SO AND I'LL HAVE ENOUGH TO GET MYSELF COMMITTED.
IF IT'S ANY CONSOLATION, ASYLUM CARE IS OFTEN QUITE EASY ON THE POCKETBOOK --
DR. ANGSTROM!

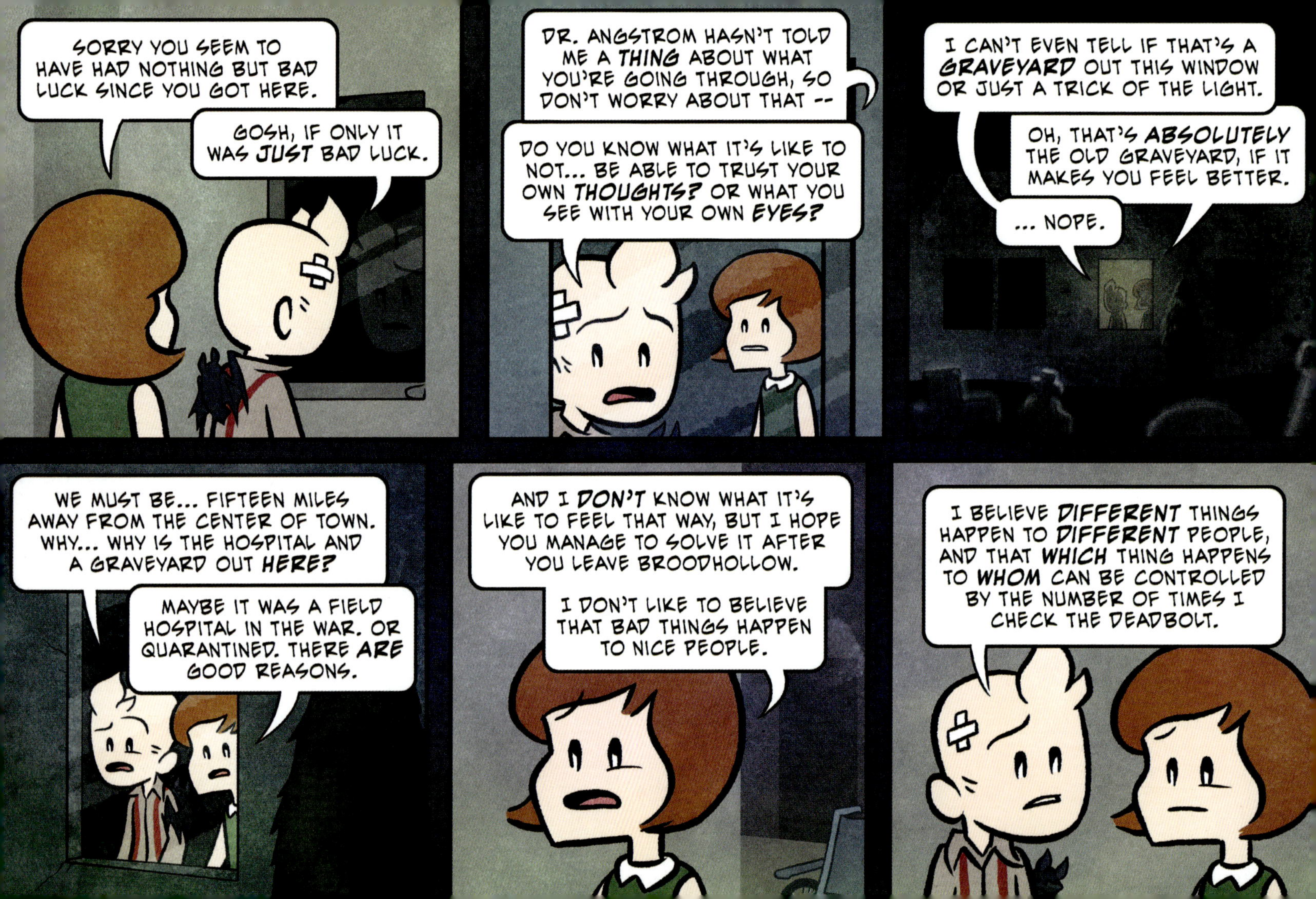
SORRY YOU SEEM TO HAVE HAD NOTHING BUT BAD LUCK SINCE YOU GOT HERE.
GOSH, IF ONLY IT WAS JUST BAD LUCK.
DR. ANGSTROM HASN'T TOLD ME A THING ABOUT WHAT YOU'RE GOING THROUGH, SO DON'T WORRY ABOUT THAT --
DO YOU KNOW WHAT IT'S LIKE TO NOT... BE ABLE TO TRUST YOUR OWN THOUGHTS? OR WHAT YOU SEE WITH YOUR OWN EYES?
I CAN'T EVEN TELL IF THAT'S A GRAVEYARD OUT THIS WINDOW OR JUST A TRICK OF THE LIGHT.
OH, THAT'S ABSOLUTELY THE OLD GRAVEYARD, IF IT MAKES YOU FEEL BETTER.
... NOPE.
WE MUST BE... FIFTEEN MILES AWAY FROM THE CENTER OF TOWN. WHY... WHY IS THE HOSPITAL AND A GRAVEYARD OUT HERE?
MAYBE IT WAS A FIELD HOSPITAL IN THE WAR. OR QUARANTINED. THERE ARE GOOD REASONS.
AND I DON'T KNOW WHAT IT'S LIKE TO FEEL THAT WAY, BUT I HOPE YOU MANAGE TO SOLVE IT AFTER YOU LEAVE BROODHOLLOW.
I DON'T LIKE TO BELIEVE THAT BAD THINGS HAPPEN TO NICE PEOPLE.
I BELIEVE DIFFERENT THINGS HAPPEN TO DIFFERENT PEOPLE, AND THAT WHICH THING HAPPENS TO WHOM CAN BE CONTROLLED BY THE NUMBER OF TIMES I CHECK THE DEADBOLT.

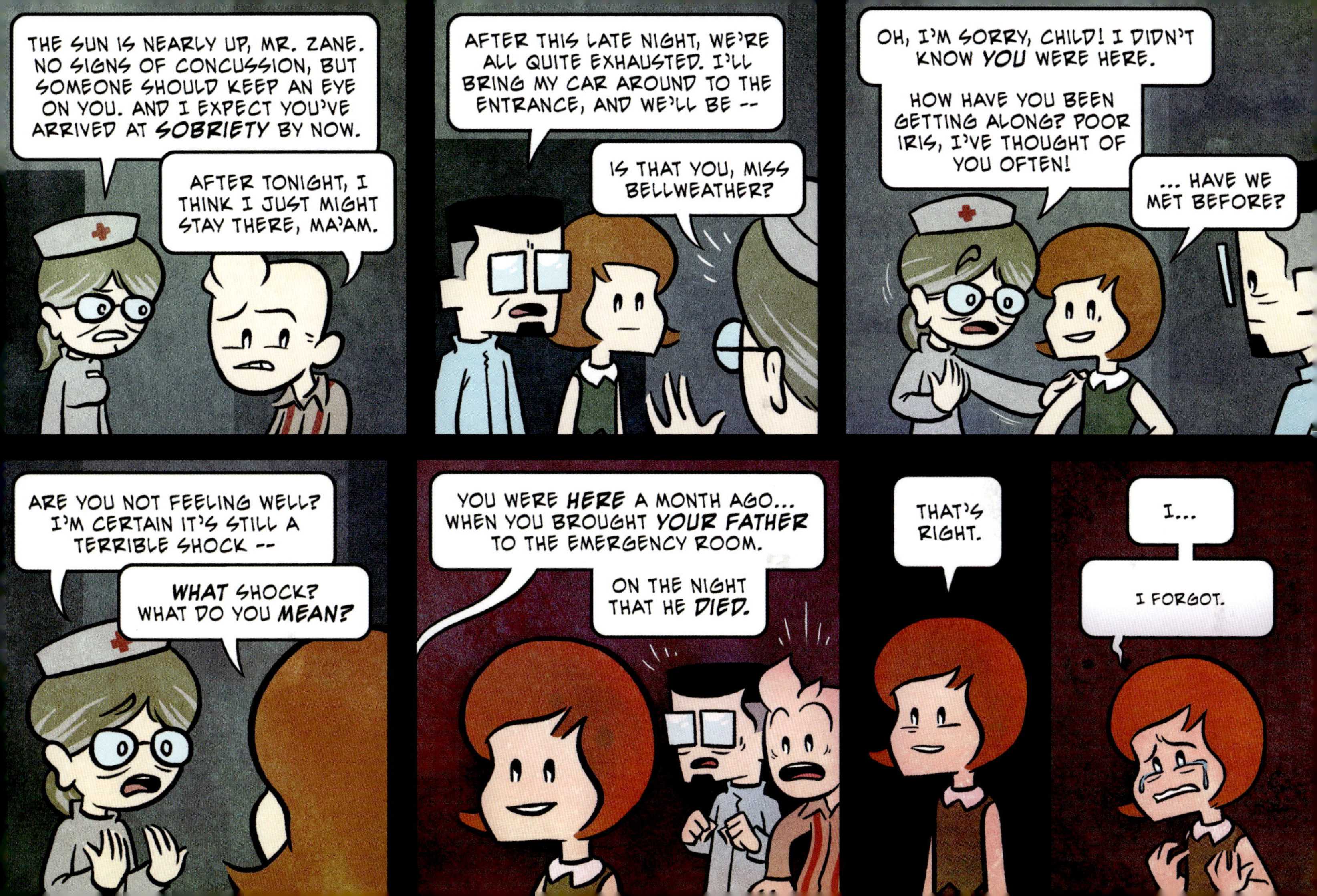
THE SUN IS NEARLY UP, MR. ZANE. NO SIGNS OF CONCUSSION, BUT SOMEONE SHOULD KEEP AN EYE ON YOU. AND I EXPECT YOU'VE ARRIVED AT *SOBRIETY* BY NOW.
AFTER TONIGHT, I THINK I JUST MIGHT STAY THERE, MA'AM.
AFTER THIS LATE NIGHT, WE'RE ALL QUITE EXHAUSTED. I'LL BRING MY CAR AROUND TO THE ENTRANCE, AND WE'LL BE --
IS THAT YOU, MISS BELLWEATHER?
OH, I'M SORRY, CHILD! I DIDN'T KNOW *YOU* WERE HERE.
HOW HAVE YOU BEEN GETTING ALONG? POOR IRIS, I'VE THOUGHT OF YOU OFTEN!
... HAVE WE MET BEFORE?
ARE YOU NOT FEELING WELL? I'M CERTAIN IT'S STILL A TERRIBLE SHOCK --
WHAT SHOCK? WHAT DO YOU *MEAN?*
YOU WERE *HERE* A MONTH AGO... WHEN YOU BROUGHT *YOUR FATHER* TO THE EMERGENCY ROOM.
ON THE NIGHT THAT HE *DIED.*
THAT'S RIGHT.
I...
I FORGOT.

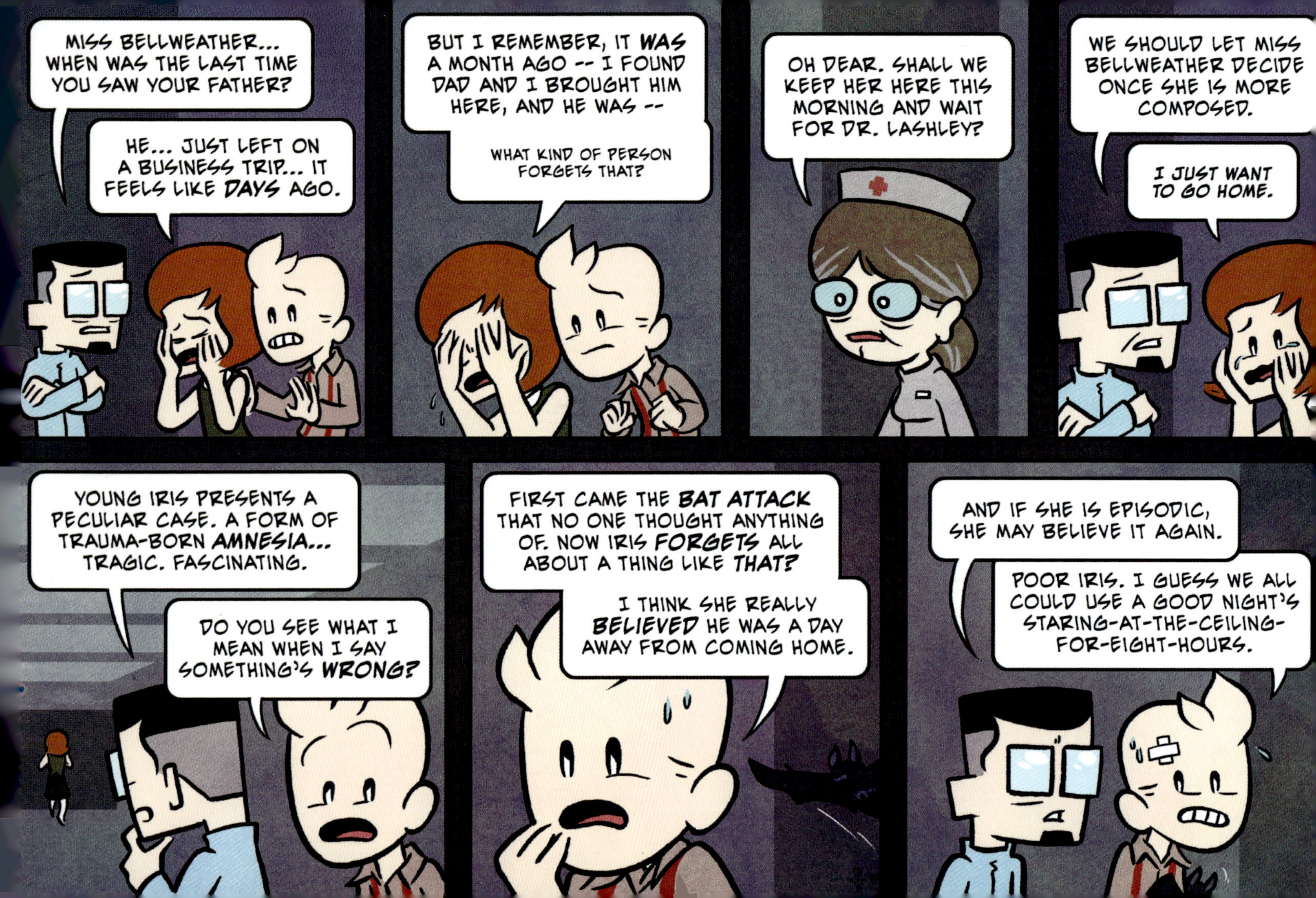
MISS BELLWEATHER... WHEN WAS THE LAST TIME YOU SAW YOUR FATHER?
HE... JUST LEFT ON A BUSINESS TRIP... IT FEELS LIKE DAYS AGO.
BUT I REMEMBER, IT WAS A MONTH AGO -- I FOUND DAD AND I BROUGHT HIM HERE, AND HE WAS --
WHAT KIND OF PERSON FORGETS THAT?
OH DEAR. SHALL WE KEEP HER HERE THIS MORNING AND WAIT FOR DR. LASHLEY?
WE SHOULD LET MISS BELLWEATHER DECIDE ONCE SHE IS MORE COMPOSED.
I JUST WANT TO GO HOME.
YOUNG IRIS PRESENTS A PECULIAR CASE. A FORM OF TRAUMA-BORN AMNESIA... TRAGIC. FASCINATING.
DO YOU SEE WHAT I MEAN WHEN I SAY SOMETHING'S WRONG?
FIRST CAME THE BAT ATTACK THAT NO ONE THOUGHT ANYTHING OF. NOW IRIS FORGETS ALL ABOUT A THING LIKE THAT?
I THINK SHE REALLY BELIEVED HE WAS A DAY AWAY FROM COMING HOME.
AND IF SHE IS EPISODIC, SHE MAY BELIEVE IT AGAIN.
POOR IRIS. I GUESS WE ALL COULD USE A GOOD NIGHT'S STARING-AT-THE-CEILING-FOR-EIGHT-HOURS.

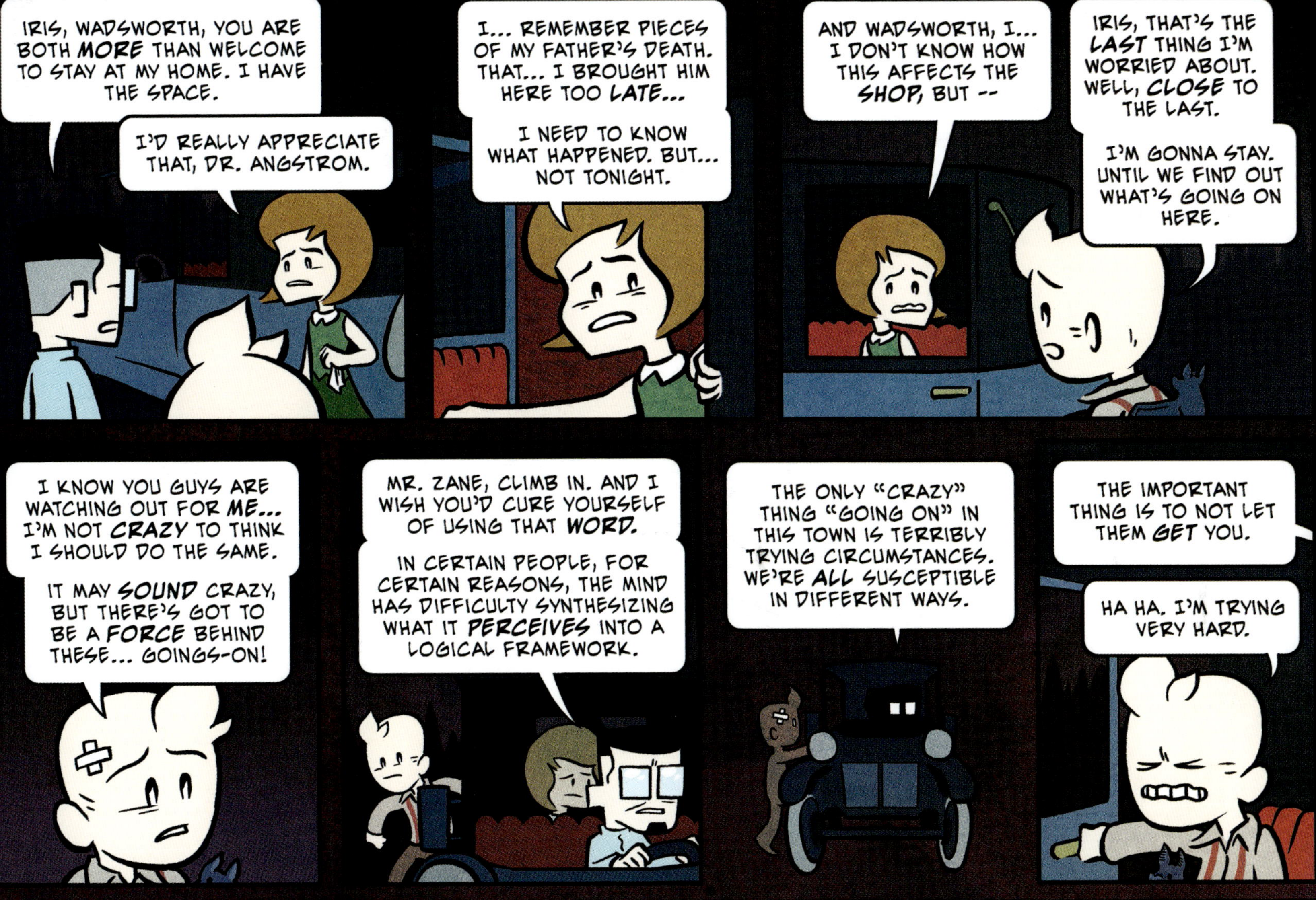
IRIS, WADSWORTH, YOU ARE BOTH MORE THAN WELCOME TO STAY AT MY HOME. I HAVE THE SPACE.
I'D REALLY APPRECIATE THAT, DR. ANGSTROM.
I... REMEMBER PIECES OF MY FATHER'S DEATH. THAT... I BROUGHT HIM HERE TOO LATE...
I NEED TO KNOW WHAT HAPPENED. BUT... NOT TONIGHT.
AND WADSWORTH, I... I DON'T KNOW HOW THIS AFFECTS THE SHOP, BUT --
IRIS, THAT'S THE LAST THING I'M WORRIED ABOUT. WELL, CLOSE TO THE LAST.
I'M GONNA STAY. UNTIL WE FIND OUT WHAT'S GOING ON HERE.
I KNOW YOU GUYS ARE WATCHING OUT FOR ME... I'M NOT CRAZY TO THINK I SHOULD DO THE SAME.
IT MAY SOUND CRAZY, BUT THERE'S GOT TO BE A FORCE BEHIND THESE... GOINGS-ON!
MR. ZANE, CLIMB IN. AND I WISH YOU'D CURE YOURSELF OF USING THAT WORD.
IN CERTAIN PEOPLE, FOR CERTAIN REASONS, THE MIND HAS DIFFICULTY SYNTHESIZING WHAT IT PERCEIVES INTO A LOGICAL FRAMEWORK.
THE ONLY "CRAZY" THING "GOING ON" IN THIS TOWN IS TERRIBLY TRYING CIRCUMSTANCES. WE'RE ALL SUSCEPTIBLE IN DIFFERENT WAYS.
THE IMPORTANT THING IS TO NOT LET THEM GET YOU.
HA HA. I'M TRYING VERY HARD.

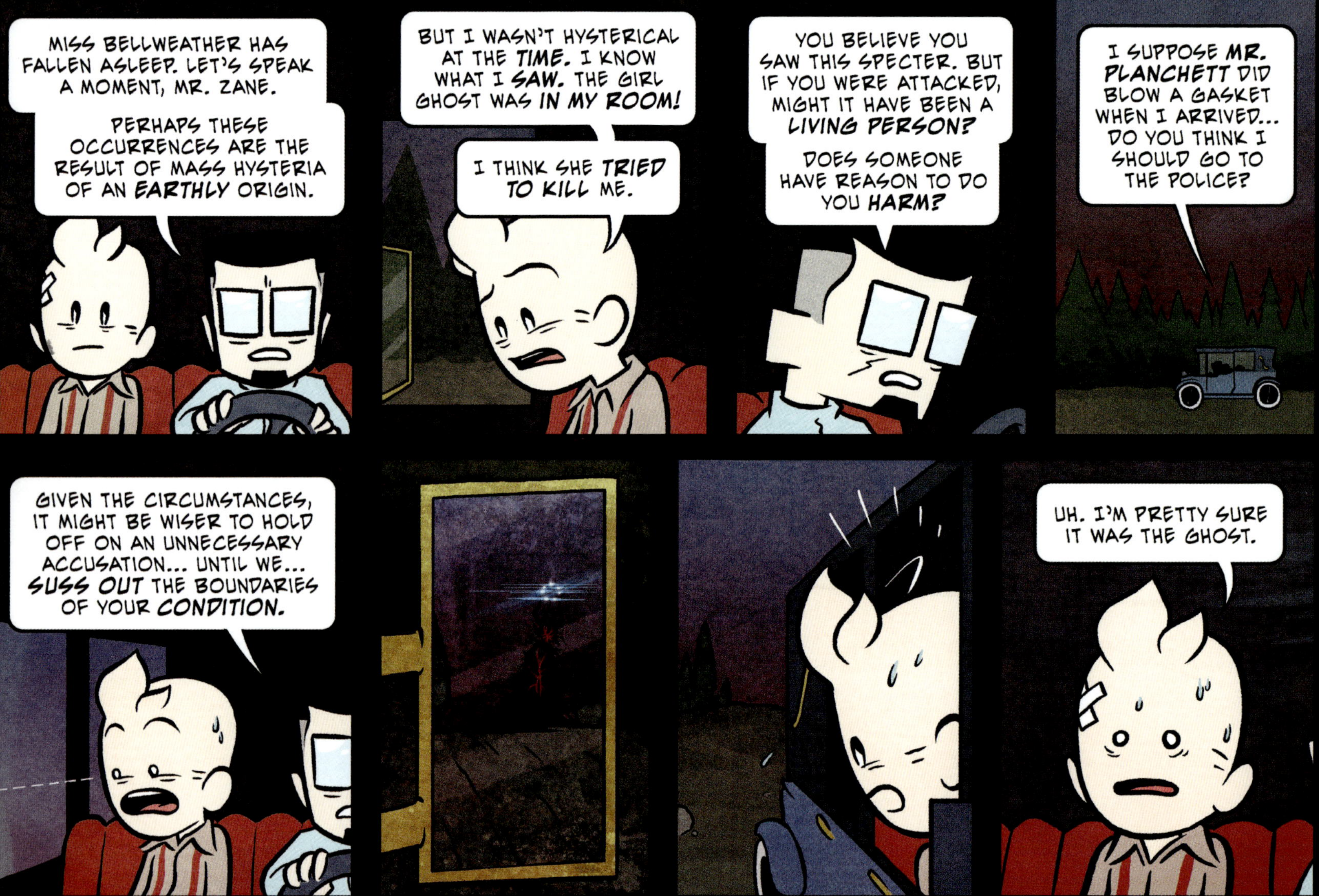
MISS BELLWEATHER HAS FALLEN ASLEEP. LET'S SPEAK A MOMENT, MR. ZANE.
PERHAPS THESE OCCURRENCES ARE THE RESULT OF MASS HYSTERIA OF AN EARTHLY ORIGIN.
BUT I WASN'T HYSTERICAL AT THE TIME. I KNOW WHAT I SAW. THE GIRL GHOST WAS IN MY ROOM!
I THINK SHE TRIED TO KILL ME.
YOU BELIEVE YOU SAW THIS SPECTER. BUT IF YOU WERE ATTACKED, MIGHT IT HAVE BEEN A LIVING PERSON?
DOES SOMEONE HAVE REASON TO DO YOU HARM?
I SUPPOSE MR. PLANCHETT DID BLOW A GASKET WHEN I ARRIVED... DO YOU THINK I SHOULD GO TO THE POLICE?
GIVEN THE CIRCUMSTANCES, IT MIGHT BE WISER TO HOLD OFF ON AN UNNECESSARY ACCUSATION... UNTIL WE... SUSS OUT THE BOUNDARIES OF YOUR CONDITION.
UH. I'M PRETTY SURE IT WAS THE GHOST.

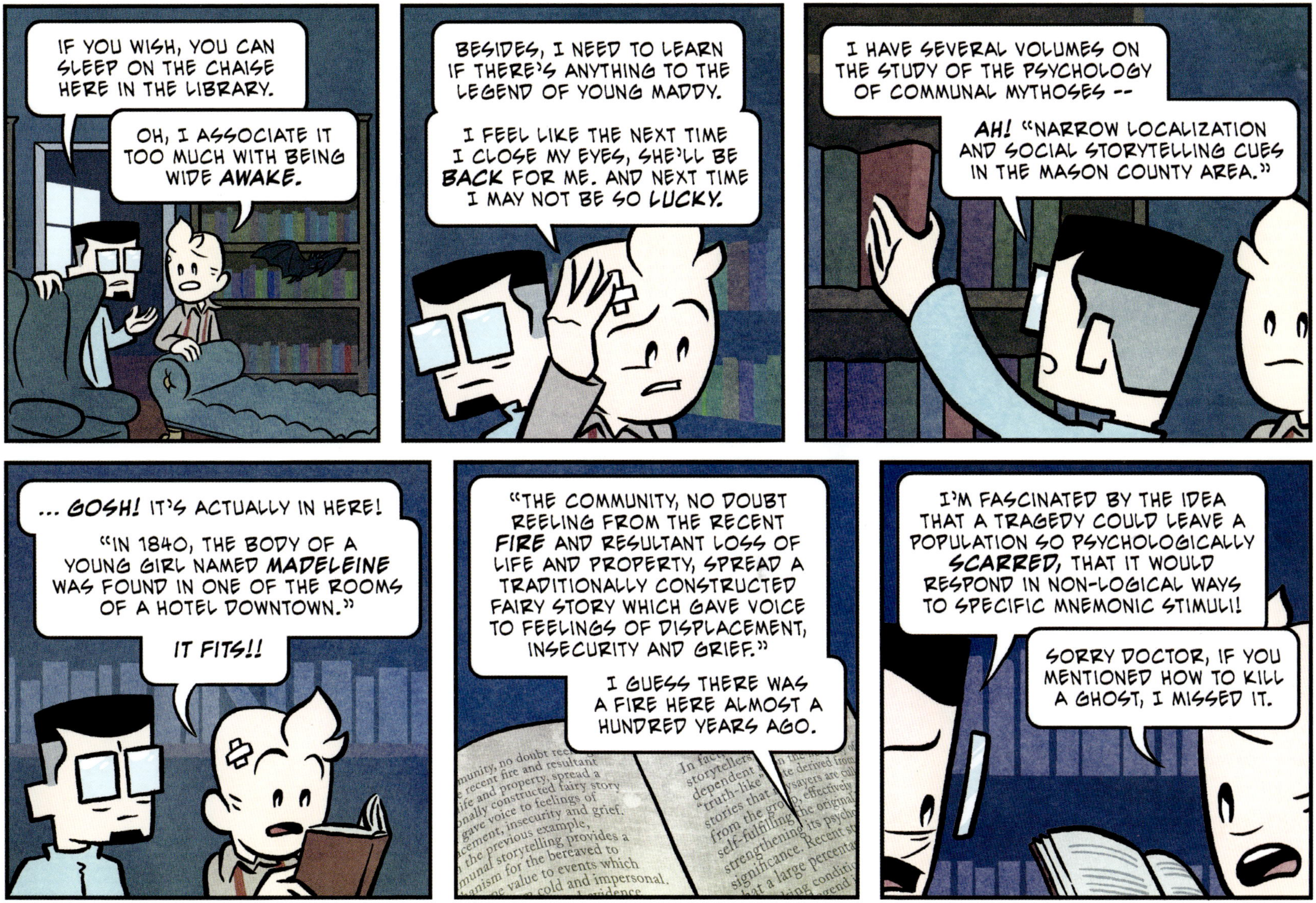
IF YOU WISH, YOU CAN SLEEP ON THE CHAISE HERE IN THE LIBRARY.
OH, I ASSOCIATE IT TOO MUCH WITH BEING WIDE **AWAKE.**
BESIDES, I NEED TO LEARN IF THERE'S ANYTHING TO THE LEGEND OF YOUNG MADDY.
I FEEL LIKE THE NEXT TIME I CLOSE MY EYES, SHE'LL BE **BACK** FOR ME. AND NEXT TIME I MAY NOT BE SO **LUCKY.**
I HAVE SEVERAL VOLUMES ON THE STUDY OF THE PSYCHOLOGY OF COMMUNAL MYTHOSES --
AH! "NARROW LOCALIZATION AND SOCIAL STORYTELLING CUES IN THE MASON COUNTY AREA."
... **GOSH!** IT'S ACTUALLY IN HERE!
"IN 1840, THE BODY OF A YOUNG GIRL NAMED **MADELEINE** WAS FOUND IN ONE OF THE ROOMS OF A HOTEL DOWNTOWN."
IT FITS!!
"THE COMMUNITY, NO DOUBT REELING FROM THE RECENT **FIRE** AND RESULTANT LOSS OF LIFE AND PROPERTY, SPREAD A TRADITIONALLY CONSTRUCTED FAIRY STORY WHICH GAVE VOICE TO FEELINGS OF DISPLACEMENT, INSECURITY AND GRIEF."
I GUESS THERE WAS A FIRE HERE ALMOST A HUNDRED YEARS AGO.
I'M FASCINATED BY THE IDEA THAT A TRAGEDY COULD LEAVE A POPULATION SO PSYCHOLOGICALLY **SCARRED,** THAT IT WOULD RESPOND IN NON-LOGICAL WAYS TO SPECIFIC MNEMONIC STIMULI!
SORRY DOCTOR, IF YOU MENTIONED HOW TO KILL A GHOST, I MISSED IT.

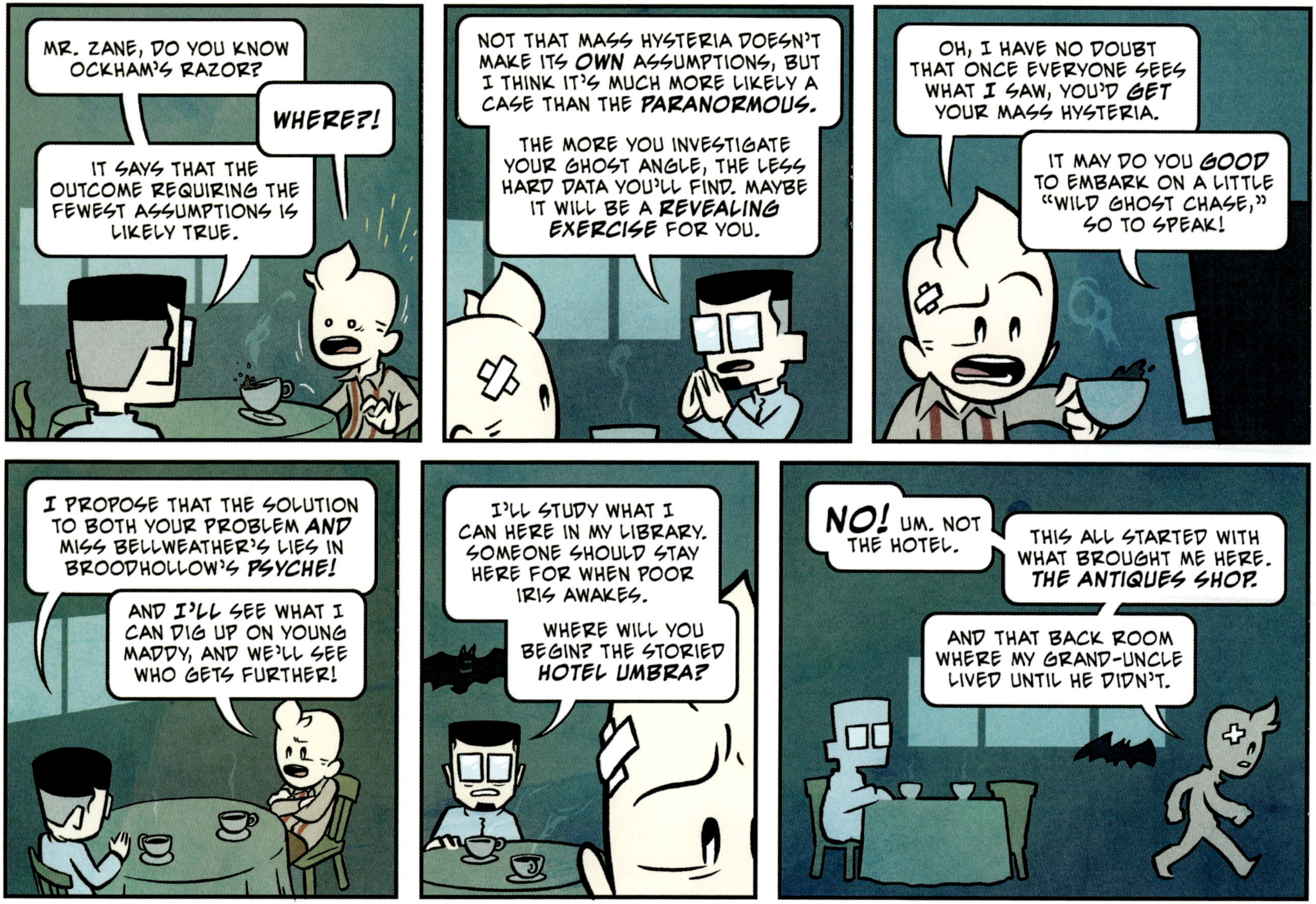
MR. ZANE, DO YOU KNOW OCKHAM'S RAZOR?
WHERE?!
IT SAYS THAT THE OUTCOME REQUIRING THE FEWEST ASSUMPTIONS IS LIKELY TRUE.
NOT THAT MASS HYSTERIA DOESN'T MAKE ITS OWN ASSUMPTIONS, BUT I THINK IT'S MUCH MORE LIKELY A CASE THAN THE PARANORMOUS.
THE MORE YOU INVESTIGATE YOUR GHOST ANGLE, THE LESS HARD DATA YOU'LL FIND. MAYBE IT WILL BE A REVEALING EXERCISE FOR YOU.
OH, I HAVE NO DOUBT THAT ONCE EVERYONE SEES WHAT I SAW, YOU'D GET YOUR MASS HYSTERIA.
IT MAY DO YOU GOOD TO EMBARK ON A LITTLE "WILD GHOST CHASE," SO TO SPEAK!
I PROPOSE THAT THE SOLUTION TO BOTH YOUR PROBLEM AND MISS BELLWEATHER'S LIES IN BROODHOLLOW'S PSYCHE!
AND I'LL SEE WHAT I CAN DIG UP ON YOUNG MADDY, AND WE'LL SEE WHO GETS FURTHER!
I'LL STUDY WHAT I CAN HERE IN MY LIBRARY. SOMEONE SHOULD STAY HERE FOR WHEN POOR IRIS AWAKES.
WHERE WILL YOU BEGIN? THE STORIED HOTEL UMBRA?
NO! UM. NOT THE HOTEL.
THIS ALL STARTED WITH WHAT BROUGHT ME HERE. THE ANTIQUES SHOP.
AND THAT BACK ROOM WHERE MY GRAND-UNCLE LIVED UNTIL HE DIDN'T.

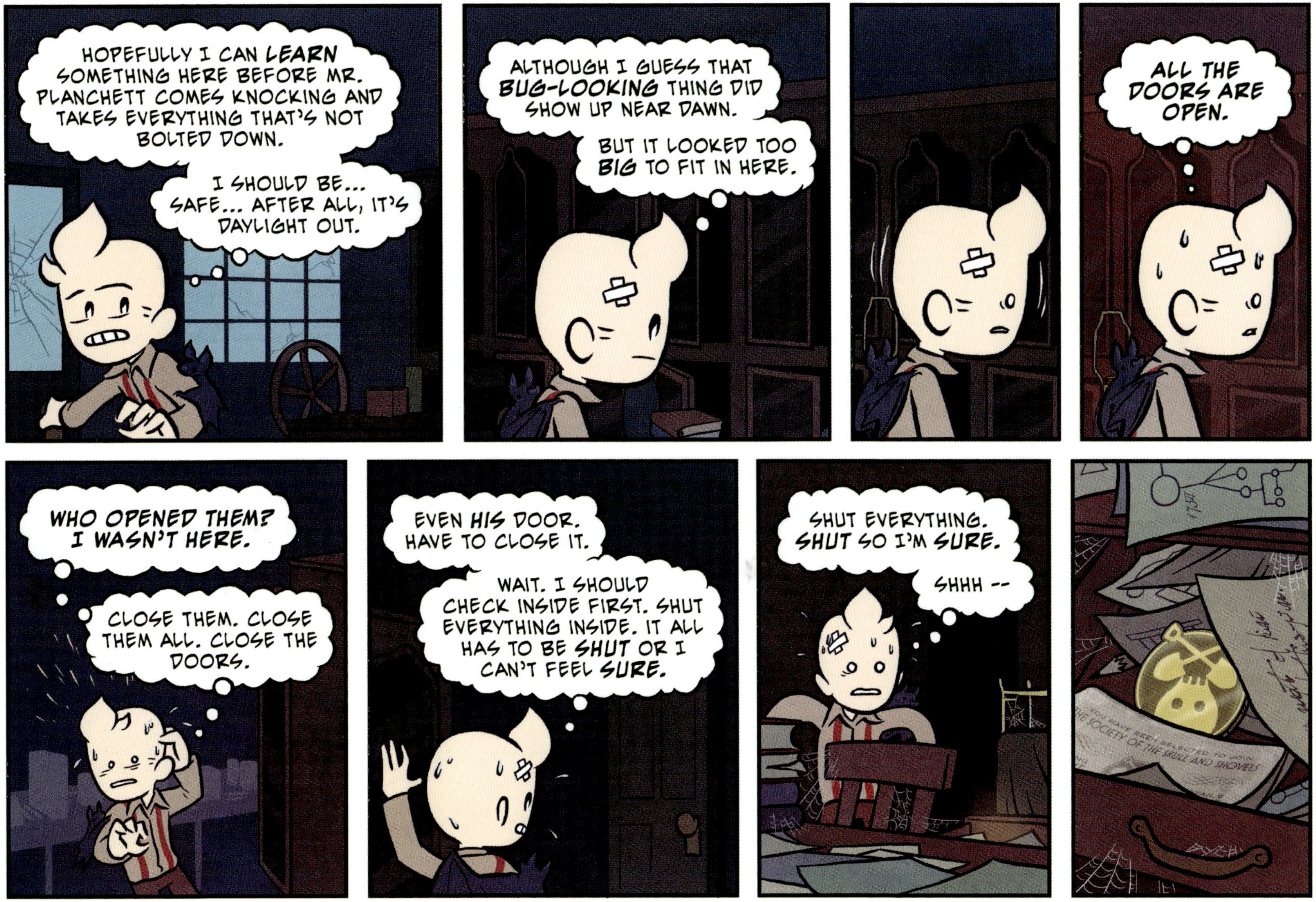
HOPEFULLY I CAN **LEARN** SOMETHING HERE BEFORE MR. PLANCHETT COMES KNOCKING AND TAKES EVERYTHING THAT'S NOT BOLTED DOWN.
I SHOULD BE... SAFE... AFTER ALL, IT'S DAYLIGHT OUT.
ALTHOUGH I GUESS THAT **BUG-LOOKING** THING DID SHOW UP NEAR DAWN.
BUT IT LOOKED TOO **BIG** TO FIT IN HERE.
ALL THE DOORS ARE OPEN.
WHO OPENED THEM? I WASN'T HERE.
CLOSE THEM. CLOSE THEM ALL. CLOSE THE DOORS.
EVEN **HIS** DOOR. HAVE TO CLOSE IT.
WAIT. I SHOULD CHECK INSIDE FIRST. SHUT EVERYTHING INSIDE. IT ALL HAS TO BE **SHUT** OR I CAN'T FEEL **SURE**.
SHUT EVERYTHING. **SHUT** SO I'M **SURE**.
SHHH --
YOU HAVE BEEN SELECTED TO JOIN
THE SOCIETY OF THE SKULL AND SHOVELS

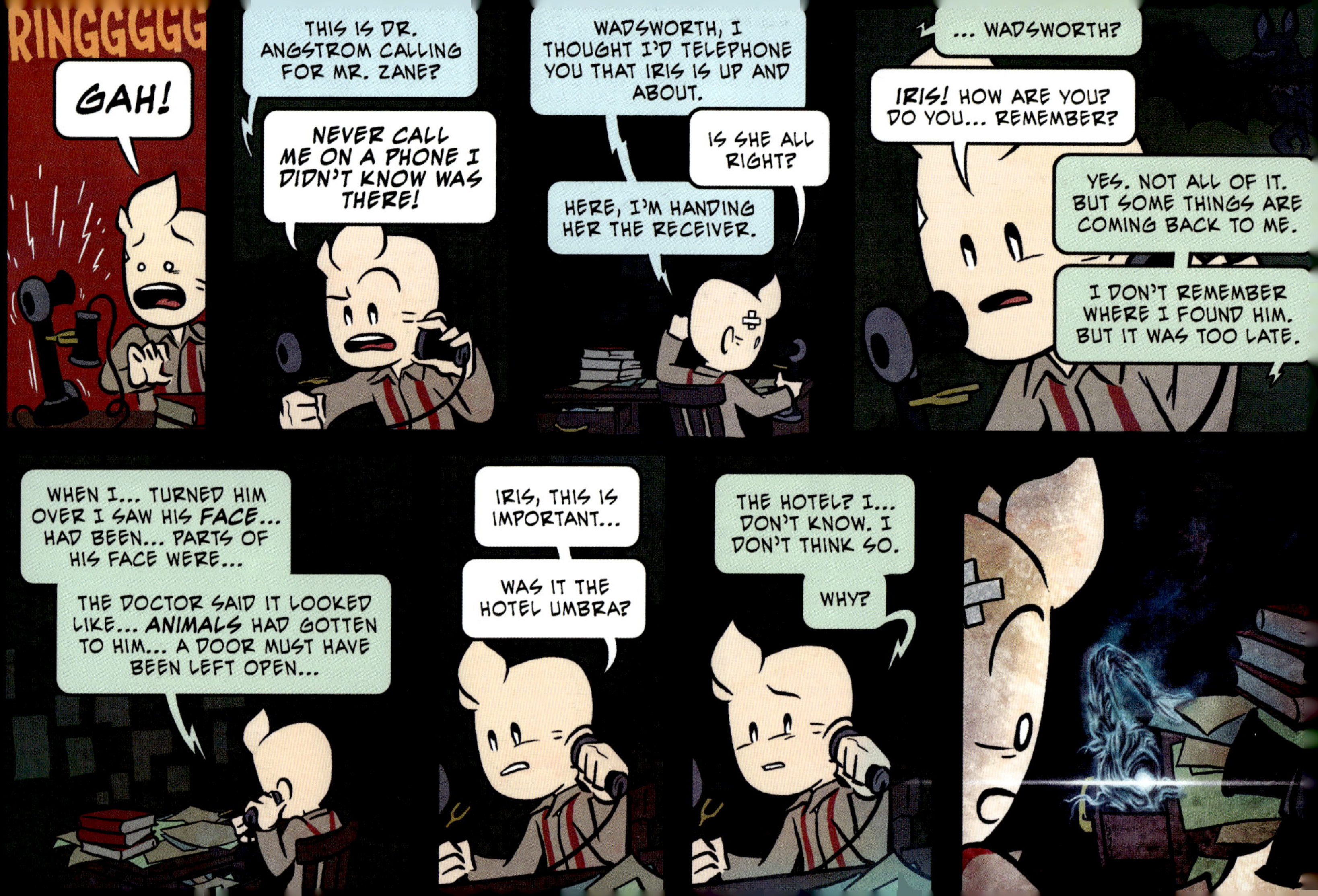

RINGGGGG
GAH!
THIS IS DR. ANGSTROM CALLING FOR MR. ZANE?
NEVER CALL ME ON A PHONE I DIDN'T KNOW WAS THERE!
WADSWORTH, I THOUGHT I'D TELEPHONE YOU THAT IRIS IS UP AND ABOUT.
IS SHE ALL RIGHT?
HERE, I'M HANDING HER THE RECEIVER.
... WADSWORTH?
IRIS! HOW ARE YOU? DO YOU... REMEMBER?
YES. NOT ALL OF IT. BUT SOME THINGS ARE COMING BACK TO ME.
I DON'T REMEMBER WHERE I FOUND HIM. BUT IT WAS TOO LATE.
WHEN I... TURNED HIM OVER I SAW HIS FACE... HAD BEEN... PARTS OF HIS FACE WERE...
THE DOCTOR SAID IT LOOKED LIKE... ANIMALS HAD GOTTEN TO HIM... A DOOR MUST HAVE BEEN LEFT OPEN...
IRIS, THIS IS IMPORTANT...
WAS IT THE HOTEL UMBRA?
THE HOTEL? I... DON'T KNOW. I DON'T THINK SO.
WHY?

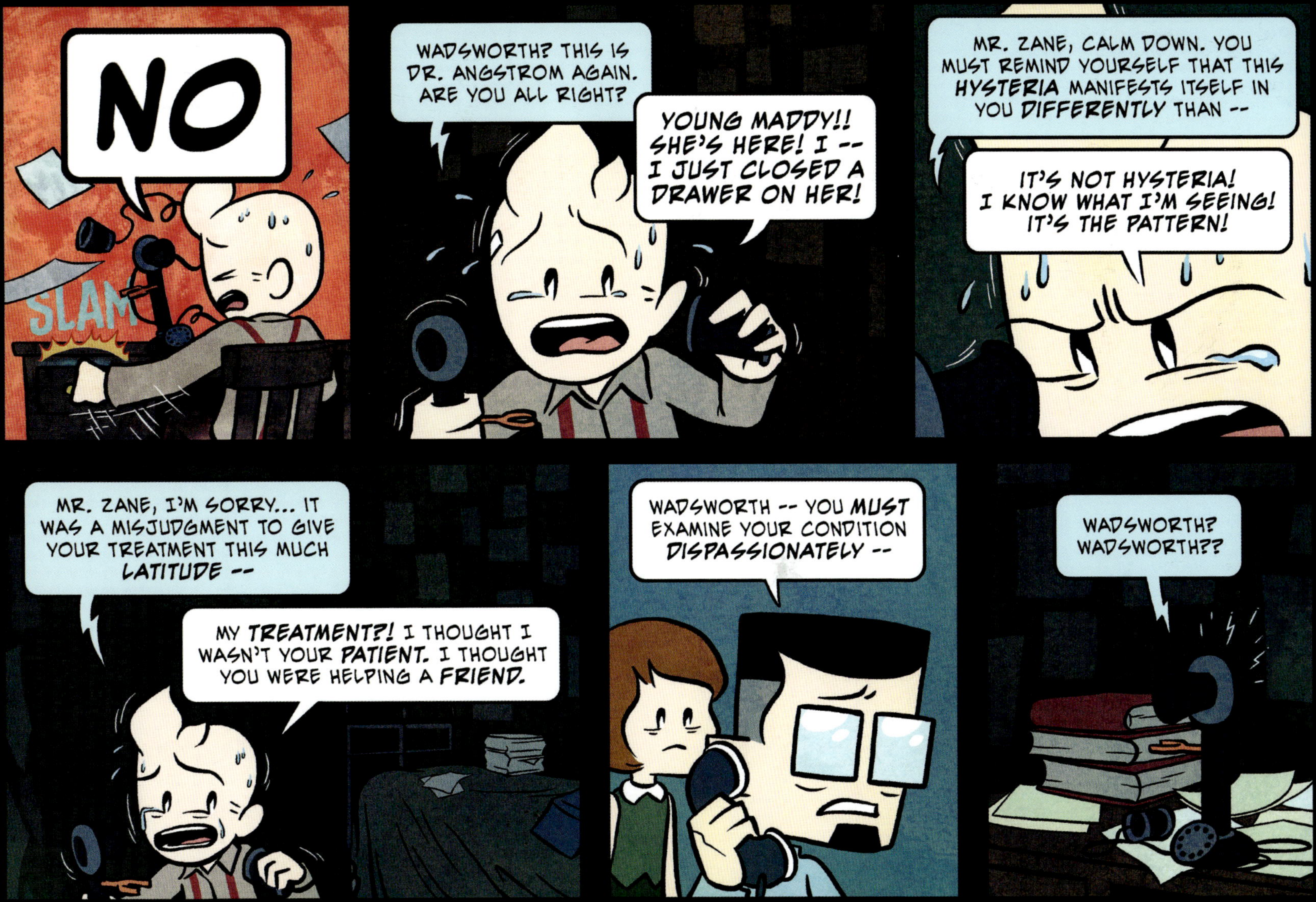
NO
SLAM
WADSWORTH? THIS IS DR. ANGSTROM AGAIN. ARE YOU ALL RIGHT?
YOUNG MADDY!! SHE'S HERE! I -- I JUST CLOSED A DRAWER ON HER!
MR. ZANE, CALM DOWN. YOU MUST REMIND YOURSELF THAT THIS HYSTERIA MANIFESTS ITSELF IN YOU DIFFERENTLY THAN --
IT'S NOT HYSTERIA! I KNOW WHAT I'M SEEING! IT'S THE PATTERN!
MR. ZANE, I'M SORRY... IT WAS A MISJUDGMENT TO GIVE YOUR TREATMENT THIS MUCH LATITUDE --
MY TREATMENT?! I THOUGHT I WASN'T YOUR PATIENT. I THOUGHT YOU WERE HELPING A FRIEND.
WADSWORTH -- YOU MUST EXAMINE YOUR CONDITION DISPASSIONATELY --
WADSWORTH? WADSWORTH??

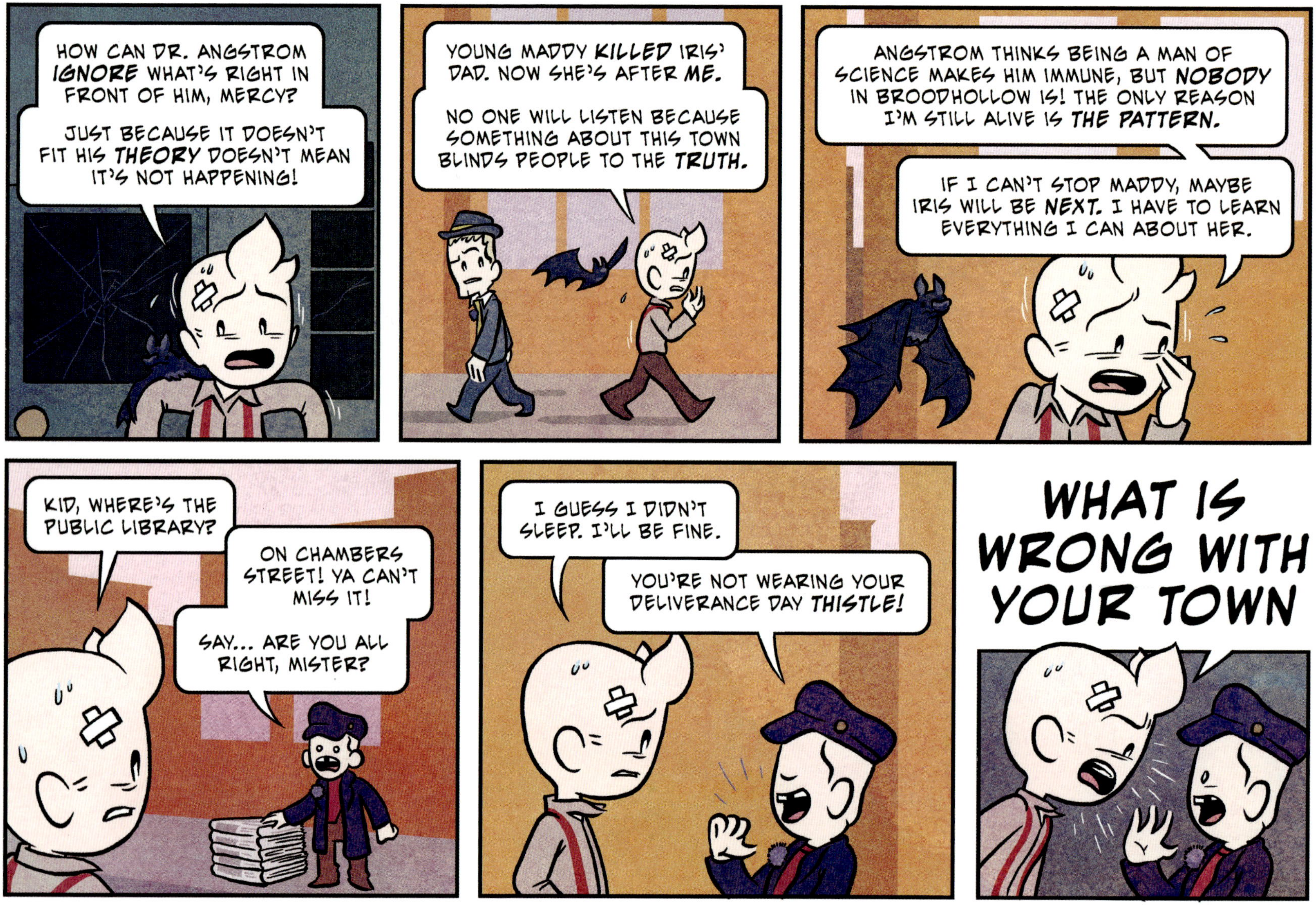

HOW CAN DR. ANGSTROM IGNORE WHAT'S RIGHT IN FRONT OF HIM, MERCY?
JUST BECAUSE IT DOESN'T FIT HIS THEORY DOESN'T MEAN IT'S NOT HAPPENING!
YOUNG MADDY KILLED IRIS' DAD. NOW SHE'S AFTER ME.
NO ONE WILL LISTEN BECAUSE SOMETHING ABOUT THIS TOWN BLINDS PEOPLE TO THE TRUTH.
ANGSTROM THINKS BEING A MAN OF SCIENCE MAKES HIM IMMUNE, BUT NOBODY IN BROODHOLLOW IS! THE ONLY REASON I'M STILL ALIVE IS THE PATTERN.
IF I CAN'T STOP MADDY, MAYBE IRIS WILL BE NEXT. I HAVE TO LEARN EVERYTHING I CAN ABOUT HER.
KID, WHERE'S THE PUBLIC LIBRARY?
ON CHAMBERS STREET! YA CAN'T MISS IT!
SAY... ARE YOU ALL RIGHT, MISTER?
I GUESS I DIDN'T SLEEP. I'LL BE FINE.
YOU'RE NOT WEARING YOUR DELIVERANCE DAY THISTLE!
WHAT IS WRONG WITH YOUR TOWN

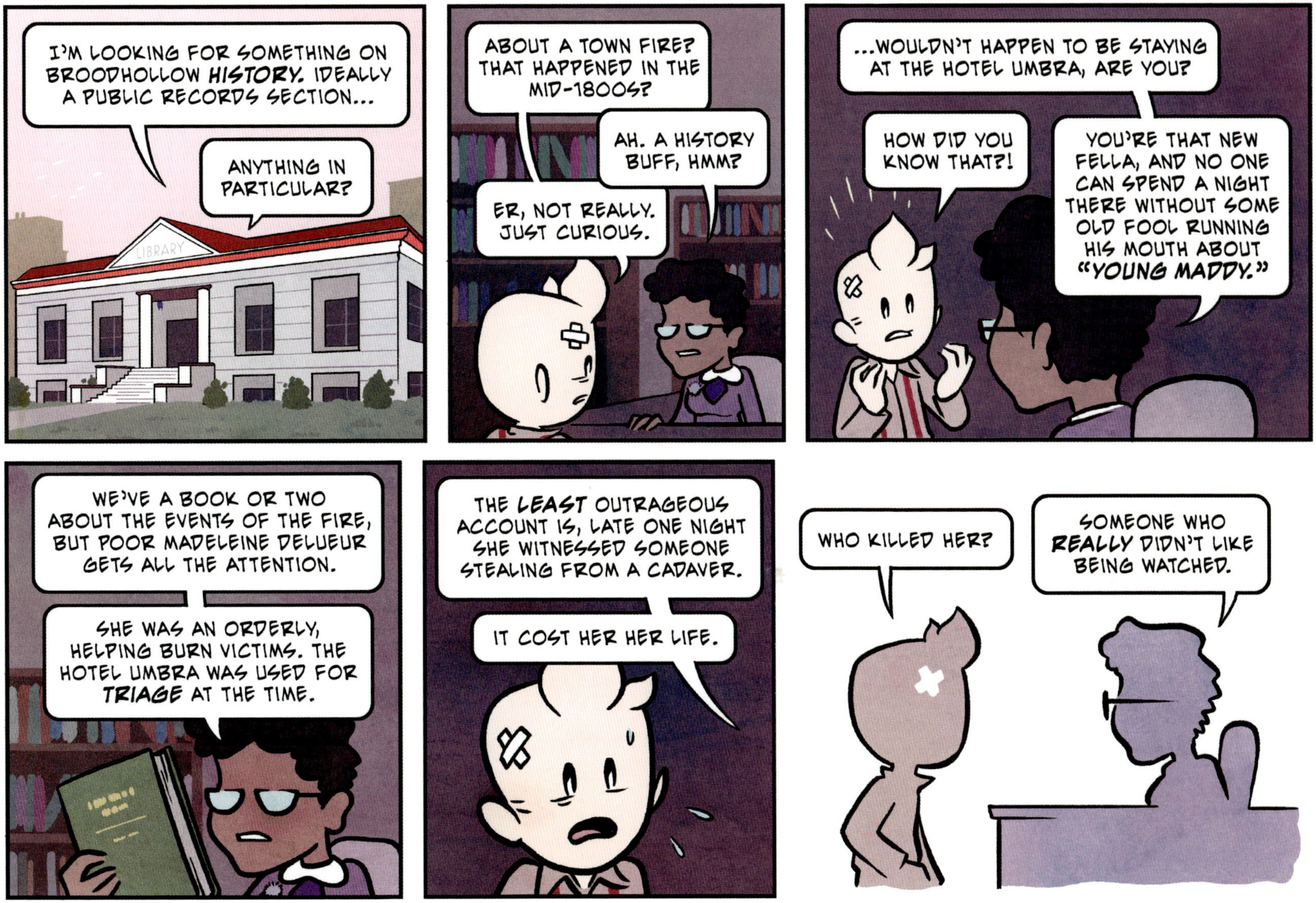
I'M LOOKING FOR SOMETHING ON BROODHOLLOW HISTORY. IDEALLY A PUBLIC RECORDS SECTION...
ANYTHING IN PARTICULAR?
LIBRARY
ABOUT A TOWN FIRE? THAT HAPPENED IN THE MID-1800S?
AH. A HISTORY BUFF, HMM?
ER, NOT REALLY. JUST CURIOUS.
...WOULDN'T HAPPEN TO BE STAYING AT THE HOTEL UMBRA, ARE YOU?
HOW DID YOU KNOW THAT?!
YOU'RE THAT NEW FELLA, AND NO ONE CAN SPEND A NIGHT THERE WITHOUT SOME OLD FOOL RUNNING HIS MOUTH ABOUT "YOUNG MADDY."
WE'VE A BOOK OR TWO ABOUT THE EVENTS OF THE FIRE, BUT POOR MADELEINE DELUEUR GETS ALL THE ATTENTION.
SHE WAS AN ORDERLY, HELPING BURN VICTIMS. THE HOTEL UMBRA WAS USED FOR TRIAGE AT THE TIME.
THE LEAST OUTRAGEOUS ACCOUNT IS, LATE ONE NIGHT SHE WITNESSED SOMEONE STEALING FROM A CADAVER.
IT COST HER HER LIFE.
WHO KILLED HER?
SOMEONE WHO REALLY DIDN'T LIKE BEING WATCHED.

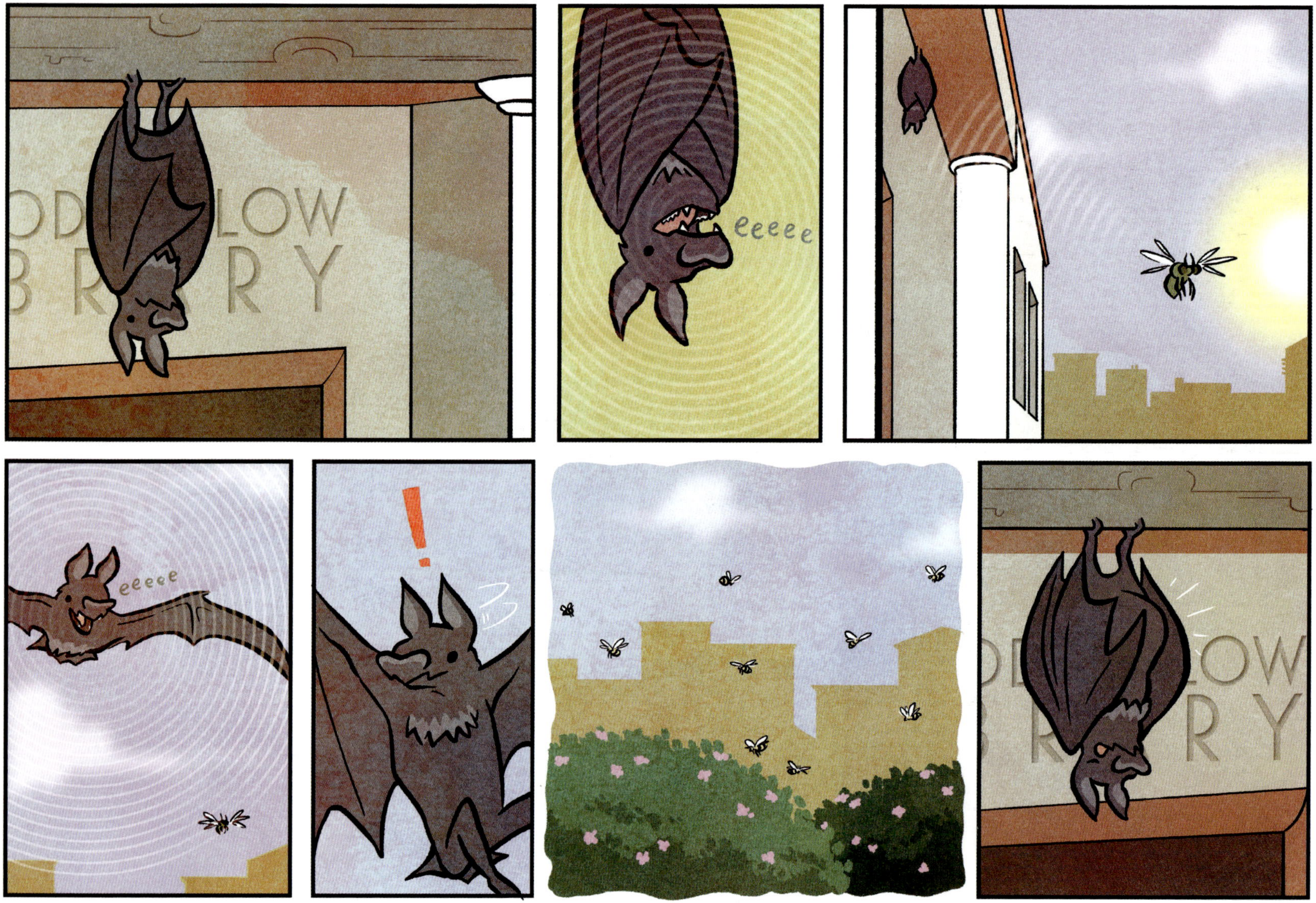
eeeee
eeeee
!

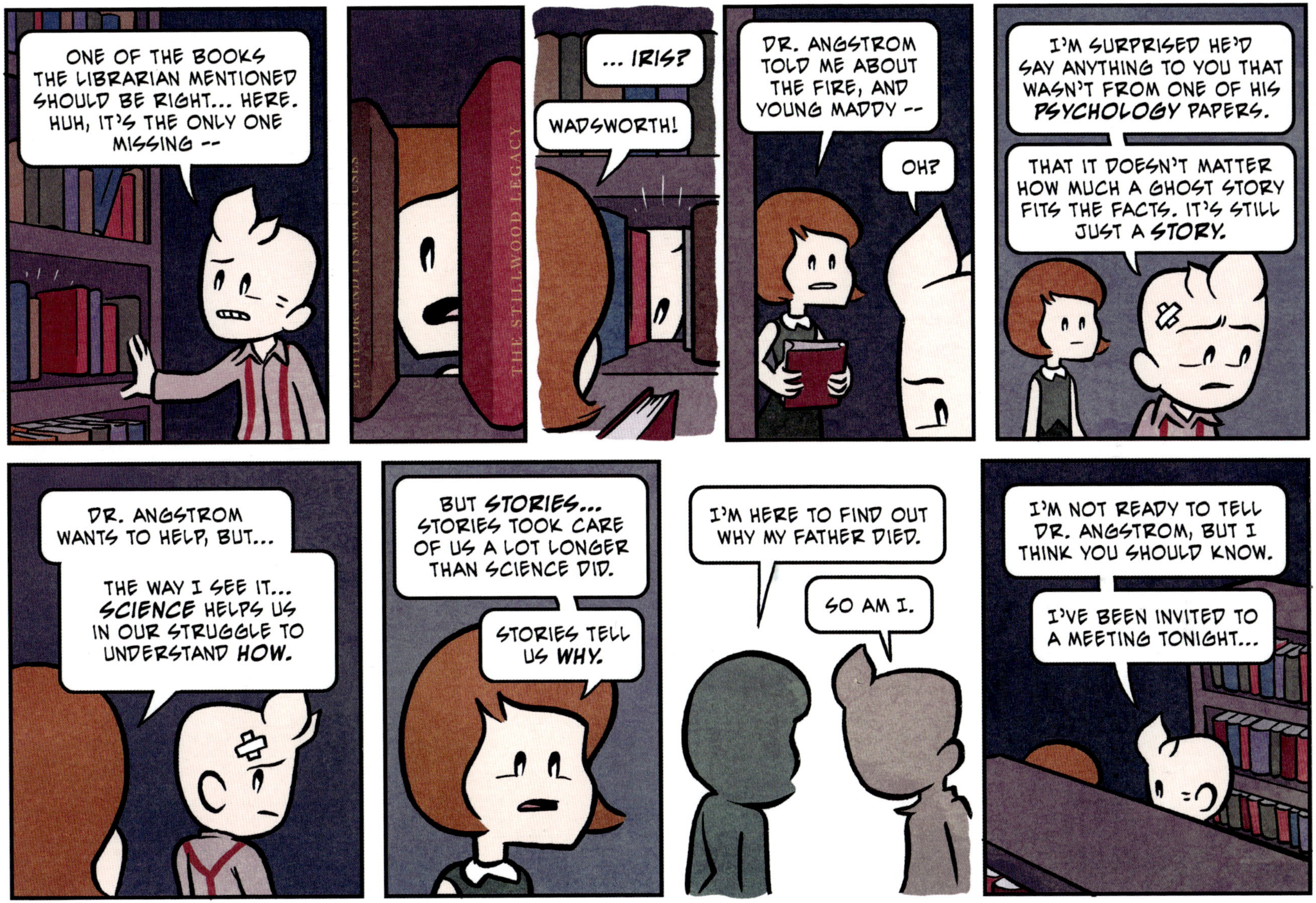
ONE OF THE BOOKS THE LIBRARIAN MENTIONED SHOULD BE RIGHT... HERE. HUH, IT'S THE ONLY ONE MISSING --
THE STILLWOOD LEGACY
... IRIS?
WADSWORTH!
DR. ANGSTROM TOLD ME ABOUT THE FIRE, AND YOUNG MADDY --
OH?
I'M SURPRISED HE'D SAY ANYTHING TO YOU THAT WASN'T FROM ONE OF HIS PSYCHOLOGY PAPERS.
THAT IT DOESN'T MATTER HOW MUCH A GHOST STORY FITS THE FACTS. IT'S STILL JUST A STORY.
DR. ANGSTROM WANTS TO HELP, BUT...
THE WAY I SEE IT... SCIENCE HELPS US IN OUR STRUGGLE TO UNDERSTAND HOW.
BUT STORIES... STORIES TOOK CARE OF US A LOT LONGER THAN SCIENCE DID.
STORIES TELL US WHY.
I'M HERE TO FIND OUT WHY MY FATHER DIED.
SO AM I.
I'M NOT READY TO TELL DR. ANGSTROM, BUT I THINK YOU SHOULD KNOW.
I'VE BEEN INVITED TO A MEETING TONIGHT...

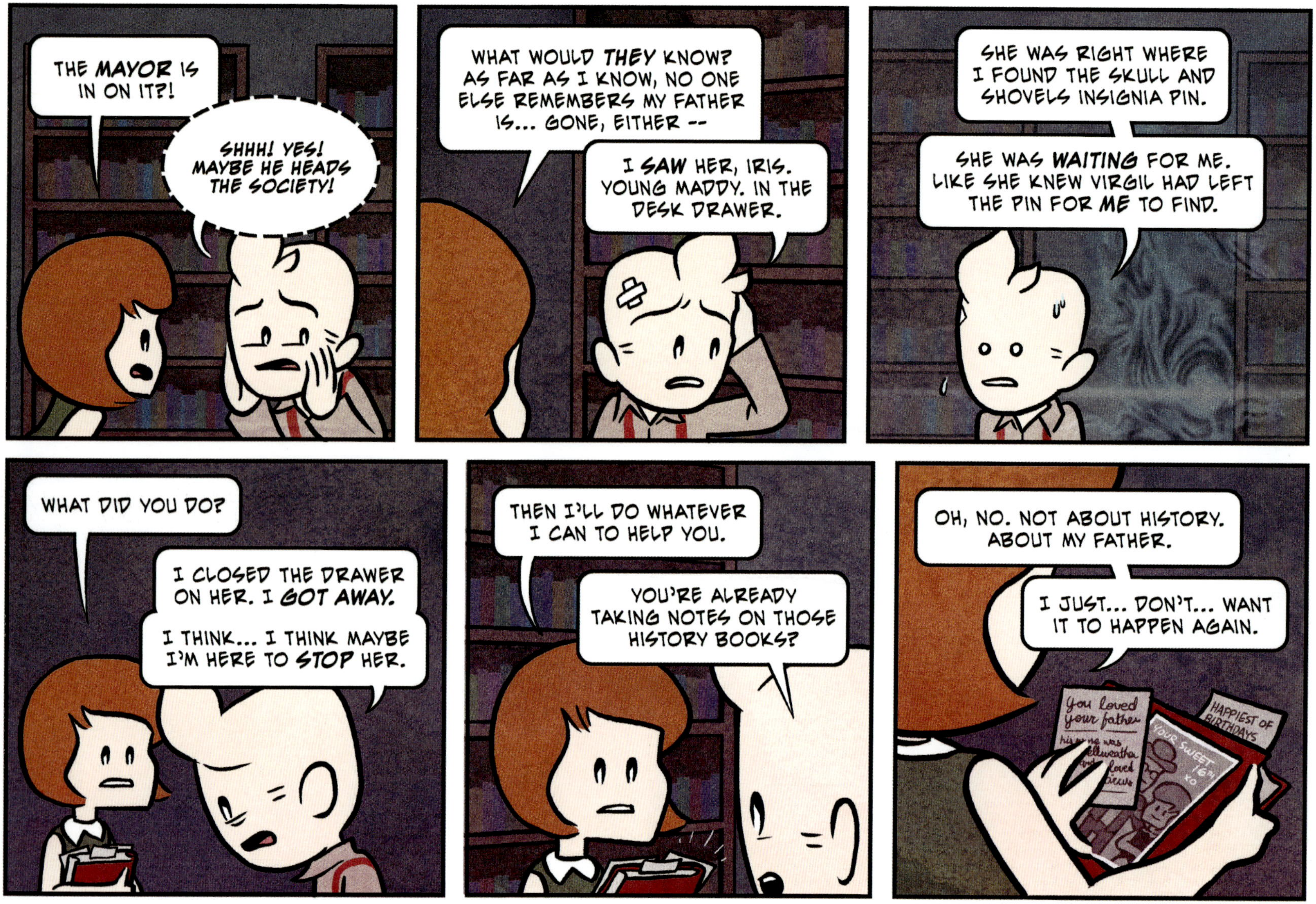
THE *MAYOR* IS IN ON IT?!
SHHH! YES! MAYBE HE HEADS THE SOCIETY!
WHAT WOULD *THEY* KNOW? AS FAR AS I KNOW, NO ONE ELSE REMEMBERS MY FATHER IS... GONE, EITHER --
I *SAW* HER, IRIS. YOUNG MADDY. IN THE DESK DRAWER.
SHE WAS RIGHT WHERE I FOUND THE SKULL AND SHOVELS INSIGNIA PIN.
SHE WAS *WAITING* FOR ME. LIKE SHE KNEW VIRGIL HAD LEFT THE PIN FOR *ME* TO FIND.
WHAT DID YOU DO?
I CLOSED THE DRAWER ON HER. I *GOT AWAY.*
I THINK... I THINK MAYBE I'M HERE TO *STOP* HER.
THEN I'LL DO WHATEVER I CAN TO HELP YOU.
YOU'RE ALREADY TAKING NOTES ON THOSE HISTORY BOOKS?
OH, NO. NOT ABOUT HISTORY. ABOUT MY FATHER.
I JUST... DON'T... WANT IT TO HAPPEN AGAIN.
You loved your father
HAPPIEST OF BIRTHDAYS
YOUR SWEET 16TH

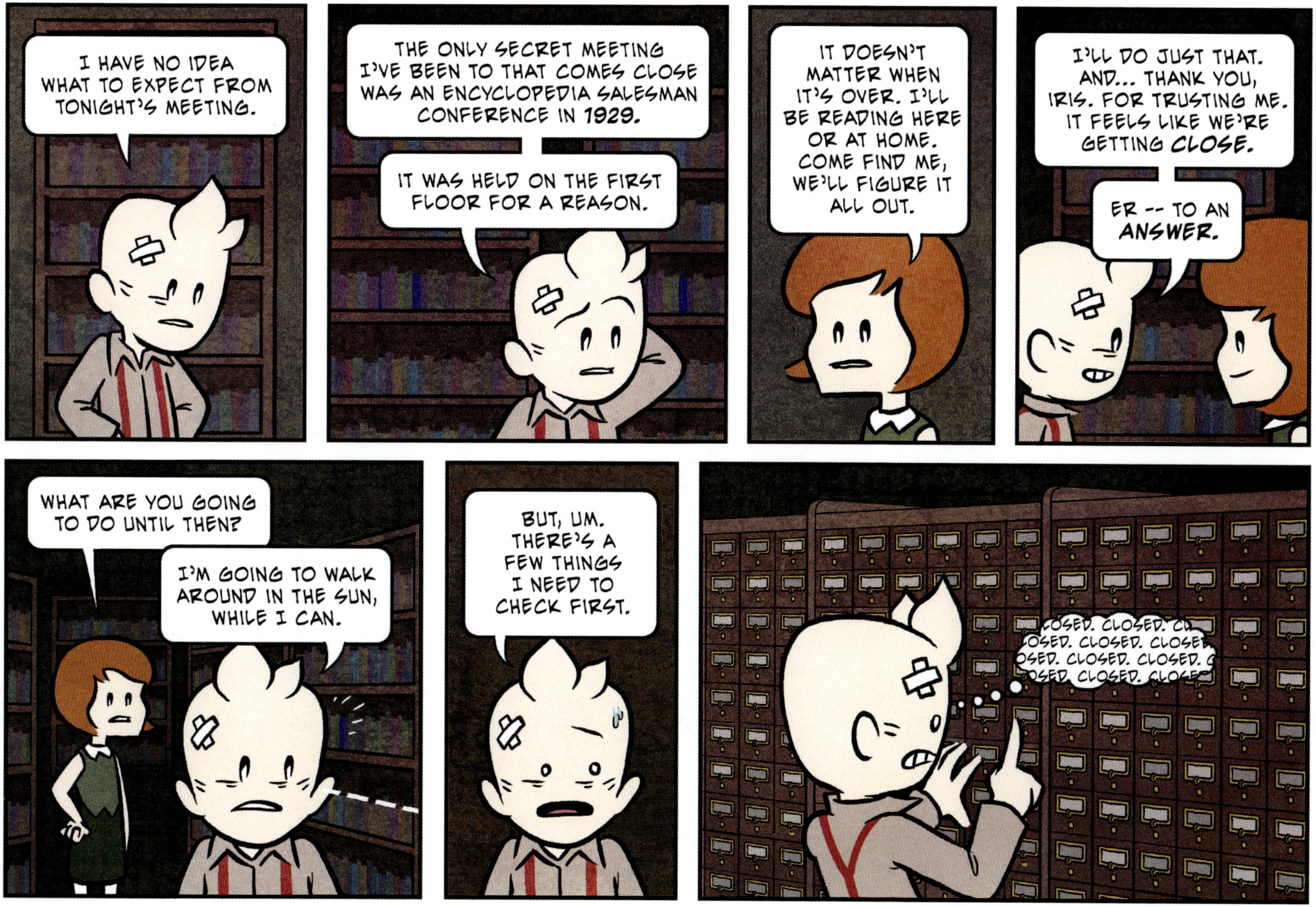
I HAVE NO IDEA WHAT TO EXPECT FROM TONIGHT'S MEETING.
THE ONLY SECRET MEETING I'VE BEEN TO THAT COMES CLOSE WAS AN ENCYCLOPEDIA SALESMAN CONFERENCE IN 1929.
IT WAS HELD ON THE FIRST FLOOR FOR A REASON.
IT DOESN'T MATTER WHEN IT'S OVER. I'LL BE READING HERE OR AT HOME. COME FIND ME, WE'LL FIGURE IT ALL OUT.
I'LL DO JUST THAT. AND... THANK YOU, IRIS. FOR TRUSTING ME. IT FEELS LIKE WE'RE GETTING **CLOSE.**
ER -- TO AN **ANSWER.**
WHAT ARE YOU GOING TO DO UNTIL THEN?
I'M GOING TO WALK AROUND IN THE SUN, WHILE I CAN.
BUT, UM. THERE'S A FEW THINGS I NEED TO CHECK FIRST.
OSED. CLOSED.
OSED. CLOSED.
OSED. CLOSED. CLOSED.
OSED. CLOSED.

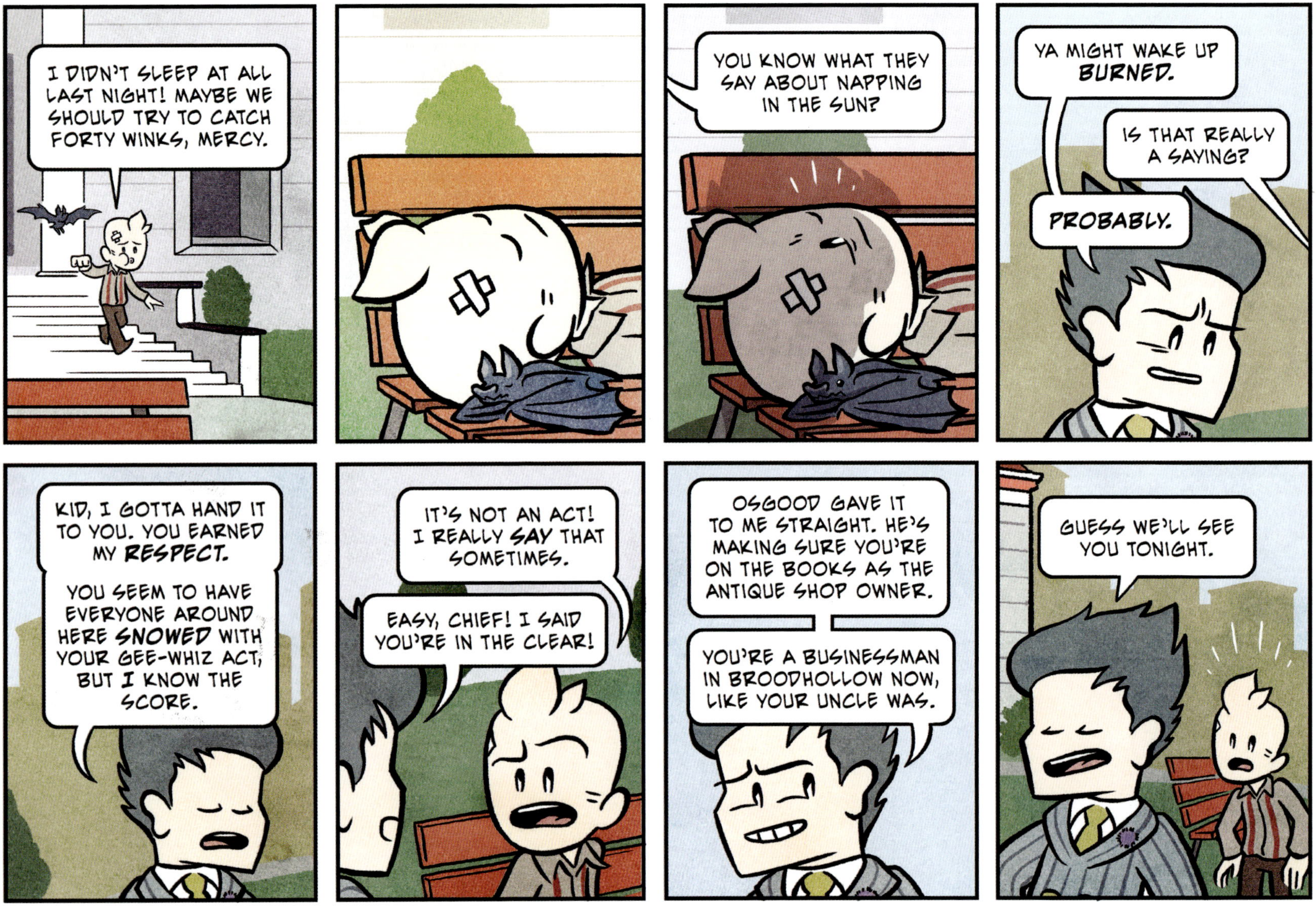

I DIDN'T SLEEP AT ALL LAST NIGHT! MAYBE WE SHOULD TRY TO CATCH FORTY WINKS, MERCY.
YOU KNOW WHAT THEY SAY ABOUT NAPPING IN THE SUN?
YA MIGHT WAKE UP **BURNED.**
IS THAT REALLY A SAYING?
PROBABLY.
KID, I GOTTA HAND IT TO YOU. YOU EARNED MY **RESPECT.**
YOU SEEM TO HAVE EVERYONE AROUND HERE **SNOWED** WITH YOUR GEE-WHIZ ACT, BUT I KNOW THE SCORE.
IT'S NOT AN ACT! I REALLY **SAY** THAT SOMETIMES.
EASY, CHIEF! I SAID YOU'RE IN THE CLEAR!
OSGOOD GAVE IT TO ME STRAIGHT. HE'S MAKING SURE YOU'RE ON THE BOOKS AS THE ANTIQUE SHOP OWNER.
YOU'RE A BUSINESSMAN IN BROODHOLLOW NOW, LIKE YOUR UNCLE WAS.
GUESS WE'LL SEE YOU TONIGHT.

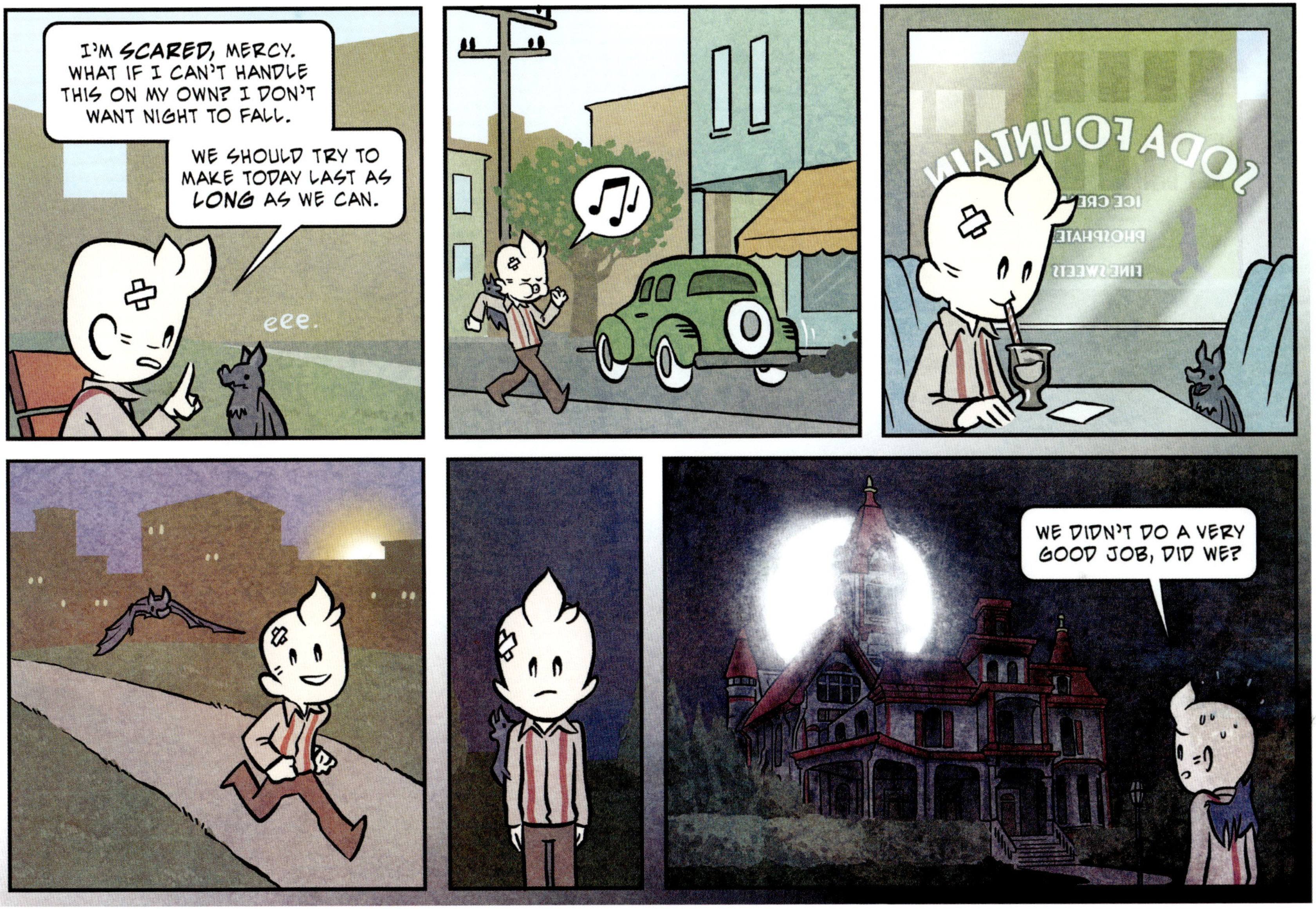

I'M SCARED, MERCY. WHAT IF I CAN'T HANDLE THIS ON MY OWN? I DON'T WANT NIGHT TO FALL.
WE SHOULD TRY TO MAKE TODAY LAST AS LONG AS WE CAN.
eee.
SODA FOUNTAIN
PHOSPHATES
FINE SWEETS
WE DIDN'T DO A VERY GOOD JOB, DID WE?

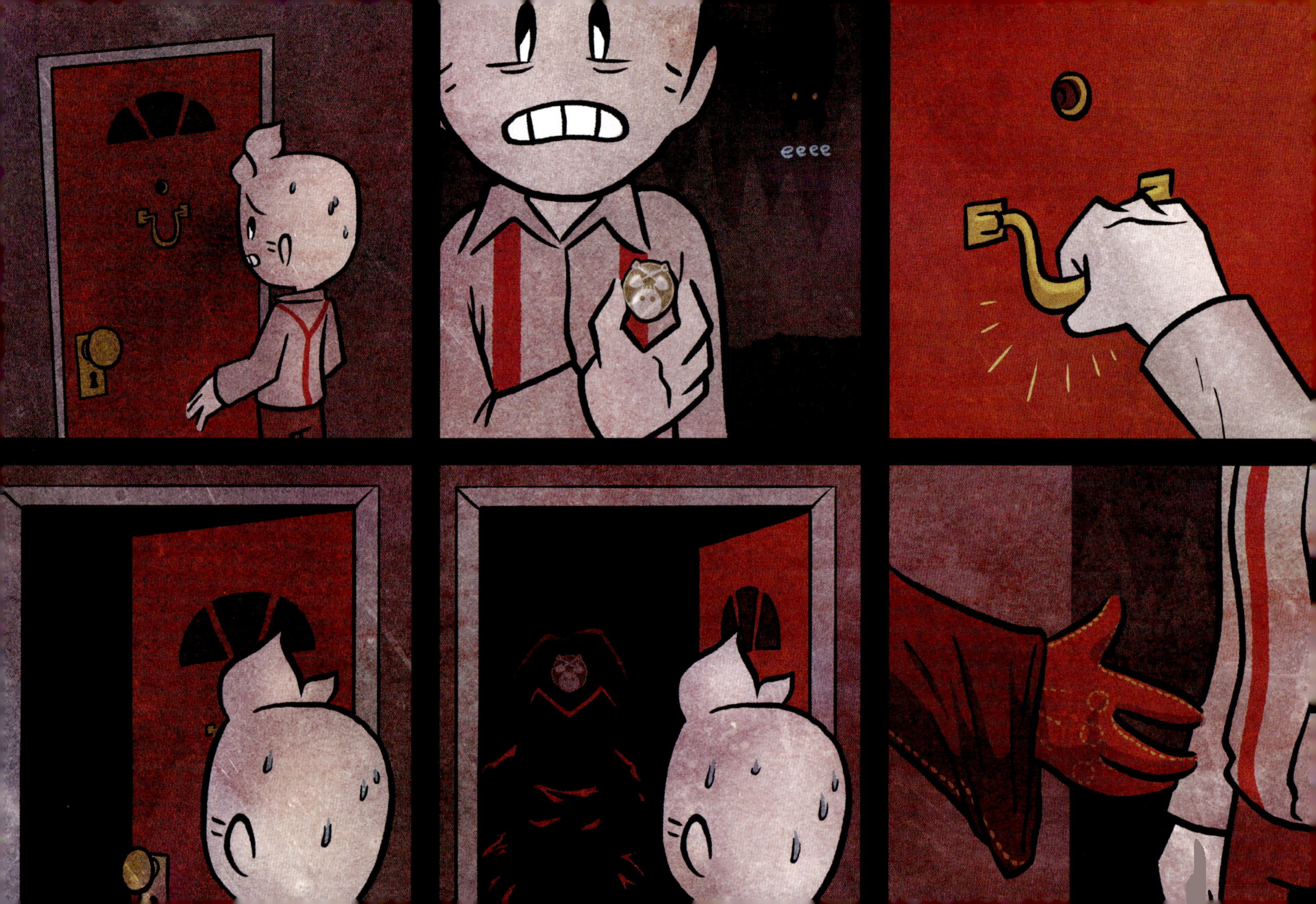
eeee

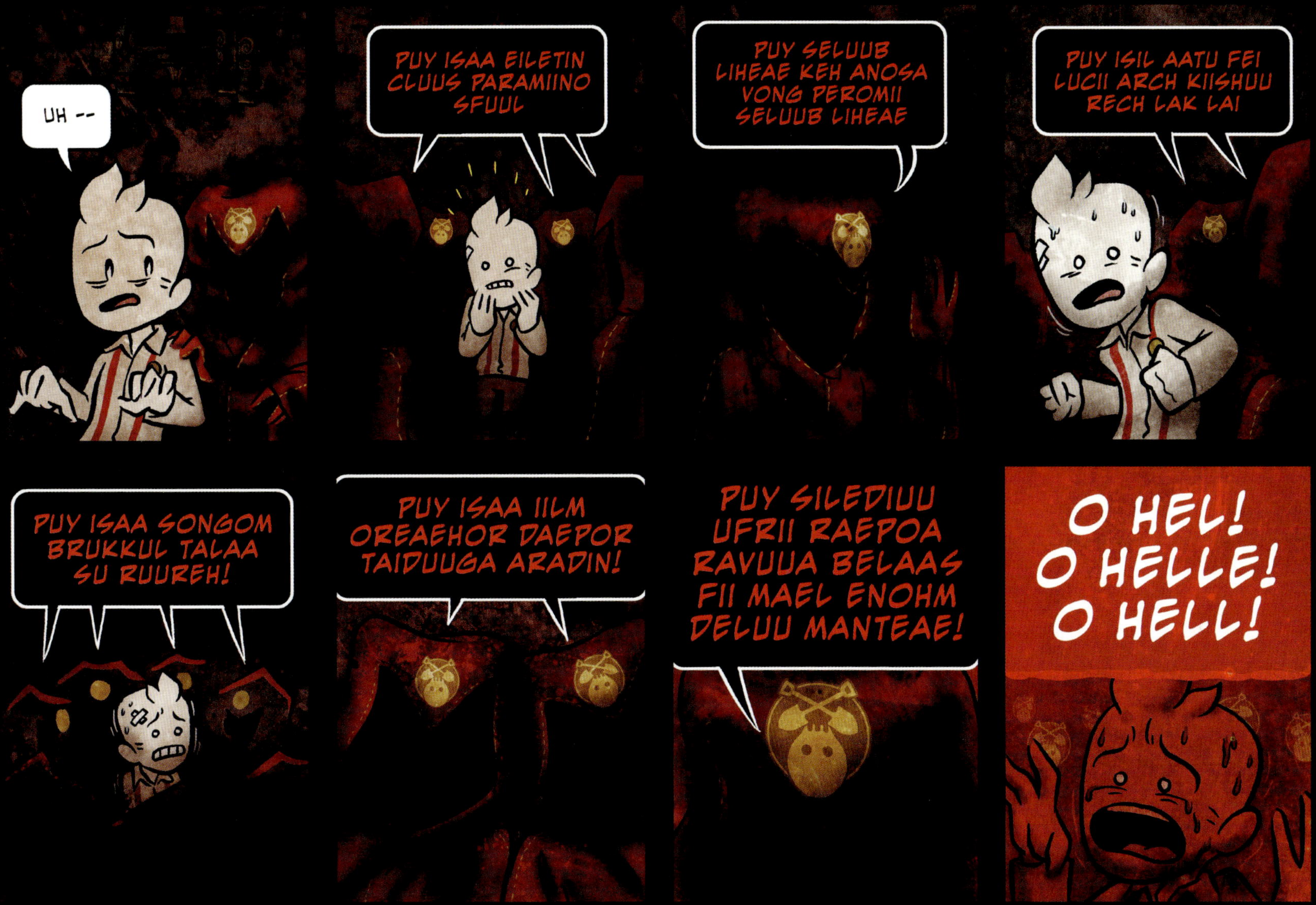
UH --
PUY ISAA EILETIN CLUUS PARAMIINO SFUUL
PUY SELUUB LIHEAE KEH ANOSA VONG PEROMII SELUUB LIHEAE
PUY ISIL AATU FEI LUCII ARCH KIISHUU RECH LAK LAI
PUY ISAA SONGOM BRUKKUL TALAA SU RUUREH!
PUY ISAA IILM OREAEHOR DAEPOR TAIDUUGA ARADIN!
PUY SILEDIUU UFRII RAEPOA RAVUUA BELAAS FII MAEL ENOHM DELUU MANTEAE!
O HEL! O HELLE! O HELL!

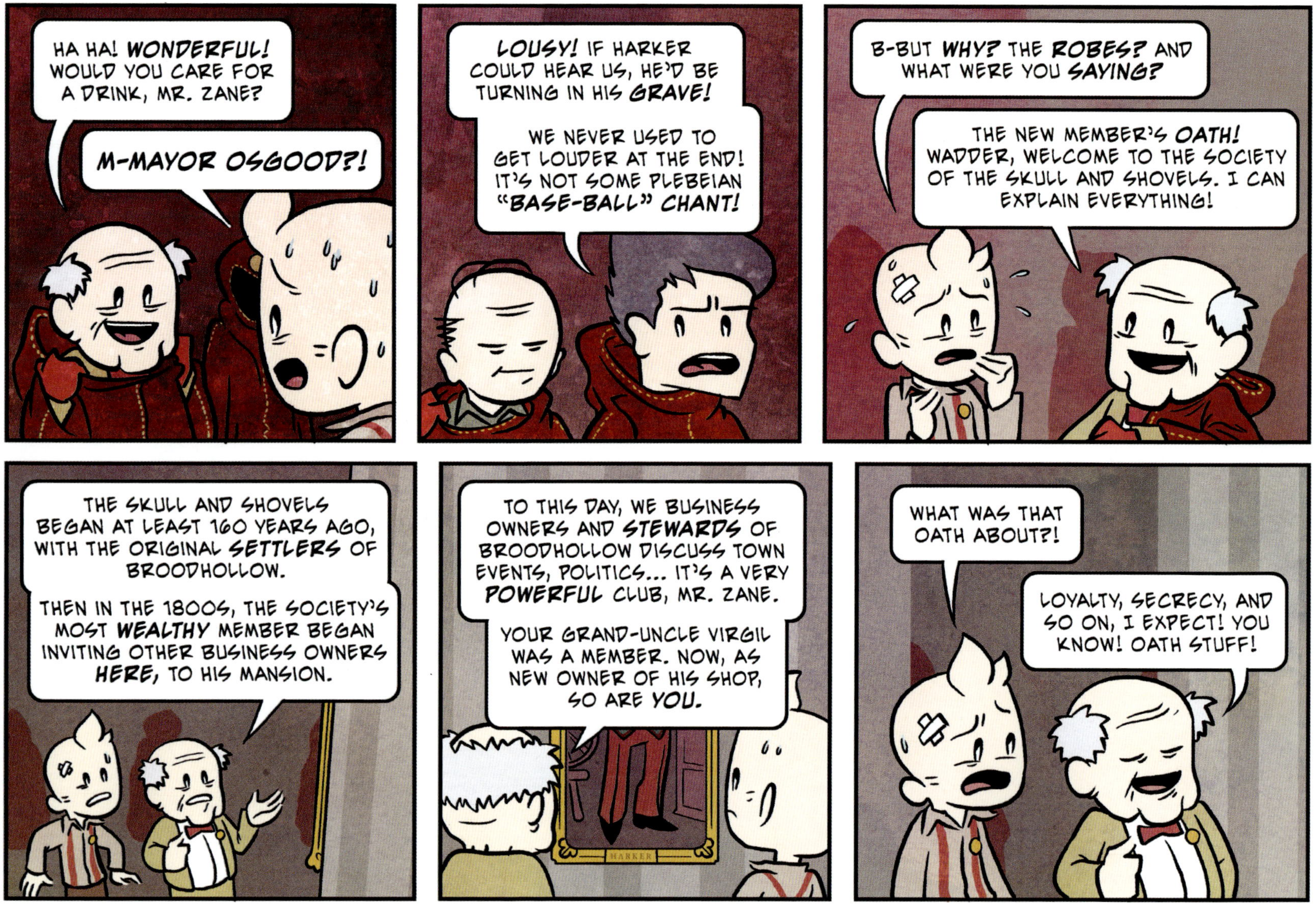
HA HA! WONDERFUL! WOULD YOU CARE FOR A DRINK, MR. ZANE?
M-MAYOR OSGOOD?!
LOUSY! IF HARKER COULD HEAR US, HE'D BE TURNING IN HIS GRAVE!
WE NEVER USED TO GET LOUDER AT THE END! IT'S NOT SOME PLEBEIAN "BASE-BALL" CHANT!
B-BUT WHY? THE ROBES? AND WHAT WERE YOU SAYING?
THE NEW MEMBER'S OATH! WADDER, WELCOME TO THE SOCIETY OF THE SKULL AND SHOVELS. I CAN EXPLAIN EVERYTHING!
THE SKULL AND SHOVELS BEGAN AT LEAST 160 YEARS AGO, WITH THE ORIGINAL SETTLERS OF BROODHOLLOW.
THEN IN THE 1800S, THE SOCIETY'S MOST WEALTHY MEMBER BEGAN INVITING OTHER BUSINESS OWNERS HERE, TO HIS MANSION.
TO THIS DAY, WE BUSINESS OWNERS AND STEWARDS OF BROODHOLLOW DISCUSS TOWN EVENTS, POLITICS... IT'S A VERY POWERFUL CLUB, MR. ZANE.
YOUR GRAND-UNCLE VIRGIL WAS A MEMBER. NOW, AS NEW OWNER OF HIS SHOP, SO ARE YOU.
HARKER
WHAT WAS THAT OATH ABOUT?!
LOYALTY, SECRECY, AND SO ON, I EXPECT! YOU KNOW! OATH STUFF!

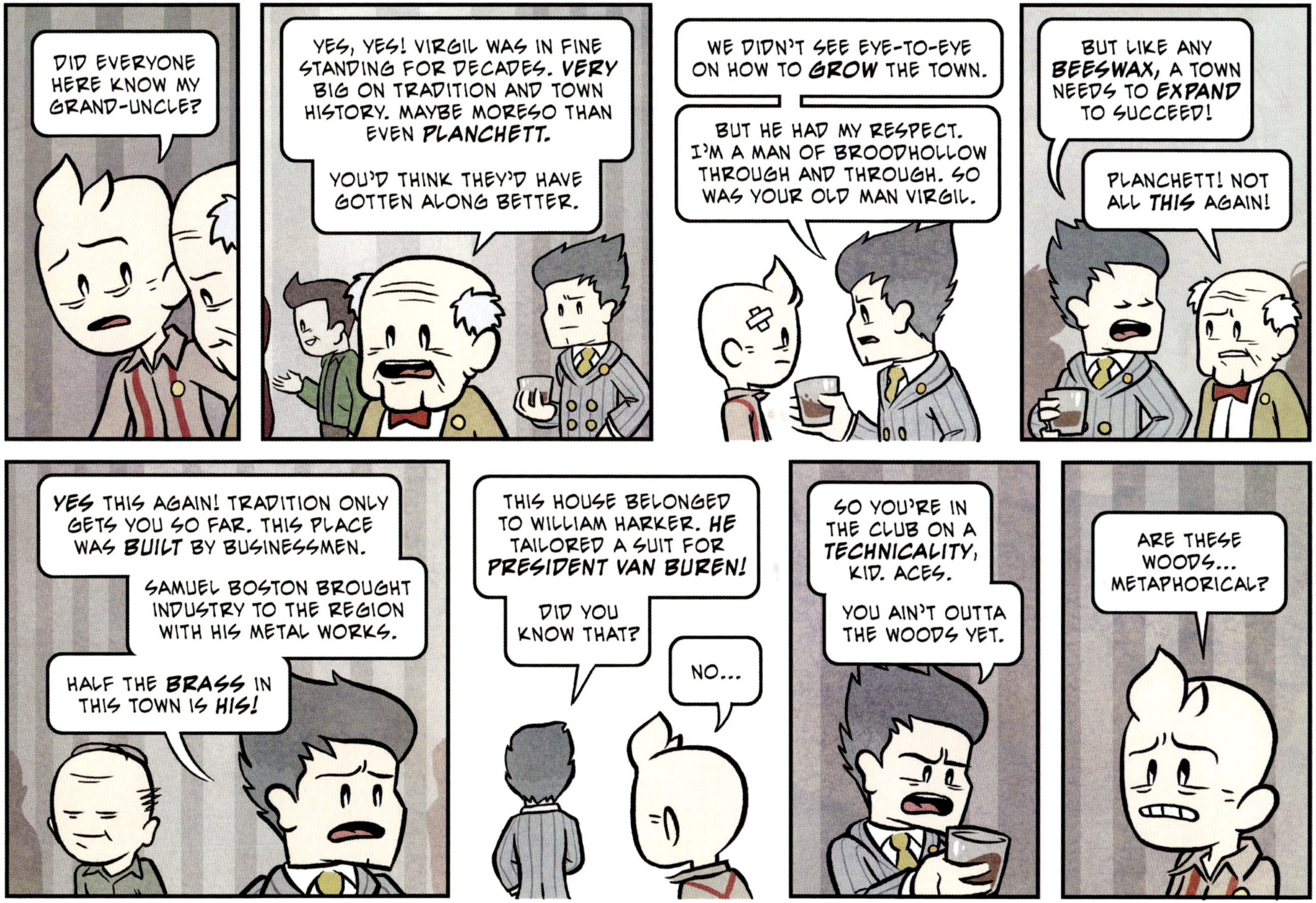
DID EVERYONE HERE KNOW MY GRAND-UNCLE?
YES, YES! VIRGIL WAS IN FINE STANDING FOR DECADES. VERY BIG ON TRADITION AND TOWN HISTORY. MAYBE MORESO THAN EVEN PLANCHETT.
YOU'D THINK THEY'D HAVE GOTTEN ALONG BETTER.
WE DIDN'T SEE EYE-TO-EYE ON HOW TO GROW THE TOWN.
BUT HE HAD MY RESPECT. I'M A MAN OF BROODHOLLOW THROUGH AND THROUGH. SO WAS YOUR OLD MAN VIRGIL.
BUT LIKE ANY BEESWAX, A TOWN NEEDS TO EXPAND TO SUCCEED!
PLANCHETT! NOT ALL THIS AGAIN!
YES THIS AGAIN! TRADITION ONLY GETS YOU SO FAR. THIS PLACE WAS BUILT BY BUSINESSMEN.
SAMUEL BOSTON BROUGHT INDUSTRY TO THE REGION WITH HIS METAL WORKS.
HALF THE BRASS IN THIS TOWN IS HIS!
THIS HOUSE BELONGED TO WILLIAM HARKER. HE TAILORED A SUIT FOR PRESIDENT VAN BUREN!
DID YOU KNOW THAT?
NO...
SO YOU'RE IN THE CLUB ON A TECHNICALITY, KID. ACES.
YOU AIN'T OUTTA THE WOODS YET.
ARE THESE WOODS... METAPHORICAL?

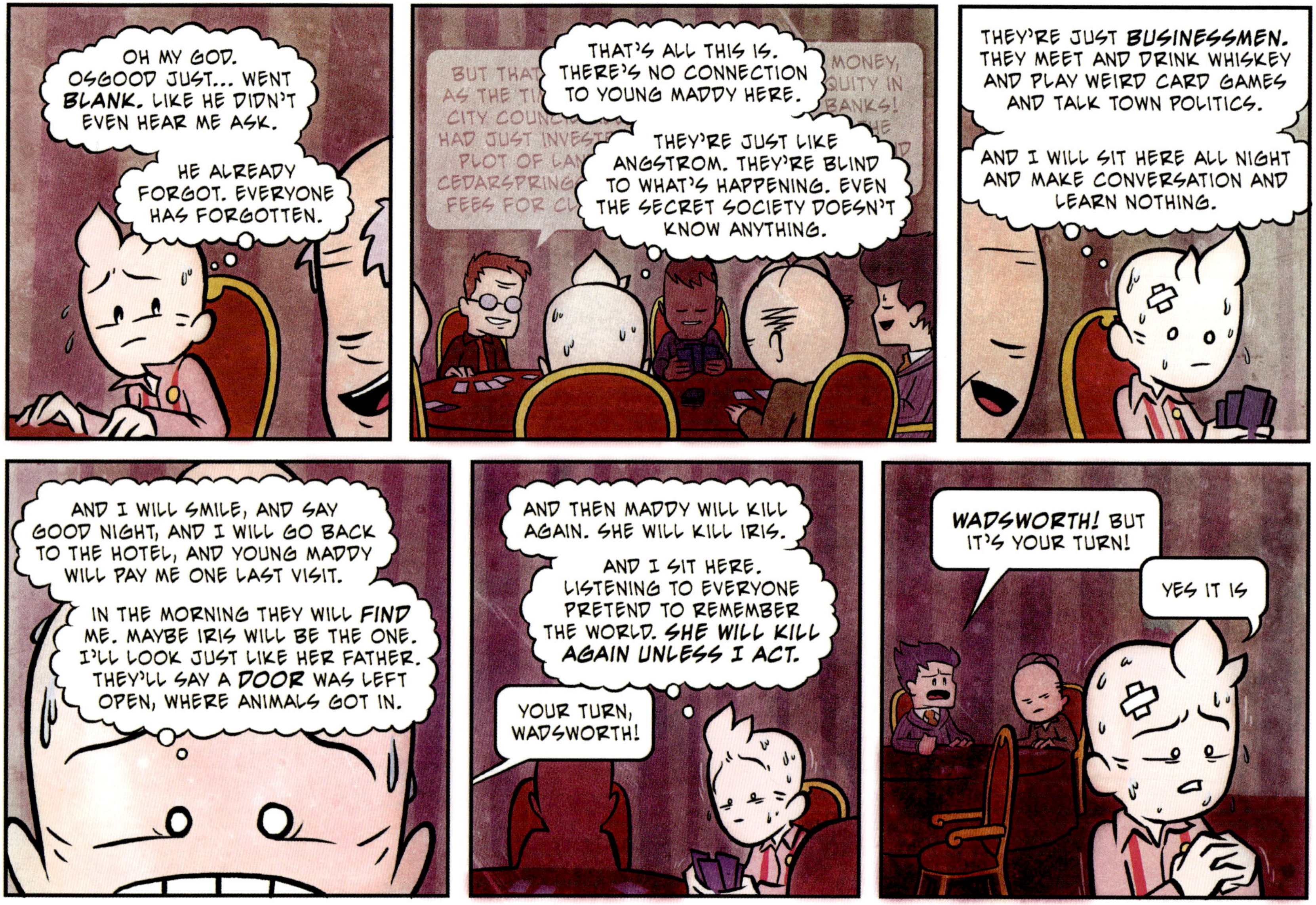

OH MY GOD. OSGOOD JUST... WENT BLANK. LIKE HE DIDN'T EVEN HEAR ME ASK.
HE ALREADY FORGOT. EVERYONE HAS FORGOTTEN.
THAT'S ALL THIS IS. THERE'S NO CONNECTION TO YOUNG MADDY HERE.
THEY'RE JUST LIKE ANGSTROM. THEY'RE BLIND TO WHAT'S HAPPENING. EVEN THE SECRET SOCIETY DOESN'T KNOW ANYTHING.
THEY'RE JUST BUSINESSMEN. THEY MEET AND DRINK WHISKEY AND PLAY WEIRD CARD GAMES AND TALK TOWN POLITICS.
AND I WILL SIT HERE ALL NIGHT AND MAKE CONVERSATION AND LEARN NOTHING.
AND I WILL SMILE, AND SAY GOOD NIGHT, AND I WILL GO BACK TO THE HOTEL, AND YOUNG MADDY WILL PAY ME ONE LAST VISIT.
IN THE MORNING THEY WILL FIND ME. MAYBE IRIS WILL BE THE ONE. I'LL LOOK JUST LIKE HER FATHER. THEY'LL SAY A DOOR WAS LEFT OPEN, WHERE ANIMALS GOT IN.
AND THEN MADDY WILL KILL AGAIN. SHE WILL KILL IRIS.
AND I SIT HERE. LISTENING TO EVERYONE PRETEND TO REMEMBER THE WORLD. SHE WILL KILL AGAIN UNLESS I ACT.
YOUR TURN, WADSWORTH!
WADSWORTH! BUT IT'S YOUR TURN!
YES IT IS

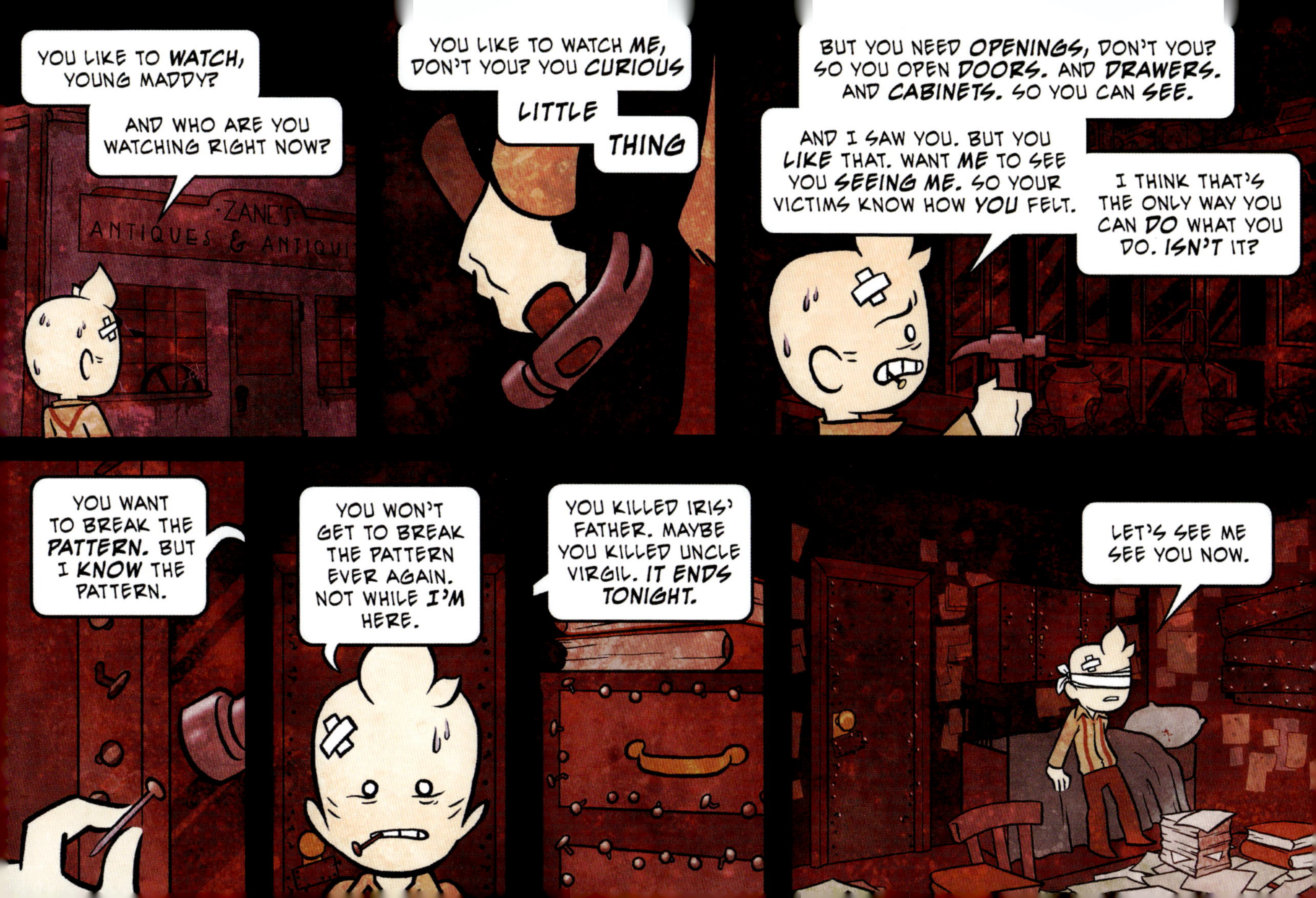
YOU LIKE TO WATCH, YOUNG MADDY?
AND WHO ARE YOU WATCHING RIGHT NOW?
ZANE'S ANTIQUES & ANTIQU
YOU LIKE TO WATCH ME, DON'T YOU? YOU CURIOUS
LITTLE
THING
BUT YOU NEED OPENINGS, DON'T YOU? SO YOU OPEN DOORS. AND DRAWERS. AND CABINETS. SO YOU CAN SEE.
AND I SAW YOU. BUT YOU LIKE THAT. WANT ME TO SEE YOU SEEING ME. SO YOUR VICTIMS KNOW HOW YOU FELT.
I THINK THAT'S THE ONLY WAY YOU CAN DO WHAT YOU DO. ISN'T IT?
YOU WANT TO BREAK THE PATTERN. BUT I KNOW THE PATTERN.
YOU WON'T GET TO BREAK THE PATTERN EVER AGAIN. NOT WHILE I'M HERE.
YOU KILLED IRIS' FATHER. MAYBE YOU KILLED UNCLE VIRGIL. IT ENDS TONIGHT.
LET'S SEE ME SEE YOU NOW.

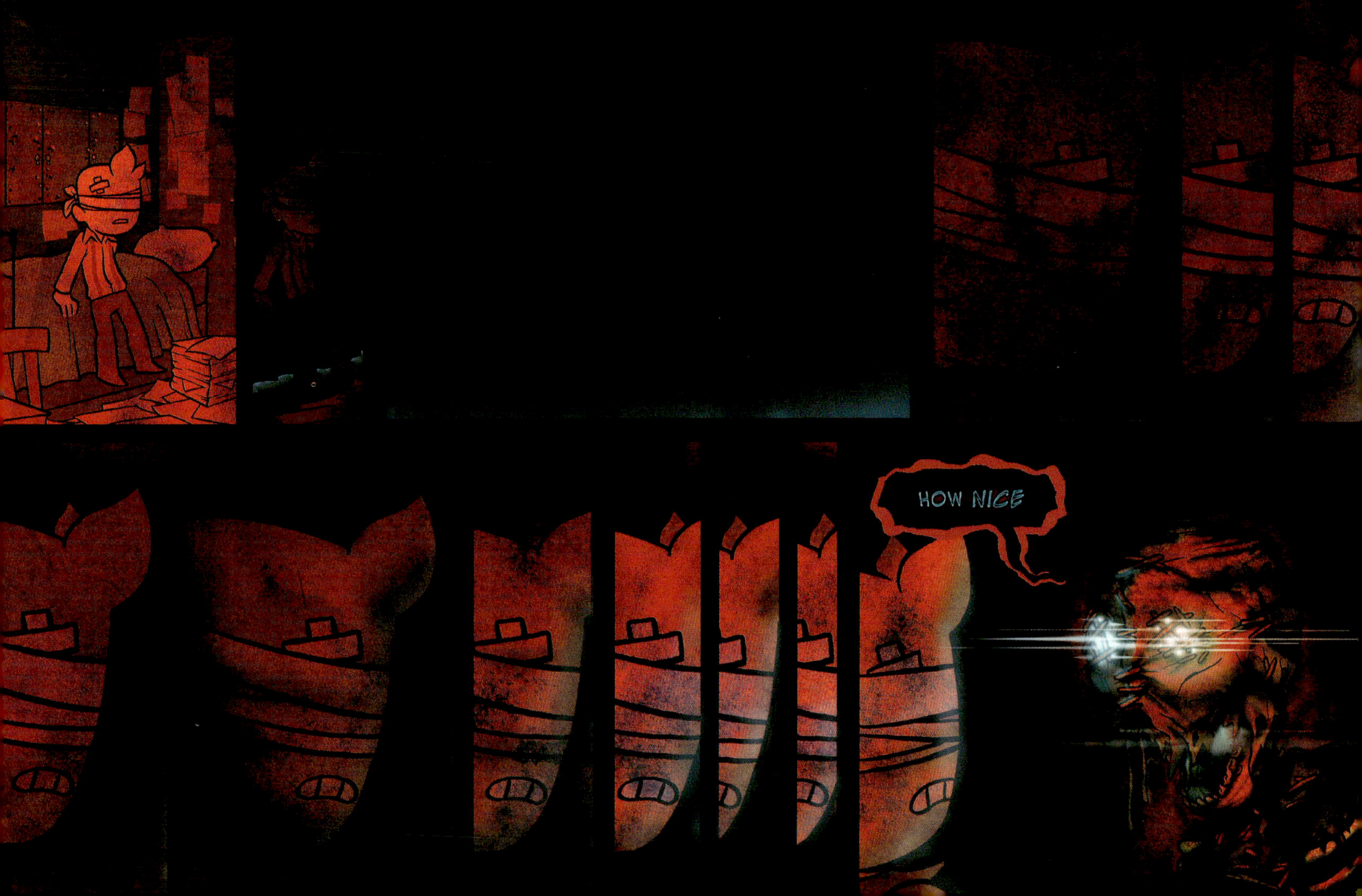
HOW NICE

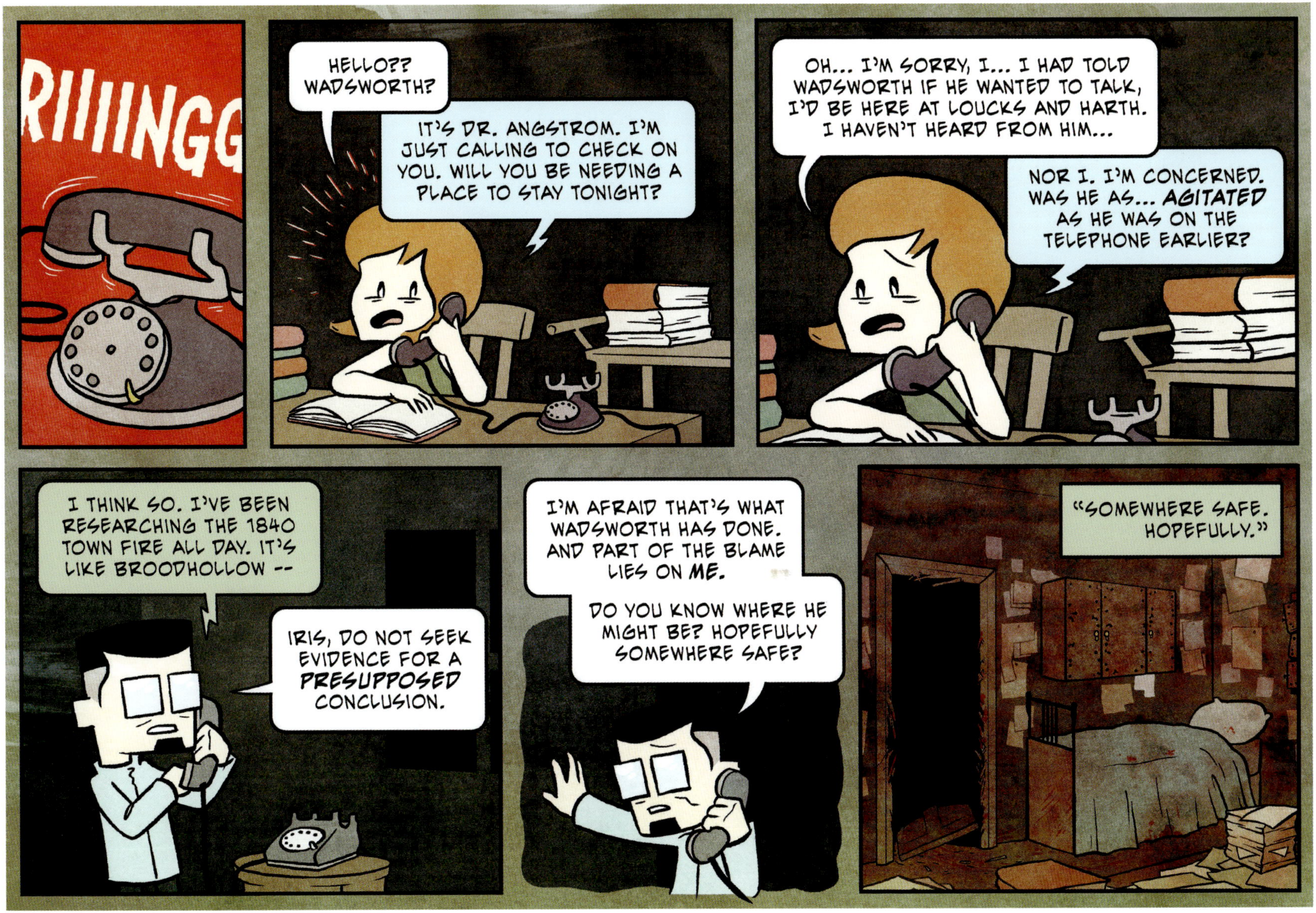
RIIINGG
HELLO?? WADSWORTH?
IT'S DR. ANGSTROM. I'M JUST CALLING TO CHECK ON YOU. WILL YOU BE NEEDING A PLACE TO STAY TONIGHT?
OH... I'M SORRY, I... I HAD TOLD WADSWORTH IF HE WANTED TO TALK, I'D BE HERE AT LOUCKS AND HARTH. I HAVEN'T HEARD FROM HIM...
NOR I. I'M CONCERNED. WAS HE AS... AGITATED AS HE WAS ON THE TELEPHONE EARLIER?
I THINK SO. I'VE BEEN RESEARCHING THE 1840 TOWN FIRE ALL DAY. IT'S LIKE BROODHOLLOW --
IRIS, DO NOT SEEK EVIDENCE FOR A PRESUPPOSED CONCLUSION.
I'M AFRAID THAT'S WHAT WADSWORTH HAS DONE. AND PART OF THE BLAME LIES ON ME.
DO YOU KNOW WHERE HE MIGHT BE? HOPEFULLY SOMEWHERE SAFE?
"SOMEWHERE SAFE. HOPEFULLY."

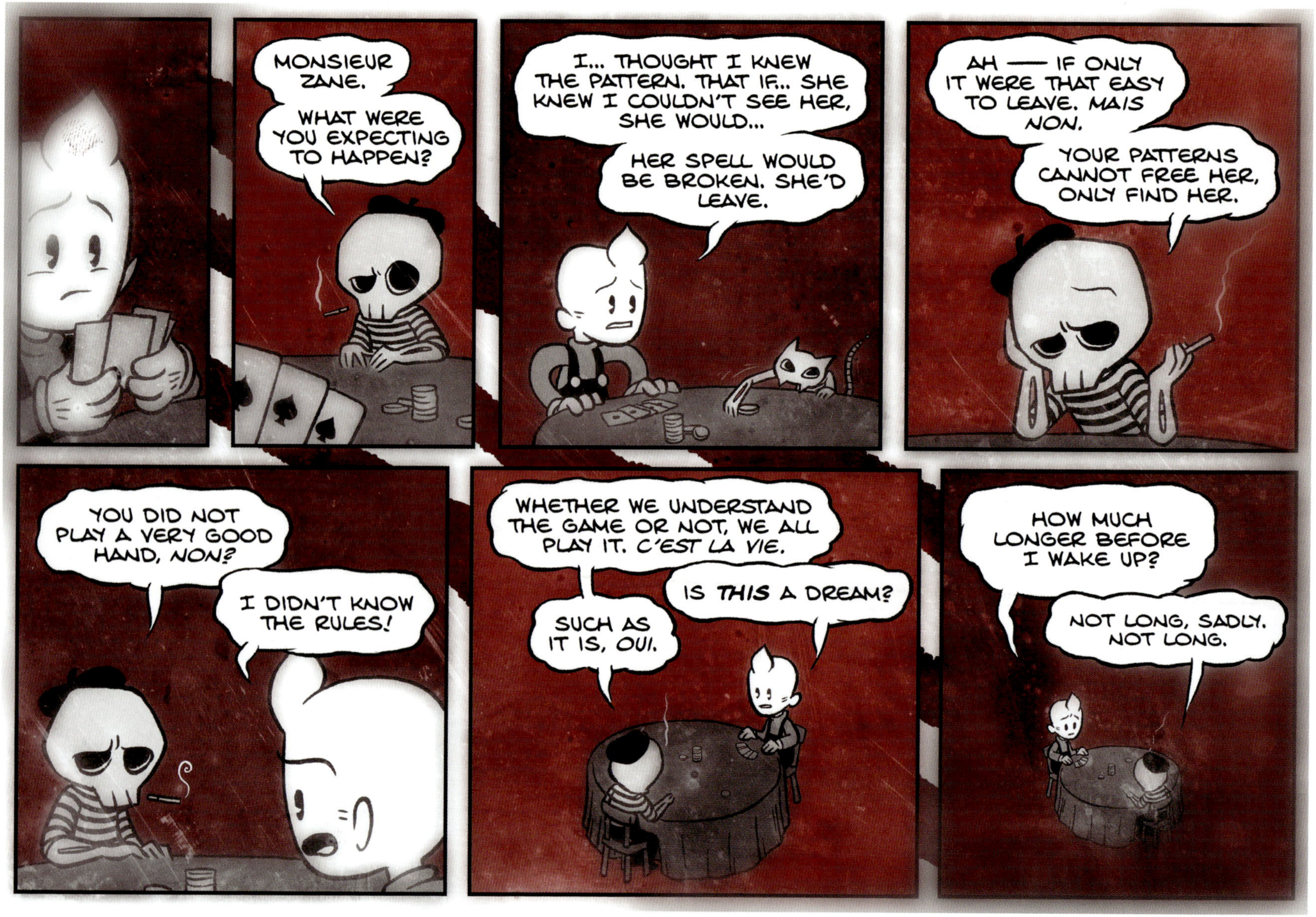

MONSIEUR ZANE.
WHAT WERE YOU EXPECTING TO HAPPEN?
I... THOUGHT I KNEW THE PATTERN. THAT IF... SHE KNEW I COULDN'T SEE HER, SHE WOULD...
HER SPELL WOULD BE BROKEN. SHE'D LEAVE.
AH — IF ONLY IT WERE THAT EASY TO LEAVE. *MAIS NON.*
YOUR PATTERNS CANNOT FREE HER, ONLY FIND HER.
YOU DID NOT PLAY A VERY GOOD HAND, *NON?*
I DIDN'T KNOW THE RULES!
WHETHER WE UNDERSTAND THE GAME OR NOT, WE ALL PLAY IT. *C'EST LA VIE.*
IS ***THIS*** A DREAM?
SUCH AS IT IS, *OUI.*
HOW MUCH LONGER BEFORE I WAKE UP?
NOT LONG, SADLY. NOT LONG.

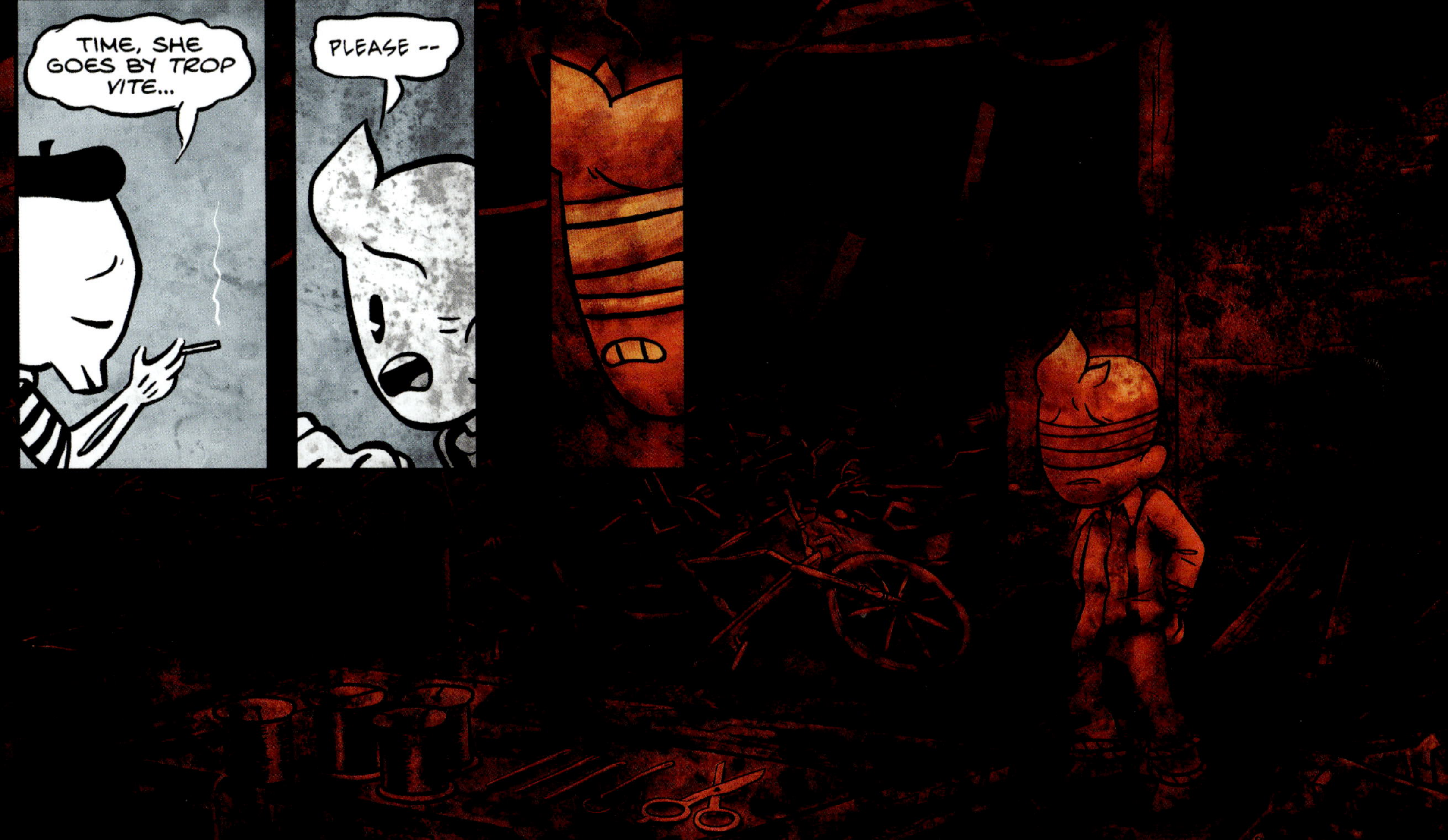
TIME, SHE GOES BY TROP VITE...
PLEASE --

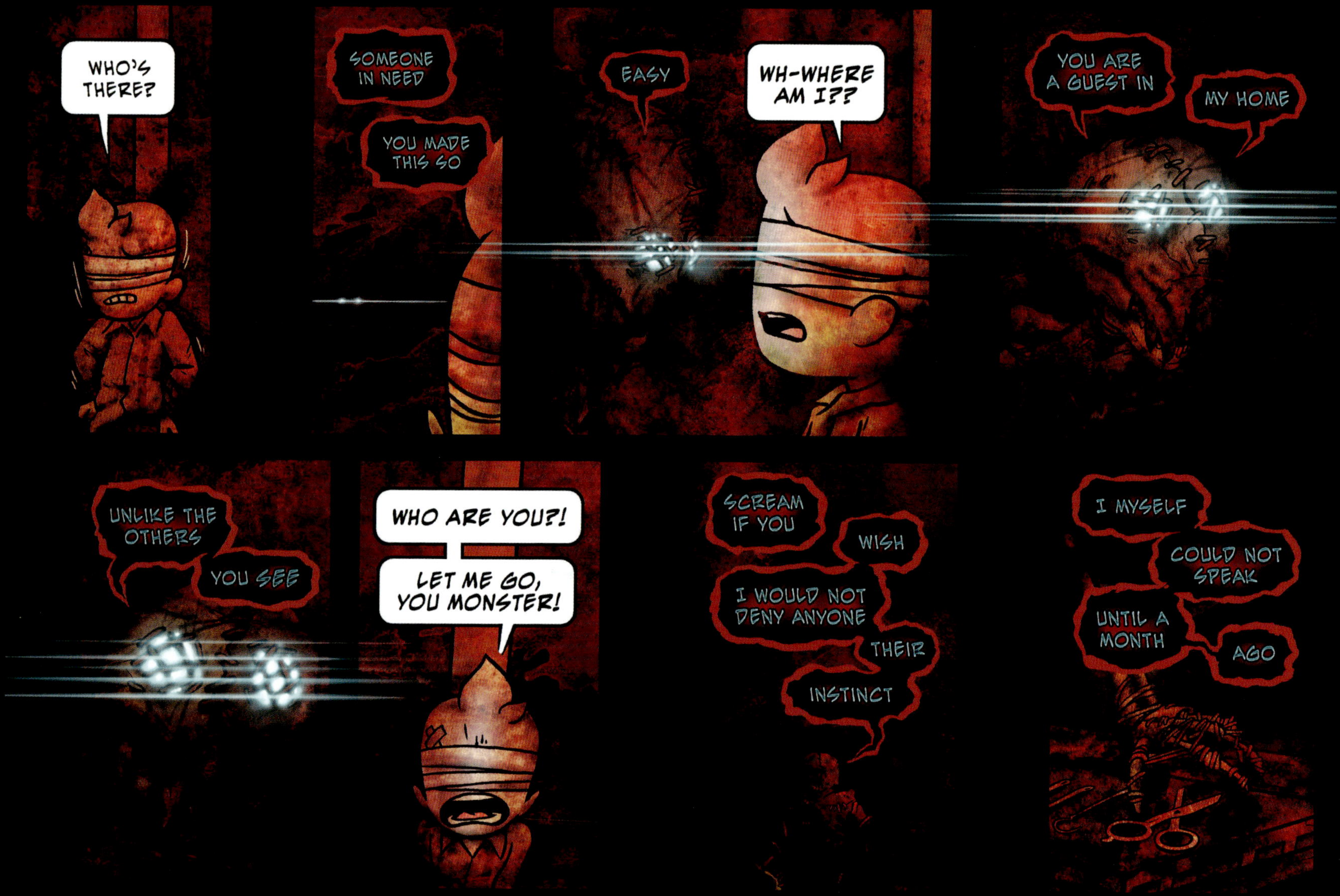
WHO'S THERE?
SOMEONE IN NEED
YOU MADE THIS SO
EASY
WH-WHERE AM I??
YOU ARE A GUEST IN
MY HOME
UNLIKE THE OTHERS
YOU SEE
WHO ARE YOU?!
LET ME GO, YOU MONSTER!
SCREAM IF YOU
WISH
I WOULD NOT DENY ANYONE
THEIR
INSTINCT
I MYSELF
COULD NOT SPEAK
UNTIL A MONTH
AGO

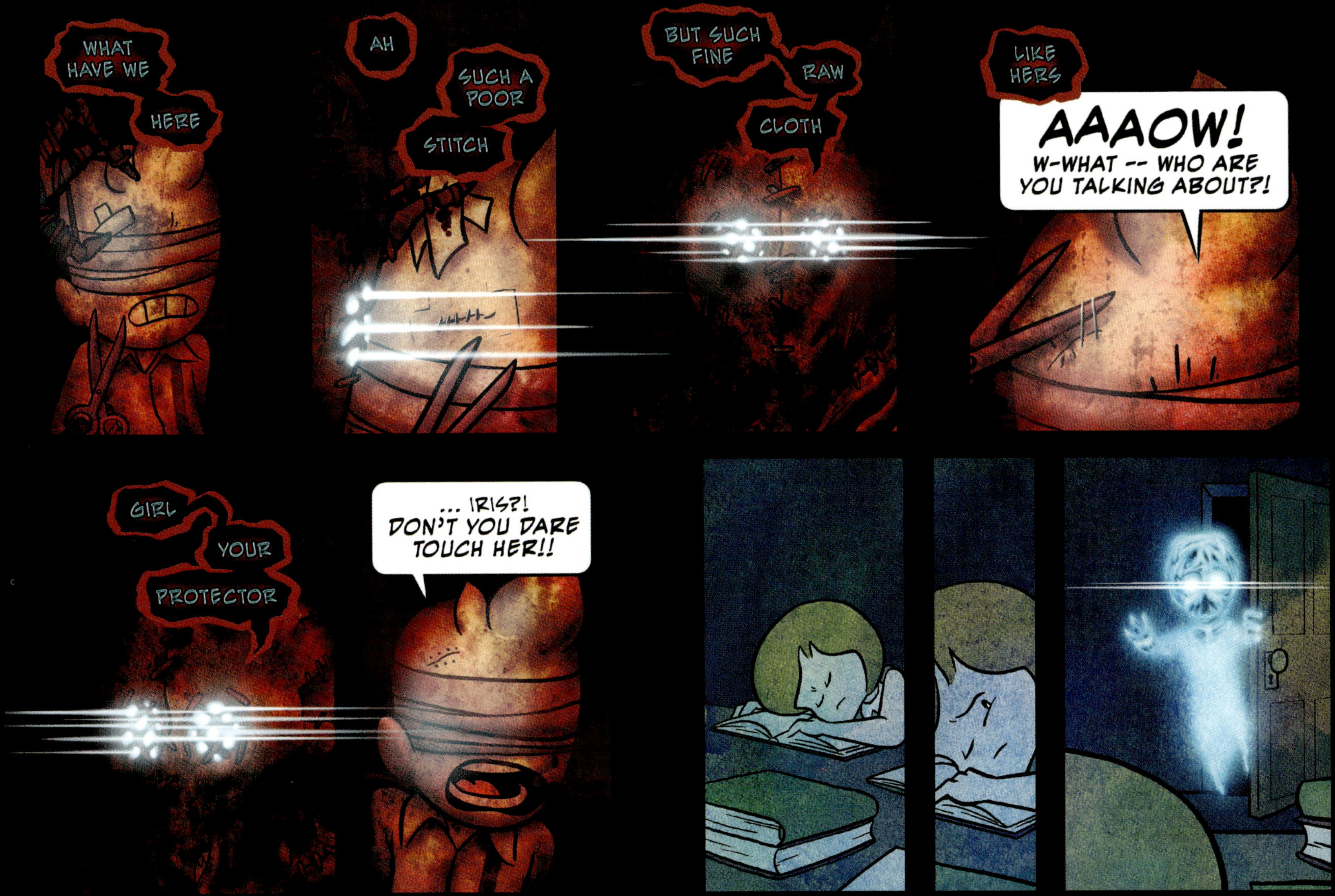
WHAT HAVE WE
HERE
AH
SUCH A POOR
STITCH
BUT SUCH FINE
RAW
CLOTH
LIKE HERS
AAAOW!
W-WHAT -- WHO ARE YOU TALKING ABOUT?!
GIRL
YOUR
PROTECTOR
... IRIS?! DON'T YOU DARE TOUCH HER!!

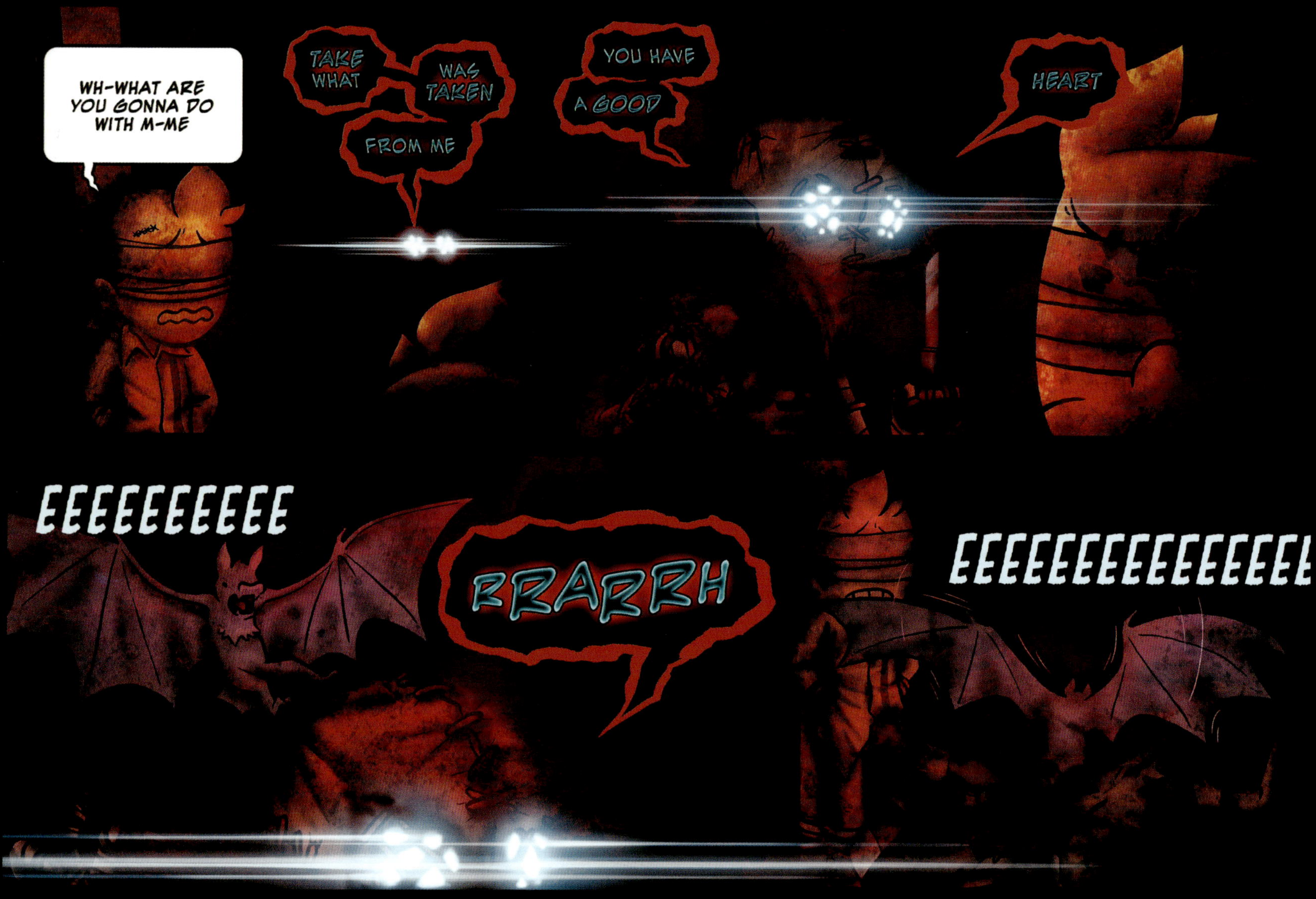
WH-WHAT ARE YOU GONNA DO WITH M-ME
TAKE WHAT
WAS TAKEN
FROM ME
YOU HAVE
A GOOD
HEART
EEEEEEEEEE
RRARRH
EEEEEEEEEEEEEEE

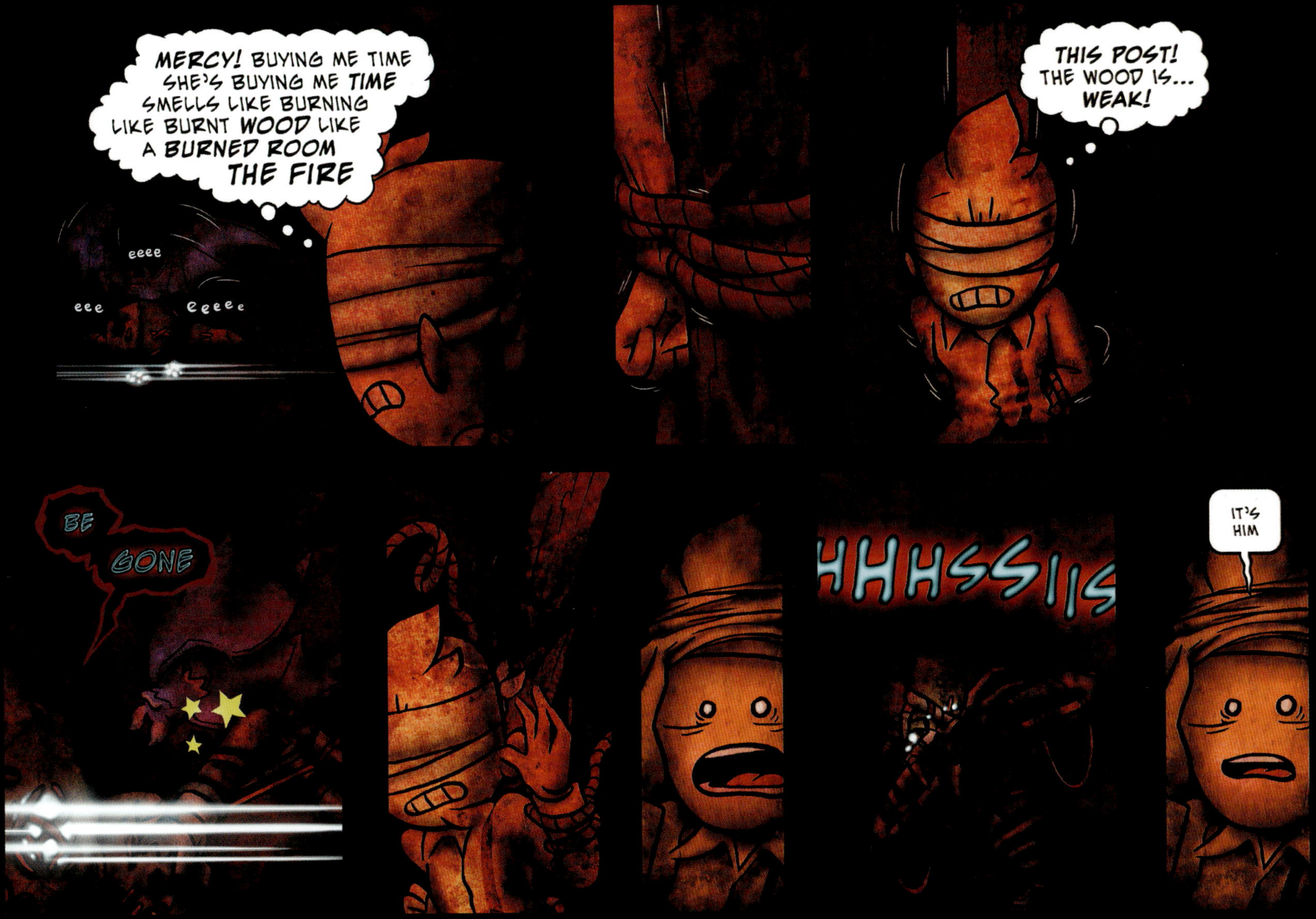
MERCY! BUYING ME TIME SHE'S BUYING ME TIME SMELLS LIKE BURNING LIKE BURNT WOOD LIKE A BURNED ROOM THE FIRE
eeee
eee
eeeee
THIS POST! THE WOOD IS... WEAK!
BE GONE
HHHSSIIS
IT'S HIM

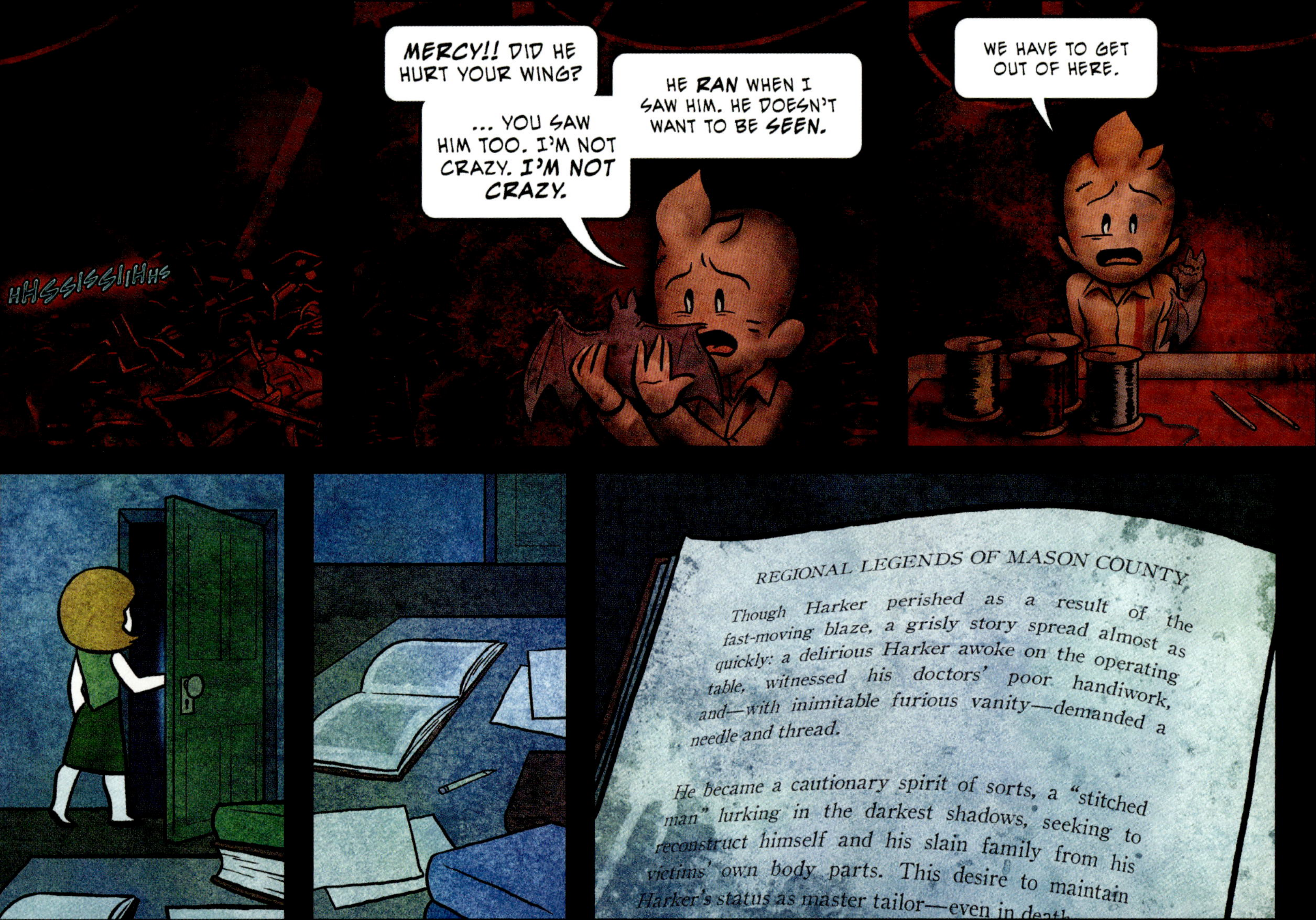
HHSSISSIIHHS
MERCY!! DID HE HURT YOUR WING?
... YOU SAW HIM TOO. I'M NOT CRAZY. I'M NOT CRAZY.
HE RAN WHEN I SAW HIM. HE DOESN'T WANT TO BE SEEN.
WE HAVE TO GET OUT OF HERE.
REGIONAL LEGENDS OF MASON COUNTY
Though Harker perished as a result of the fast-moving blaze, a grisly story spread almost as quickly: a delirious Harker awoke on the operating table, witnessed his doctors' poor handiwork, and—with inimitable furious vanity—demanded a needle and thread.
He became a cautionary spirit of sorts, a "stitched man" lurking in the darkest shadows, seeking to reconstruct himself and his slain family from his victims' own body parts. This desire to maintain Harker's status as master tailor—even in death

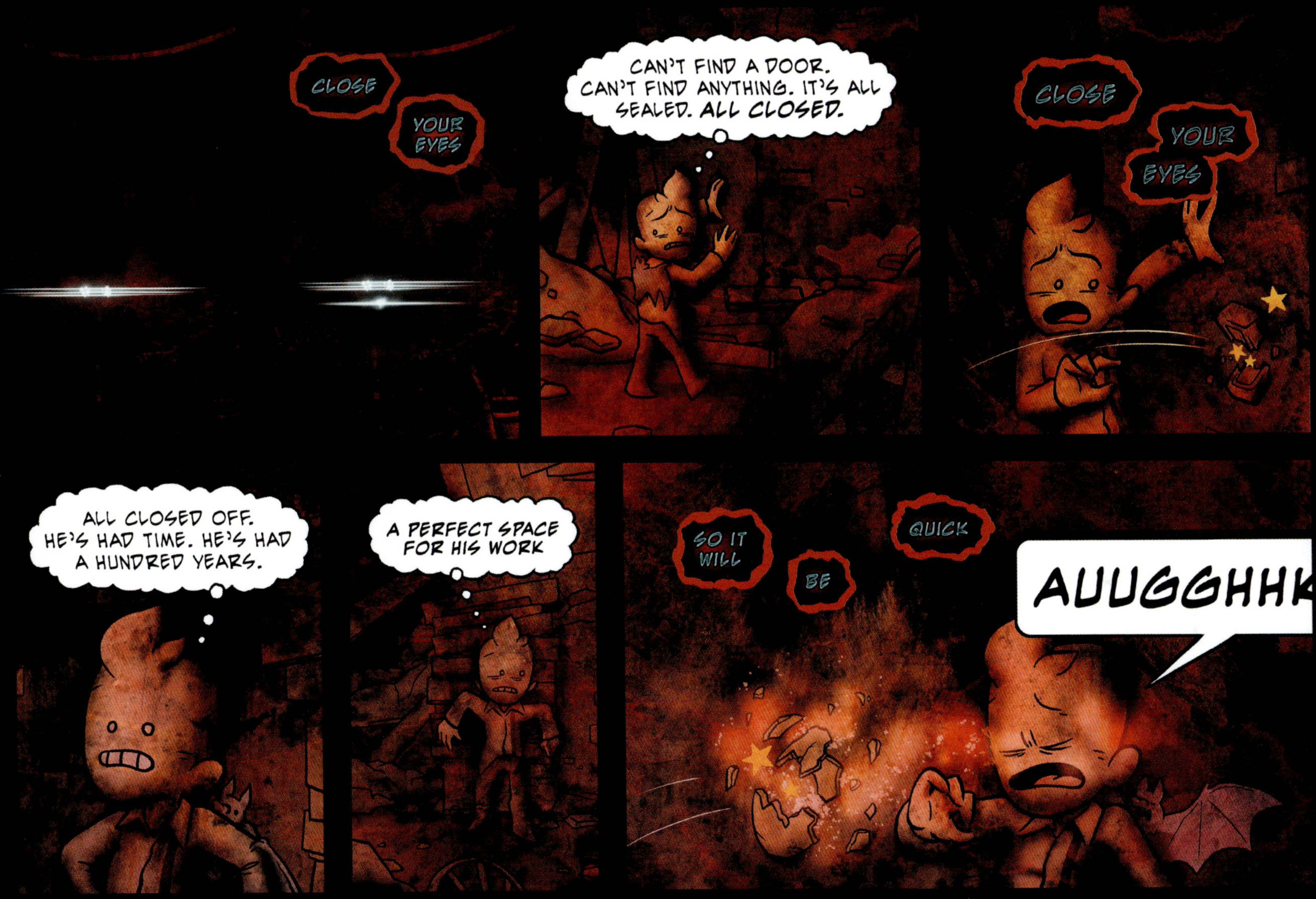
CLOSE
YOUR EYES
CAN'T FIND A DOOR. CAN'T FIND ANYTHING. IT'S ALL SEALED. ALL CLOSED.
CLOSE
YOUR
EYES
ALL CLOSED OFF. HE'S HAD TIME. HE'S HAD A HUNDRED YEARS.
A PERFECT SPACE FOR HIS WORK
SO IT WILL
BE
QUICK
AUUGGHHK

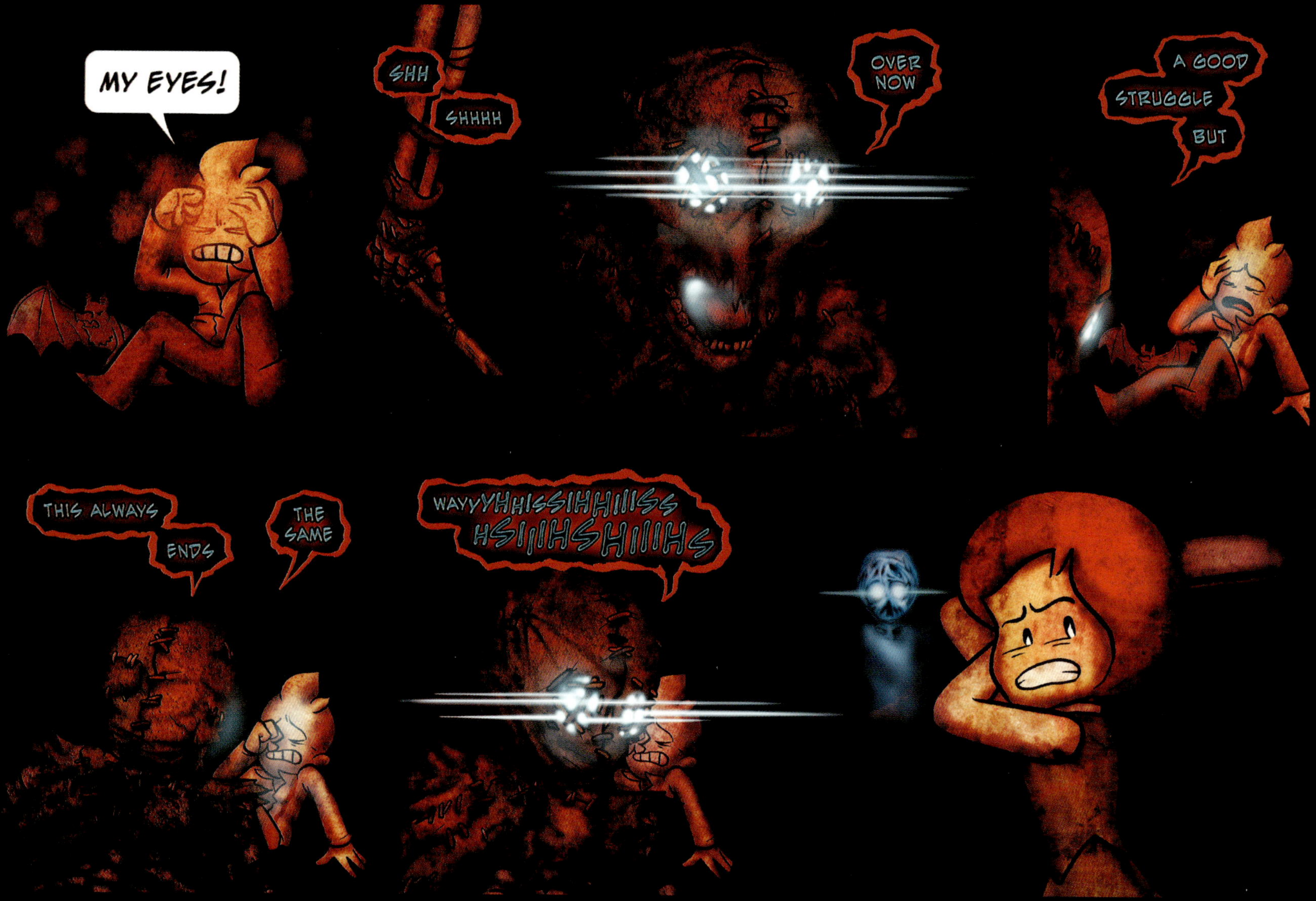
MY EYES!
SHH
SHHHH
OVER NOW
A GOOD STRUGGLE BUT
THIS ALWAYS ENDS
THE SAME
WAYYYHHISSIHHIIISS HSIIIHSHIIIHS

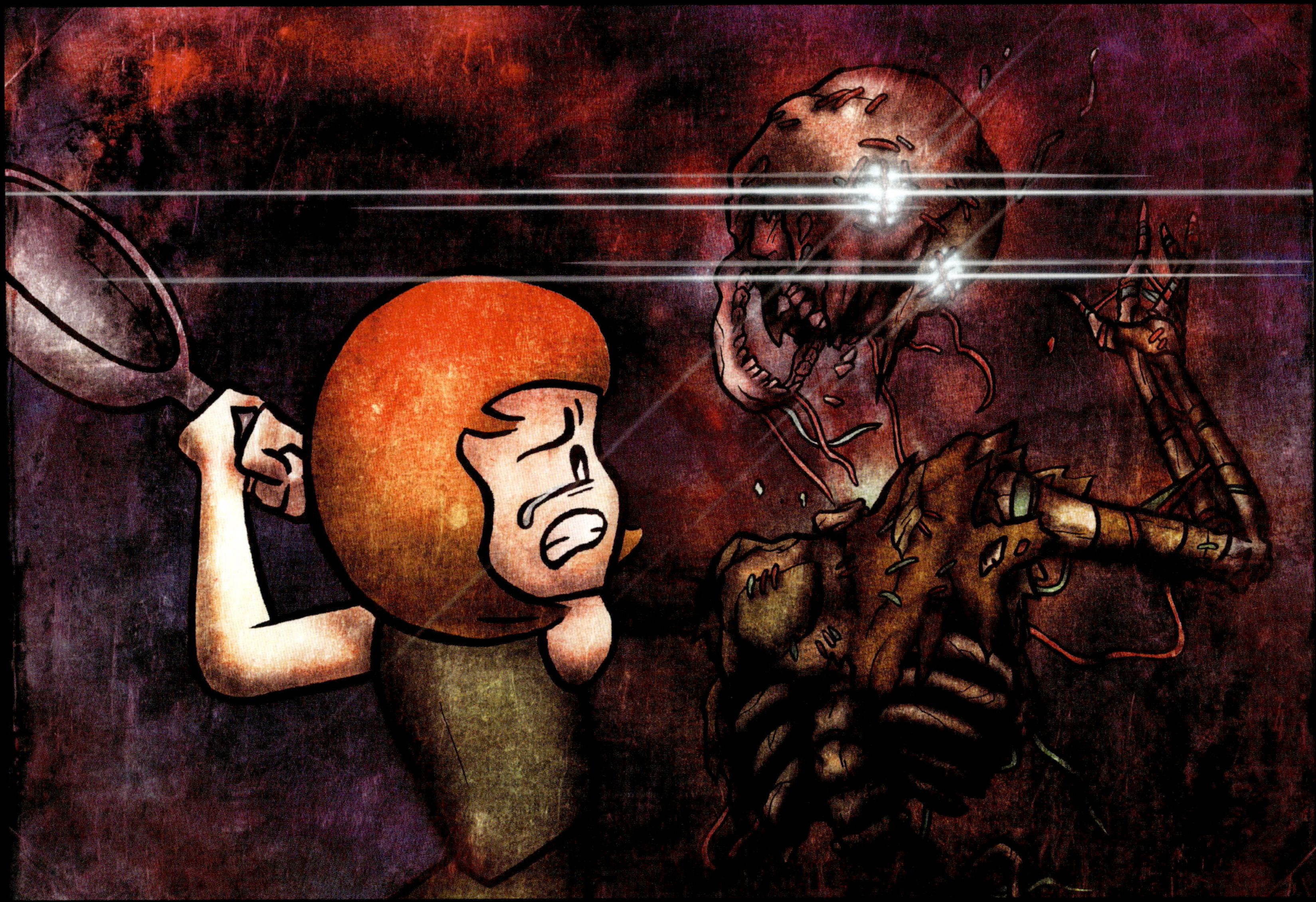

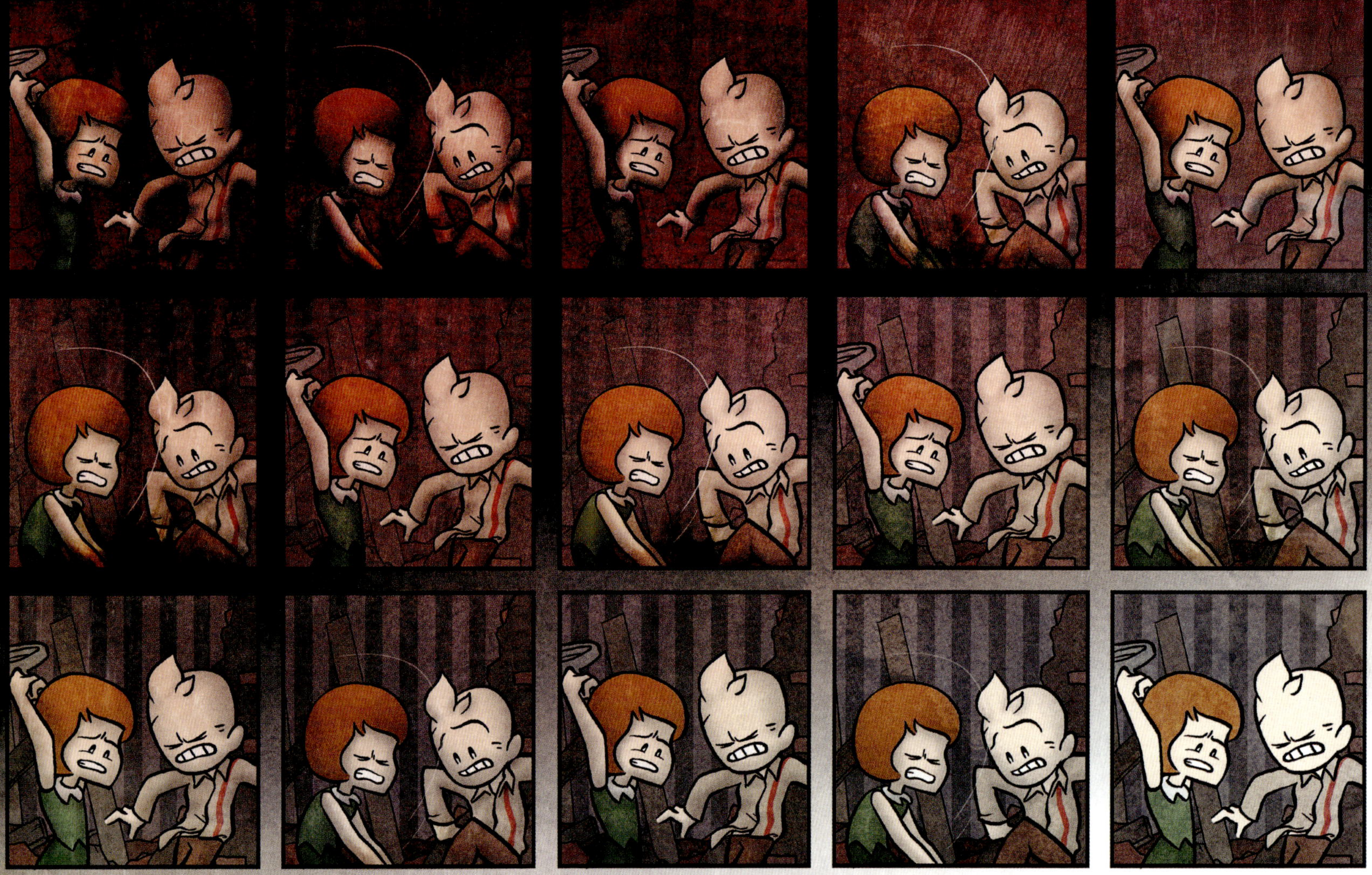

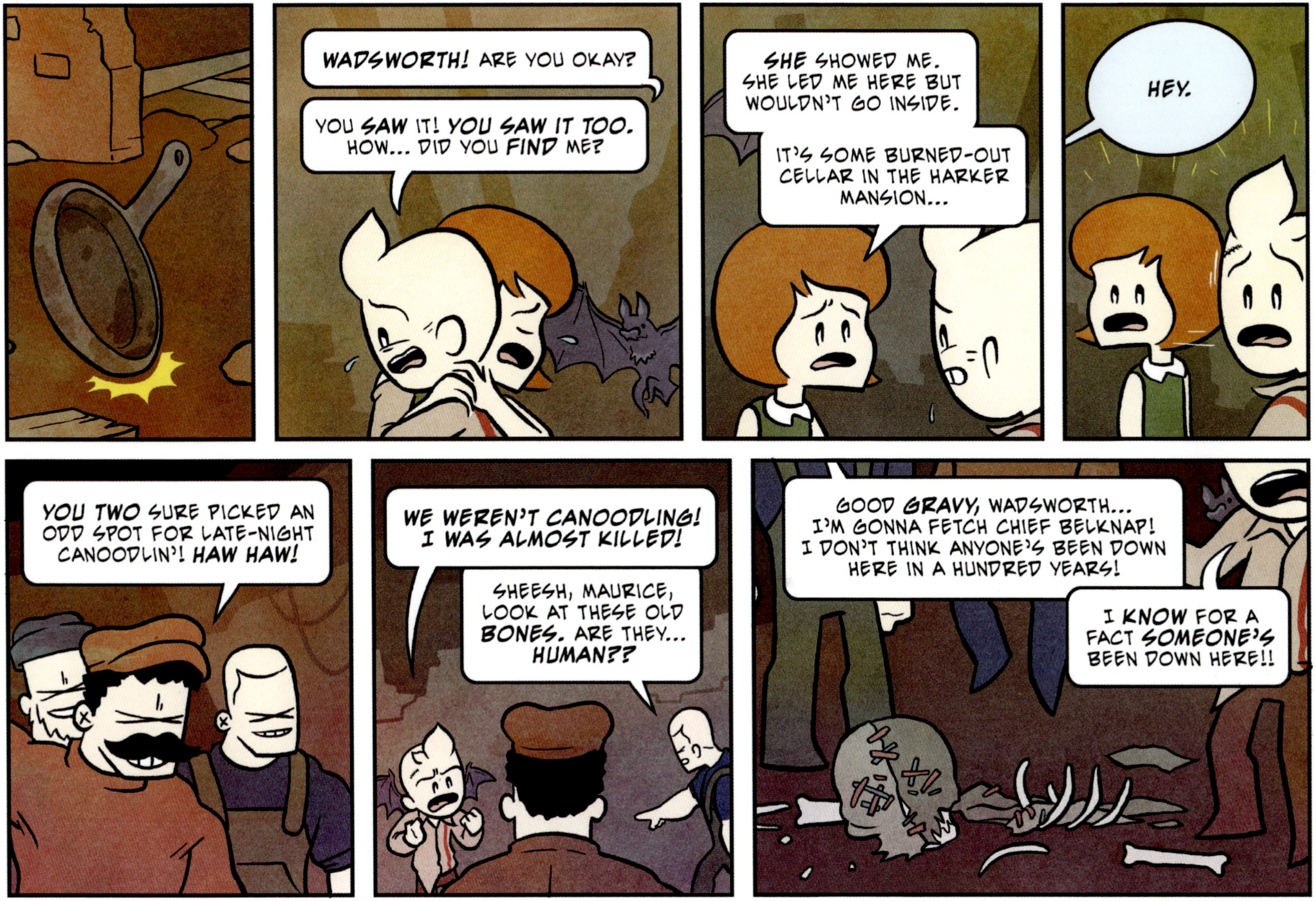
WADSWORTH! ARE YOU OKAY?
YOU SAW IT! YOU SAW IT TOO. HOW... DID YOU FIND ME?
SHE SHOWED ME. SHE LED ME HERE BUT WOULDN'T GO INSIDE.
IT'S SOME BURNED-OUT CELLAR IN THE HARKER MANSION...
HEY.
YOU TWO SURE PICKED AN ODD SPOT FOR LATE-NIGHT CANOODLIN'! HAW HAW!
WE WEREN'T CANOODLING! I WAS ALMOST KILLED!
SHEESH, MAURICE, LOOK AT THESE OLD BONES. ARE THEY... HUMAN??
GOOD GRAVY, WADSWORTH... I'M GONNA FETCH CHIEF BELKNAP! I DON'T THINK ANYONE'S BEEN DOWN HERE IN A HUNDRED YEARS!
I KNOW FOR A FACT SOMEONE'S BEEN DOWN HERE!!

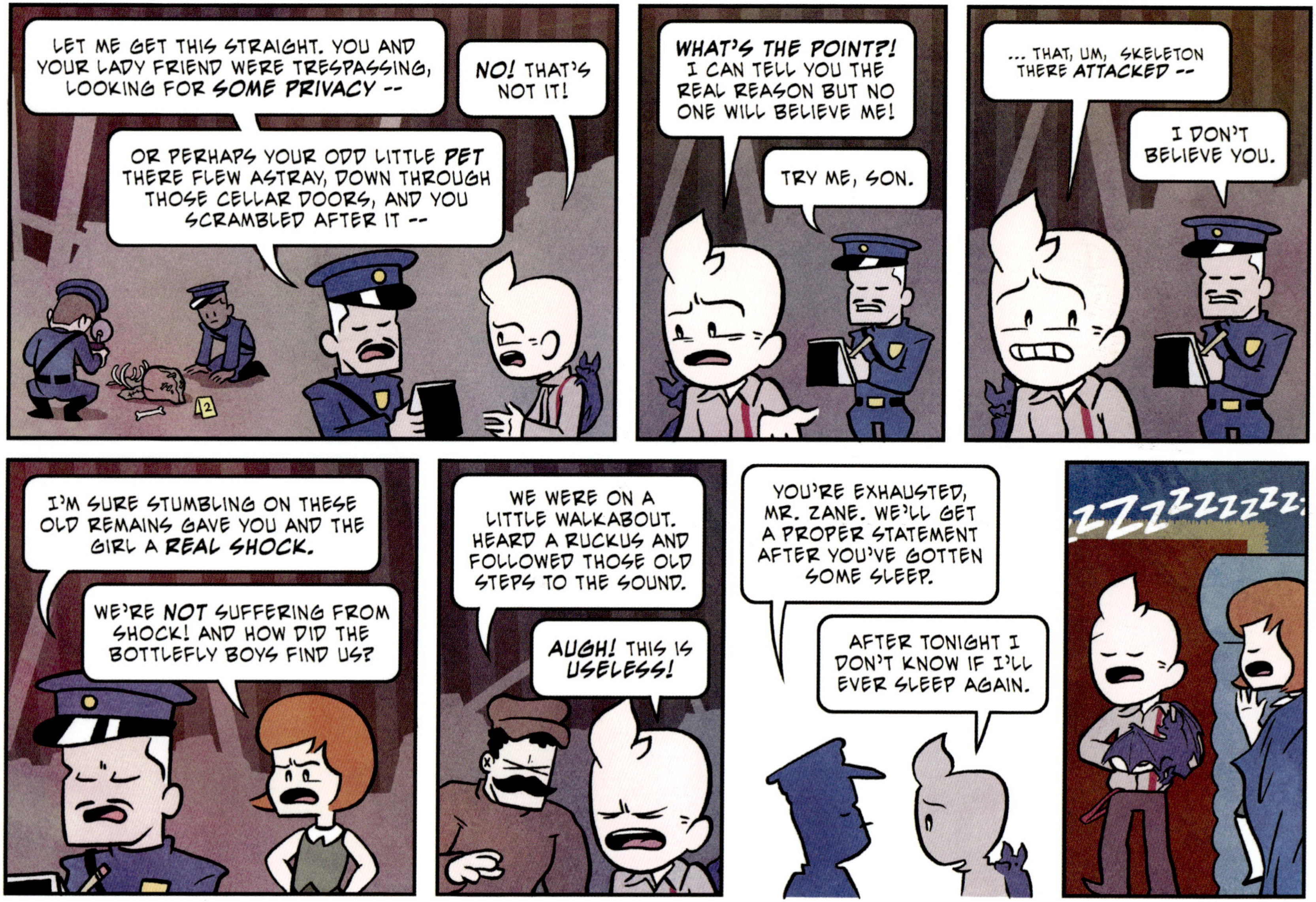
LET ME GET THIS STRAIGHT. YOU AND YOUR LADY FRIEND WERE TRESPASSING, LOOKING FOR SOME PRIVACY --
OR PERHAPS YOUR ODD LITTLE PET THERE FLEW ASTRAY, DOWN THROUGH THOSE CELLAR DOORS, AND YOU SCRAMBLED AFTER IT --
NO! THAT'S NOT IT!
WHAT'S THE POINT?! I CAN TELL YOU THE REAL REASON BUT NO ONE WILL BELIEVE ME!
TRY ME, SON.
... THAT, UM, SKELETON THERE ATTACKED --
I DON'T BELIEVE YOU.
I'M SURE STUMBLING ON THESE OLD REMAINS GAVE YOU AND THE GIRL A REAL SHOCK.
WE'RE NOT SUFFERING FROM SHOCK! AND HOW DID THE BOTTLEFLY BOYS FIND US?
WE WERE ON A LITTLE WALKABOUT. HEARD A RUCKUS AND FOLLOWED THOSE OLD STEPS TO THE SOUND.
AUGH! THIS IS USELESS!
YOU'RE EXHAUSTED, MR. ZANE. WE'LL GET A PROPER STATEMENT AFTER YOU'VE GOTTEN SOME SLEEP.
AFTER TONIGHT I DON'T KNOW IF I'LL EVER SLEEP AGAIN.
ZZZZZZZZZ

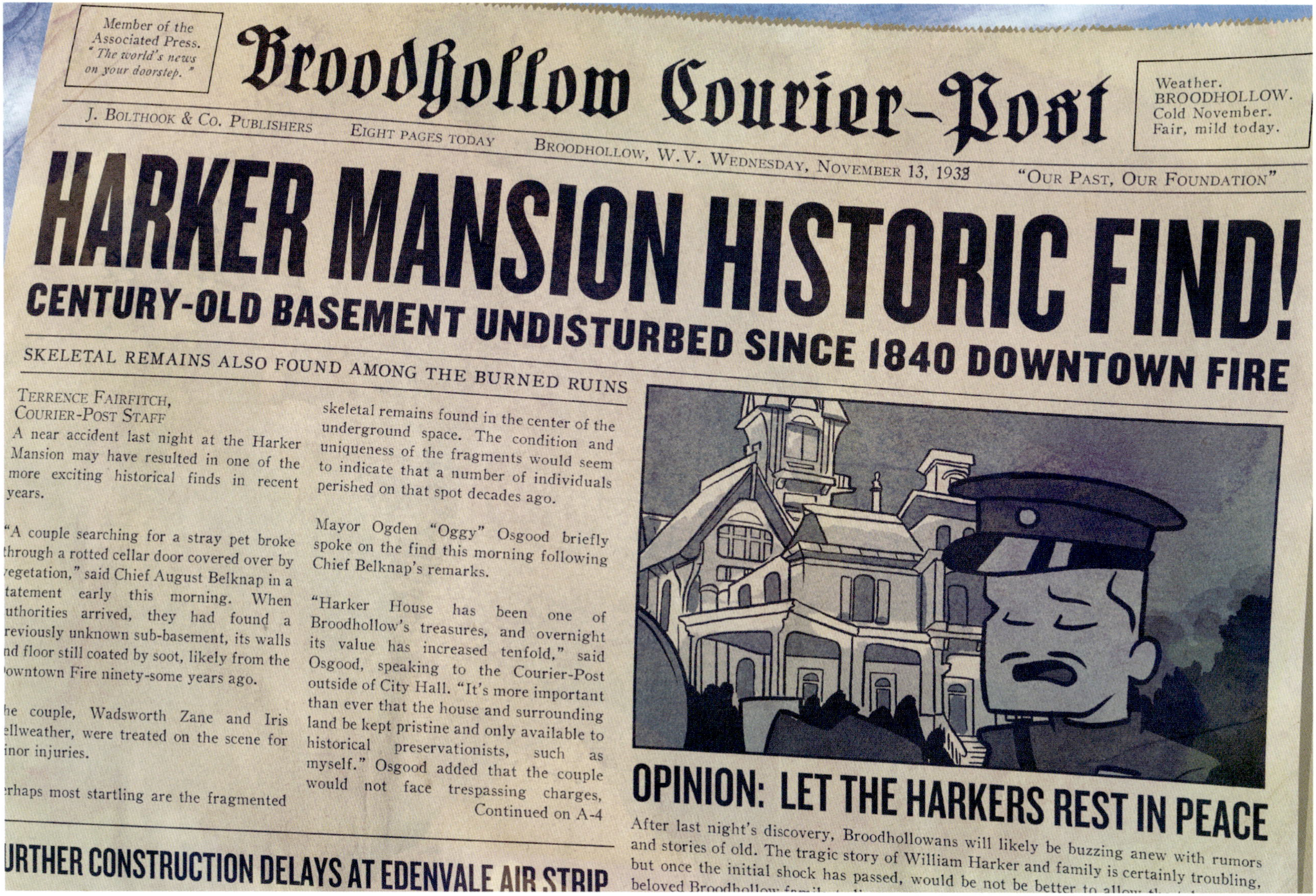

Member of the Associated Press. "The world's news on your doorstep."

Broodhollow Courier-Post

Weather. BROODHOLLOW. Cold November. Fair, mild today.

J. BOLTHOOK & CO. PUBLISHERS EIGHT PAGES TODAY BROODHOLLOW, W.V. WEDNESDAY, NOVEMBER 13, 1932 "OUR PAST, OUR FOUNDATION"

HARKER MANSION HISTORIC FIND!

CENTURY-OLD BASEMENT UNDISTURBED SINCE 1840 DOWNTOWN FIRE

SKELETAL REMAINS ALSO FOUND AMONG THE BURNED RUINS

TERRENCE FAIRFITCH, COURIER-POST STAFF

A near accident last night at the Harker Mansion may have resulted in one of the more exciting historical finds in recent years.

"A couple searching for a stray pet broke through a rotted cellar door covered over by egetation," said Chief August Belknap in a tatement early this morning. When uthorities arrived, they had found a reviously unknown sub-basement, its walls nd floor still coated by soot, likely from the owntown Fire ninety-some years ago.

he couple, Wadsworth Zane and Iris ellweather, were treated on the scene for inor injuries.

erhaps most startling are the fragmented skeletal remains found in the center of the underground space. The condition and uniqueness of the fragments would seem to indicate that a number of individuals perished on that spot decades ago.

Mayor Ogden "Oggy" Osgood briefly spoke on the find this morning following Chief Belknap's remarks.

"Harker House has been one of Broodhollow's treasures, and overnight its value has increased tenfold," said Osgood, speaking to the Courier-Post outside of City Hall. "It's more important than ever that the house and surrounding land be kept pristine and only available to historical preservationists, such as myself." Osgood added that the couple would not face trespassing charges,

Continued on A-4

OPINION: LET THE HARKERS REST IN PEACE

After last night's discovery, Broodhollowans will likely be buzzing anew with rumors and stories of old. The tragic story of William Harker and family is certainly troubling, but once the initial shock has passed, would be not be better to allow

URTHER CONSTRUCTION DELAYS AT EDENVALE AIR STRIP

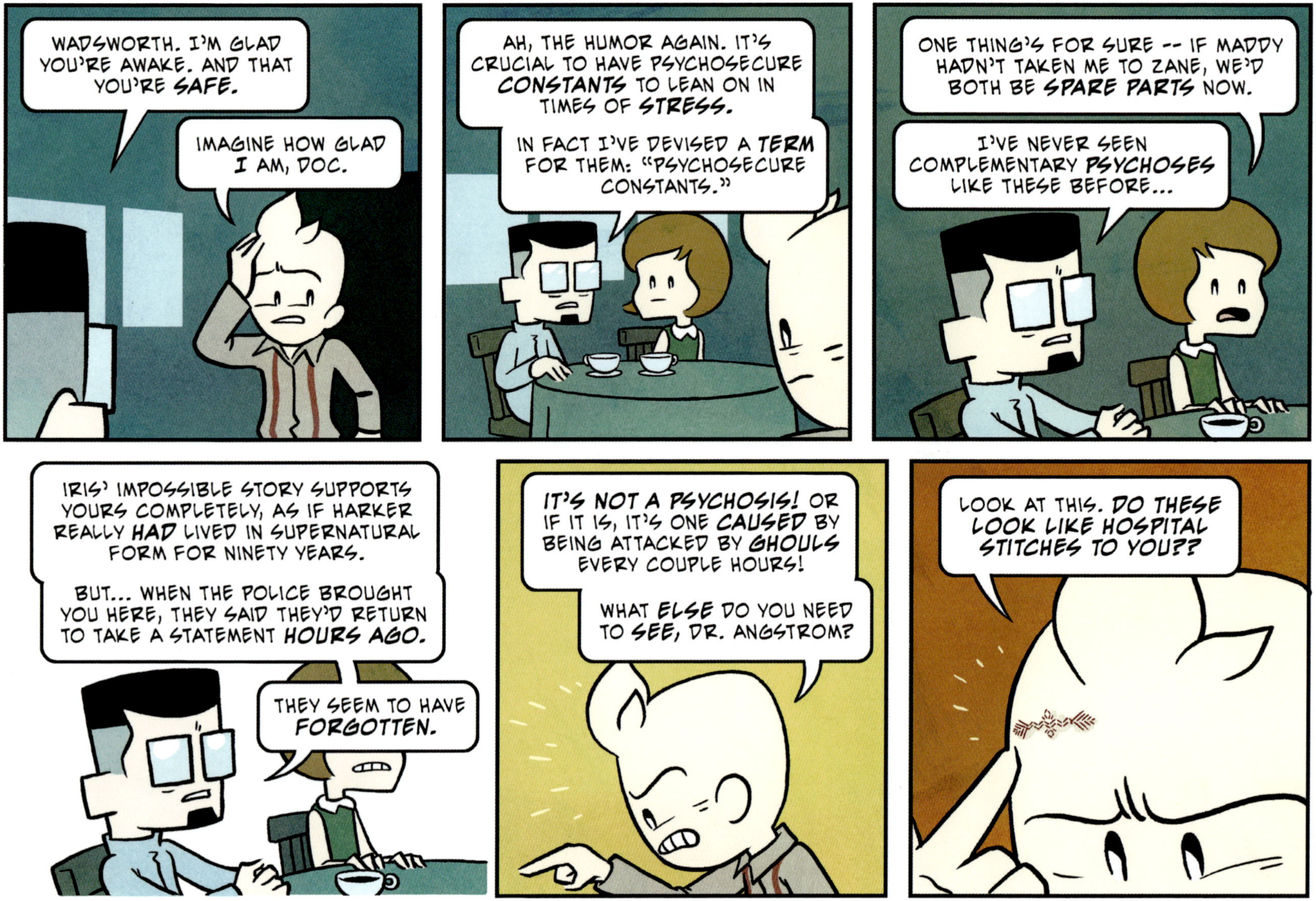
WADSWORTH. I'M GLAD YOU'RE AWAKE. AND THAT YOU'RE SAFE.
IMAGINE HOW GLAD I AM, DOC.
AH, THE HUMOR AGAIN. IT'S CRUCIAL TO HAVE PSYCHOSECURE CONSTANTS TO LEAN ON IN TIMES OF STRESS.
IN FACT I'VE DEVISED A TERM FOR THEM: "PSYCHOSECURE CONSTANTS."
ONE THING'S FOR SURE -- IF MADDY HADN'T TAKEN ME TO ZANE, WE'D BOTH BE SPARE PARTS NOW.
I'VE NEVER SEEN COMPLEMENTARY PSYCHOSES LIKE THESE BEFORE...
IRIS' IMPOSSIBLE STORY SUPPORTS YOURS COMPLETELY, AS IF HARKER REALLY HAD LIVED IN SUPERNATURAL FORM FOR NINETY YEARS.
BUT... WHEN THE POLICE BROUGHT YOU HERE, THEY SAID THEY'D RETURN TO TAKE A STATEMENT HOURS AGO.
THEY SEEM TO HAVE FORGOTTEN.
IT'S NOT A PSYCHOSIS! OR IF IT IS, IT'S ONE CAUSED BY BEING ATTACKED BY GHOULS EVERY COUPLE HOURS!
WHAT ELSE DO YOU NEED TO SEE, DR. ANGSTROM?
LOOK AT THIS. DO THESE LOOK LIKE HOSPITAL STITCHES TO YOU??

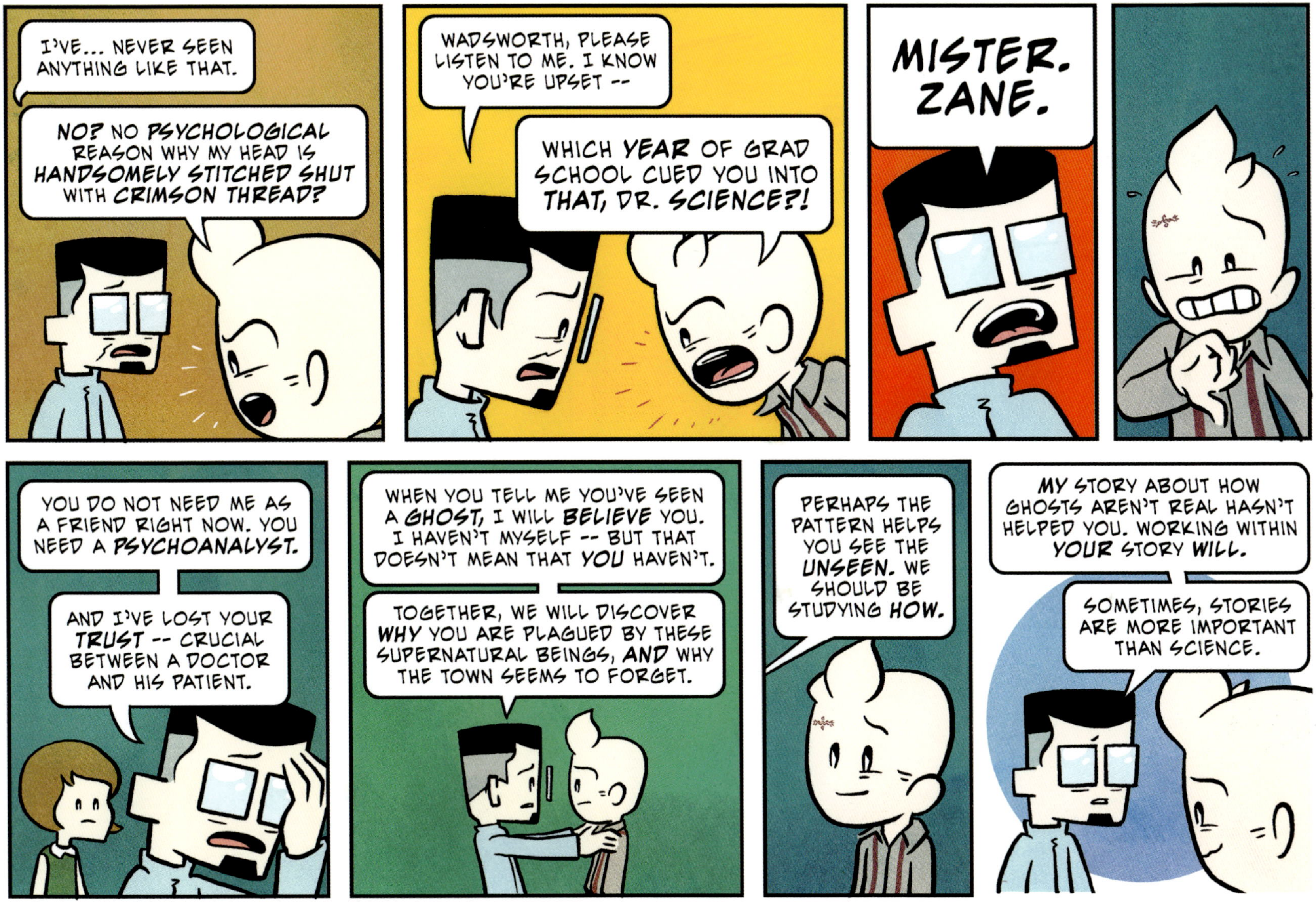
I'VE... NEVER SEEN ANYTHING LIKE THAT.
NO? NO PSYCHOLOGICAL REASON WHY MY HEAD IS HANDSOMELY STITCHED SHUT WITH CRIMSON THREAD?
WADSWORTH, PLEASE LISTEN TO ME. I KNOW YOU'RE UPSET --
WHICH YEAR OF GRAD SCHOOL CUED YOU INTO THAT, DR. SCIENCE?!
MISTER. ZANE.
YOU DO NOT NEED ME AS A FRIEND RIGHT NOW. YOU NEED A PSYCHOANALYST.
AND I'VE LOST YOUR TRUST -- CRUCIAL BETWEEN A DOCTOR AND HIS PATIENT.
WHEN YOU TELL ME YOU'VE SEEN A GHOST, I WILL BELIEVE YOU. I HAVEN'T MYSELF -- BUT THAT DOESN'T MEAN THAT YOU HAVEN'T.
TOGETHER, WE WILL DISCOVER WHY YOU ARE PLAGUED BY THESE SUPERNATURAL BEINGS, AND WHY THE TOWN SEEMS TO FORGET.
PERHAPS THE PATTERN HELPS YOU SEE THE UNSEEN. WE SHOULD BE STUDYING HOW.
MY STORY ABOUT HOW GHOSTS AREN'T REAL HASN'T HELPED YOU. WORKING WITHIN YOUR STORY WILL.
SOMETIMES, STORIES ARE MORE IMPORTANT THAN SCIENCE.

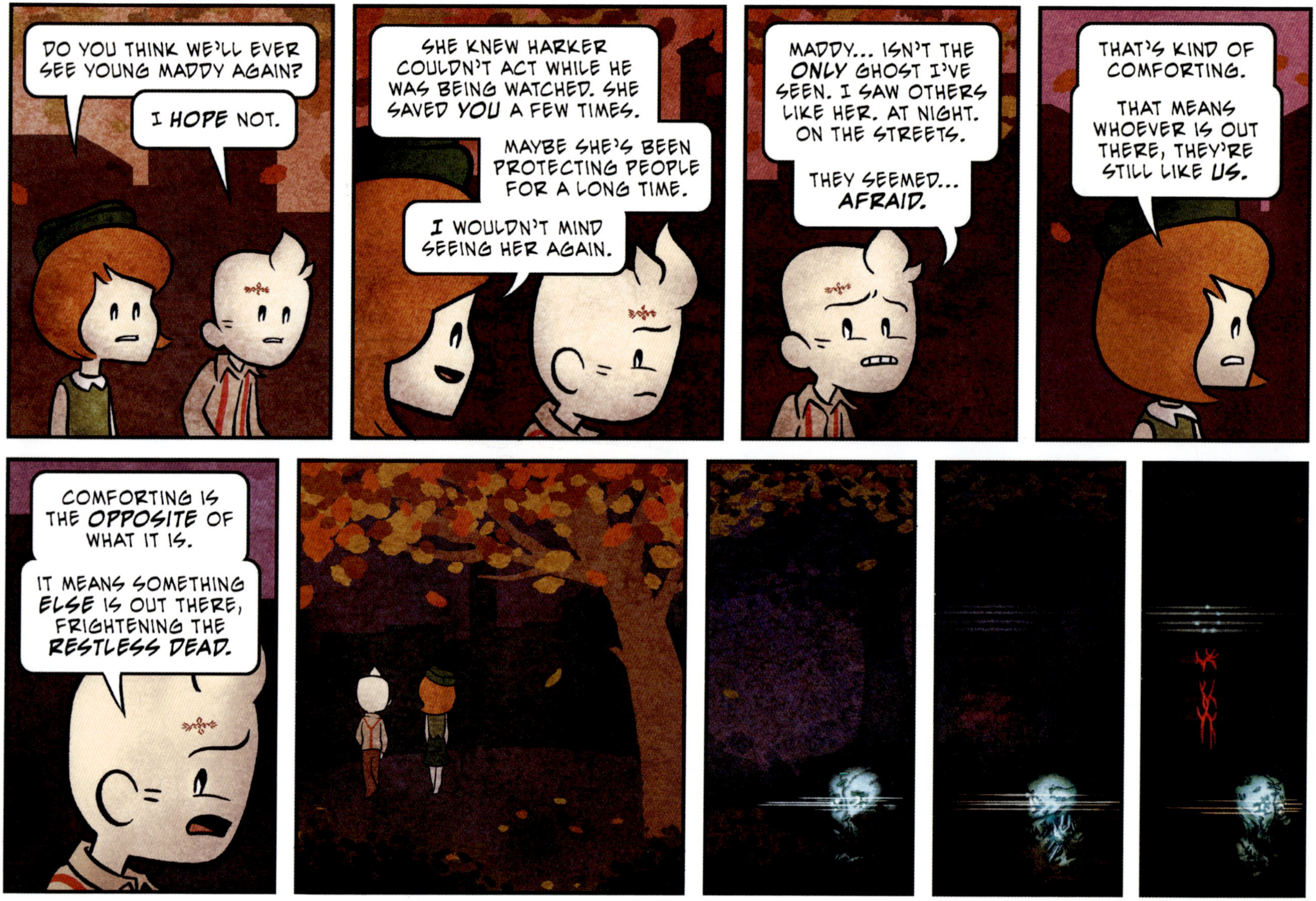
DO YOU THINK WE'LL EVER SEE YOUNG MADDY AGAIN?
I HOPE NOT.
SHE KNEW HARKER COULDN'T ACT WHILE HE WAS BEING WATCHED. SHE SAVED YOU A FEW TIMES.
MAYBE SHE'S BEEN PROTECTING PEOPLE FOR A LONG TIME.
I WOULDN'T MIND SEEING HER AGAIN.
MADDY... ISN'T THE ONLY GHOST I'VE SEEN. I SAW OTHERS LIKE HER. AT NIGHT. ON THE STREETS.
THEY SEEMED... AFRAID.
THAT'S KIND OF COMFORTING.
THAT MEANS WHOEVER IS OUT THERE, THEY'RE STILL LIKE US.
COMFORTING IS THE OPPOSITE OF WHAT IT IS.
IT MEANS SOMETHING ELSE IS OUT THERE, FRIGHTENING THE RESTLESS DEAD.

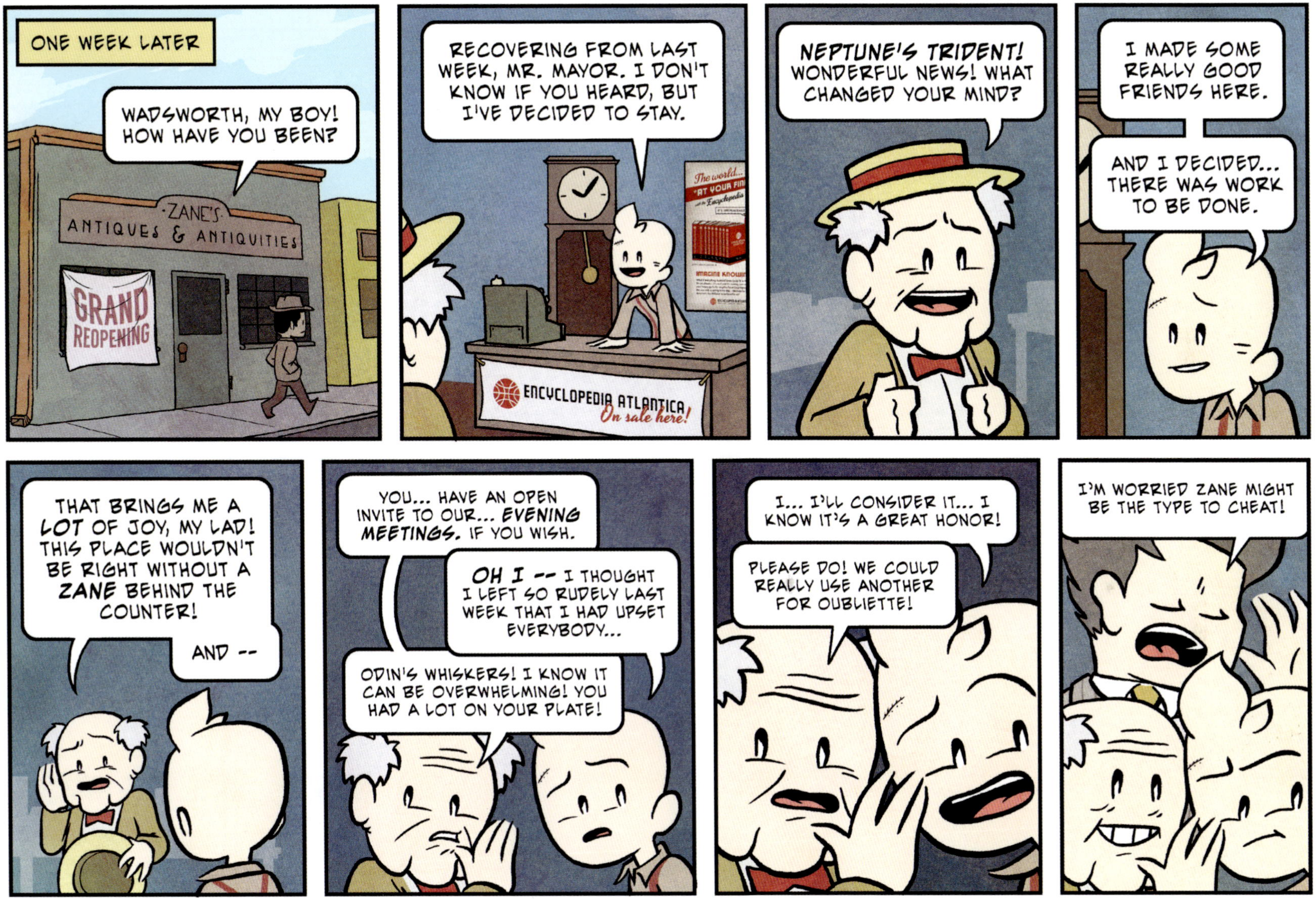
ONE WEEK LATER
WADSWORTH, MY BOY! HOW HAVE YOU BEEN?
ZANE'S ANTIQUES & ANTIQUITIES
GRAND REOPENING
RECOVERING FROM LAST WEEK, MR. MAYOR. I DON'T KNOW IF YOU HEARD, BUT I'VE DECIDED TO STAY.
ENCYCLOPEDIA ATLANTICA On sale here!
NEPTUNE'S TRIDENT! WONDERFUL NEWS! WHAT CHANGED YOUR MIND?
I MADE SOME REALLY GOOD FRIENDS HERE.
AND I DECIDED... THERE WAS WORK TO BE DONE.
THAT BRINGS ME A LOT OF JOY, MY LAD! THIS PLACE WOULDN'T BE RIGHT WITHOUT A ZANE BEHIND THE COUNTER!
AND --
YOU... HAVE AN OPEN INVITE TO OUR... EVENING MEETINGS. IF YOU WISH.
OH I -- I THOUGHT I LEFT SO RUDELY LAST WEEK THAT I HAD UPSET EVERYBODY...
ODIN'S WHISKERS! I KNOW IT CAN BE OVERWHELMING! YOU HAD A LOT ON YOUR PLATE!
I... I'LL CONSIDER IT... I KNOW IT'S A GREAT HONOR!
PLEASE DO! WE COULD REALLY USE ANOTHER FOR OUBLIETTE!
I'M WORRIED ZANE MIGHT BE THE TYPE TO CHEAT!

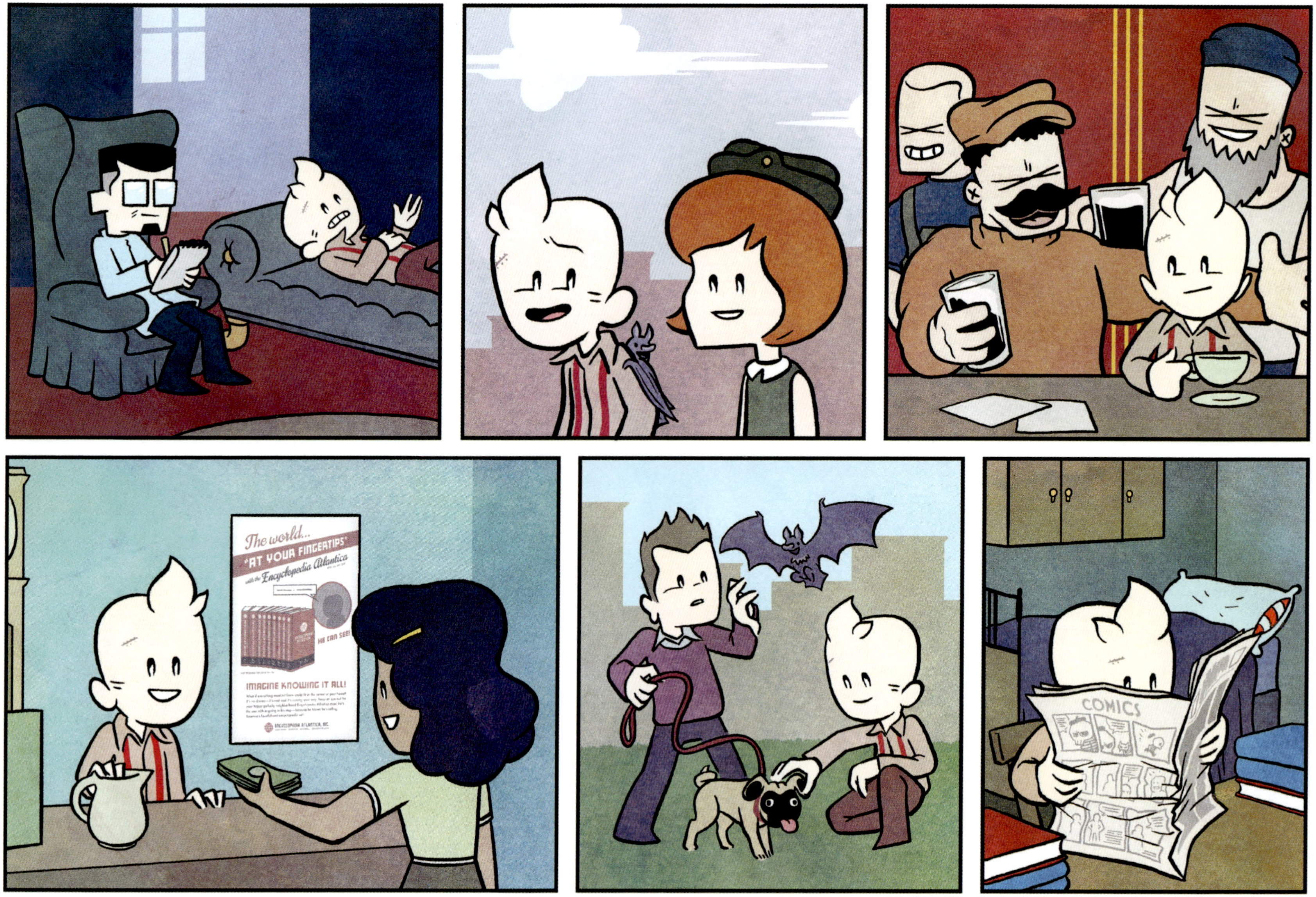
The world...
"AT YOUR FINGERTIPS"
with the Encyclopedia Atlantica
HE CAN SEE!
IMAGINE KNOWING IT ALL!
ENCYCLOPEDIA ATLANTICA, INC.
COMICS

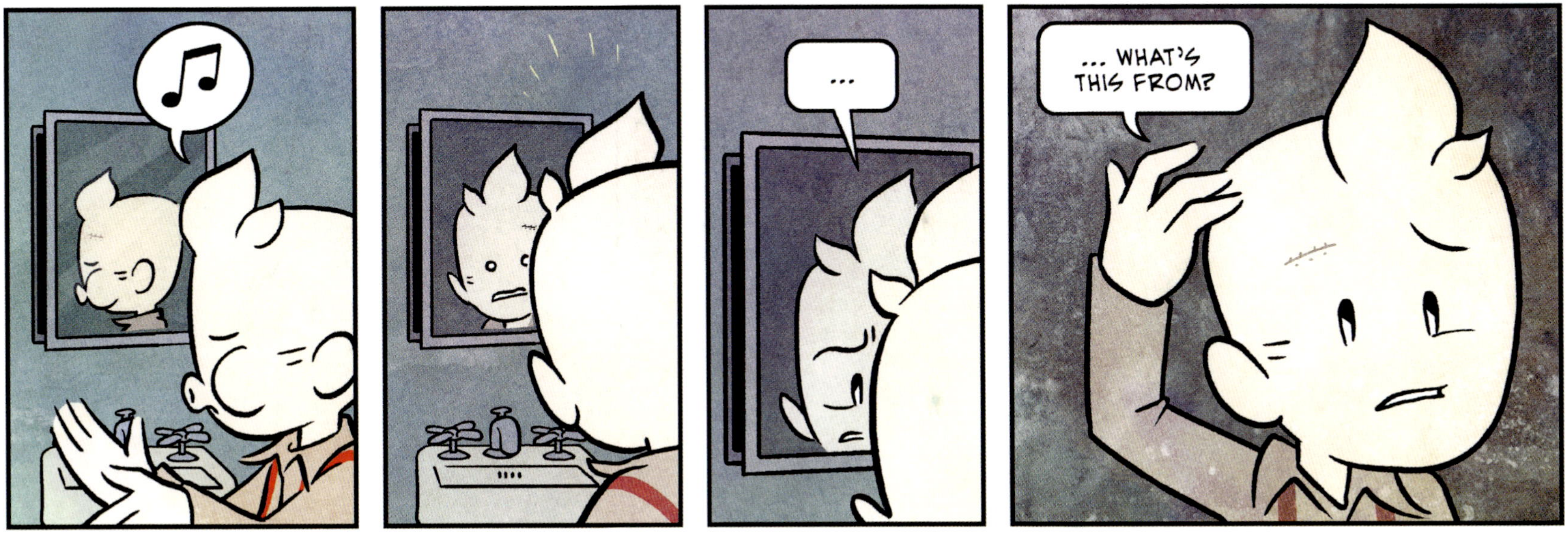
...
... WHAT'S THIS FROM?

BROODHOLLOW

18 11

OUR PAST
OUR FOUNDATION

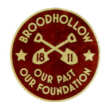

CURIOUS LITTLE THING

Between 2007 and 2009, I published a number of short horror stories online, set in and around the fictional Ichor Falls. One of the stories, Candle Cove, achieved popularity as a hoax due to its internet forum-style formatting. The rest of the stories are much more traditionally written, including this one, which became the inspiration for the first Broodhollow arc. This Curious Little Thing ends very differently.

I have an odd habit a friend recently picked up on, a habit I developed about a year ago. He noticed that when I enter a room — any room — and shut the door, I turn my face away from it and close my eyes until I hear the lock click. Only after the door is fully closed will I open my eyes. He gave me a hard time about it until I told him why it started.

I work for a water-seal company in St. Paul. We produce sealant for exposed wood — decks, boats, that kind of thing. You hear about sealant being a dirty word in the Ashland-Ichor Falls-Ironton area, but not all those companies were part of the infamous "Ethylor summer" that wiped out the local economy in the '50s. I got sent to an industrial park outside of Ichor Falls on business.

I checked into this dismal hotel, the Hotel Umbra, that looked like the decor hadn't been changed since 1930. The lobby wallpaper had gone yellow from decades of cigarette smoke, and everything had a fine layer of dust, including the old man behind the front desk. I hoped that the room would be in better shape. Mine was on the fourth floor.

Being an old place, the hotel had a rickety cable elevator, the kind with the double set of enclosures: one of those flexing metal gates, and a solid outer pair of doors. I shut the gate and latched it, and pressed the tiny black button for my floor.

Just as the outer elevator doors were about to close, I was startled by the face of a young woman rushing at the gap between them. She was too late; the doors shut, and after a moment the elevator ascended.

I thought nothing of it, until I needed to take the elevator back down for one of my bags. I entered, pushed the button for the lobby, and pressed my tired back to the elevator wall opposite the doors. They had nearly completely shut when again I was surprised by a woman's face moving towards the gap, staring into the elevator through the gate, too late to put her hand through to stop the doors from closing. This time I sprang forward and held the "Door Open" button, and after a moment the doors lurched and slid open.

I waited a moment. From the opening I could see partly down the hallway: no one in sight. Still holding the button down, I slid open the metal gate and craned my head into the hallway to look down the other direction.

No one. No trace of the girl, no recently shut hotel room door, no footsteps, no jingle of keys.

I released the button, but did not lean back against the wall. I stood directly in front of the spot where the

elevator doors would meet. After a pause, the doors again began to slide shut, to move towards each other until the space between them was the width of a young girl's face.

In that quarter-second several fingertips appeared, followed immediately by her face again, rushing from around the corner, staring at me as the doors met. I had been watching the gap where I thought she might be, so this time I saw her clearly — she was about thirteen years old, and very plain, almost homely, with a pale complexion and neck-length dark brown hair that looked mussed or slightly dirty.

I didn't have time to glance down at her visible shoulder, to see what she was wearing. From her behavior I wondered if she was a runaway, or a homeless person who had gotten into the building. She had a glassy, blank expression, tinged with desperation, some distant desire or need. A look that could easily be accompanied by the words "Please help."

The next time I passed the front desk, I asked the old man if he'd seen a young girl running through.

"Heard the stories, then," he said between throat-clearings, rocking gently in his seat. "Young Maddy has been here a long time. Takes a liking to gentlemen guests. Always been shy. Never says a word, not a word. Just curious."

I told him I hadn't heard any stories, and that there had been a girl taking the stairs and standing in front of my elevator on every floor.

"That's our Maddy," he said. "She likes you then. Sweet on you. She just wants to see, that's all, just to see. All she ever does. Curious little thing. Just wants to see."

I stayed at the Hotel Umbra for three nights. It was a four-night business trip; the last night I tried sleeping in my car. It didn't help.

Let me tell you about Young Maddy.

You only catch glimpses of her, of a face with a resigned look of quiet desperation, dominated by a pair of wide, dark eyes. Locked doors, barricades, nothing made a difference. She gets inside.

I never saw her longer than half a second. Every time I laid eyes on her she retreated instantly, only to appear again an hour or two later. An hour or two if I was lucky.

Let me tell you about where I saw Young Maddy.

Every time I shut the door to my bathroom, in my hotel room, I saw her. If I watched as I shut it, at the last possible second I'd see the crescent of her face moving fast at the gap. I'd throw the door open to find nothing.

Every time I closed the closet door I saw her. If I watched that gap, she'd suddenly be inside the closet, leaning her head to watch me just as it shut. It's as if she knew where to go, where to be, so that my eye would meet hers. But there was never an impact, never a moment when she'd make contact with the door or the wall.

The first time I sat at that writing table I saw her. As I closed the large bottom drawer. She rushed at the gap from inside the drawer, her wide eyes pleading for something I could not give. I pulled the drawer from its rails and threw it to the floor.

I spent that last night in my car, but like I said, it did no good. Tossing and turning on that rental car seat, the back ratcheted as flat as I could get it, I'd have to open my eyes sometimes, and if there was a place for her to dart from my view when I opened them, she did. In the side-view mirror, or peeking over the hood of my car — once upside-down, at the top of the windshield, as if she was on the roof.

I'm back in St. Paul again, and I've been back for a year. But Maddy hasn't stopped. If I keep my eyes open long enough, if I watch a place long enough, I'll eventually catch sight of movement — near the copier in my office, a pile of boxes in an alley, a column in a quiet parking lot — and my eye will get there just in time to see her eye retreating from view. There's never anything there when I go to look, so I've stopped looking.

That's how I've had to change things since the Hotel Umbra. I've stopped looking. I keep my eyes shut when I close doors, when I shut drawers and cabinets, fridges, coolers, the trunk of my car. Not all spaces. Just ones that are big enough.

At least, that used to work. I was getting ready for bed a few nights ago, standing in front of my bathroom mirror, door shut, cabinets shut. Watching myself floss. I opened up wide to get my molars.

I swear I saw fingertips retreat down the back of my throat.

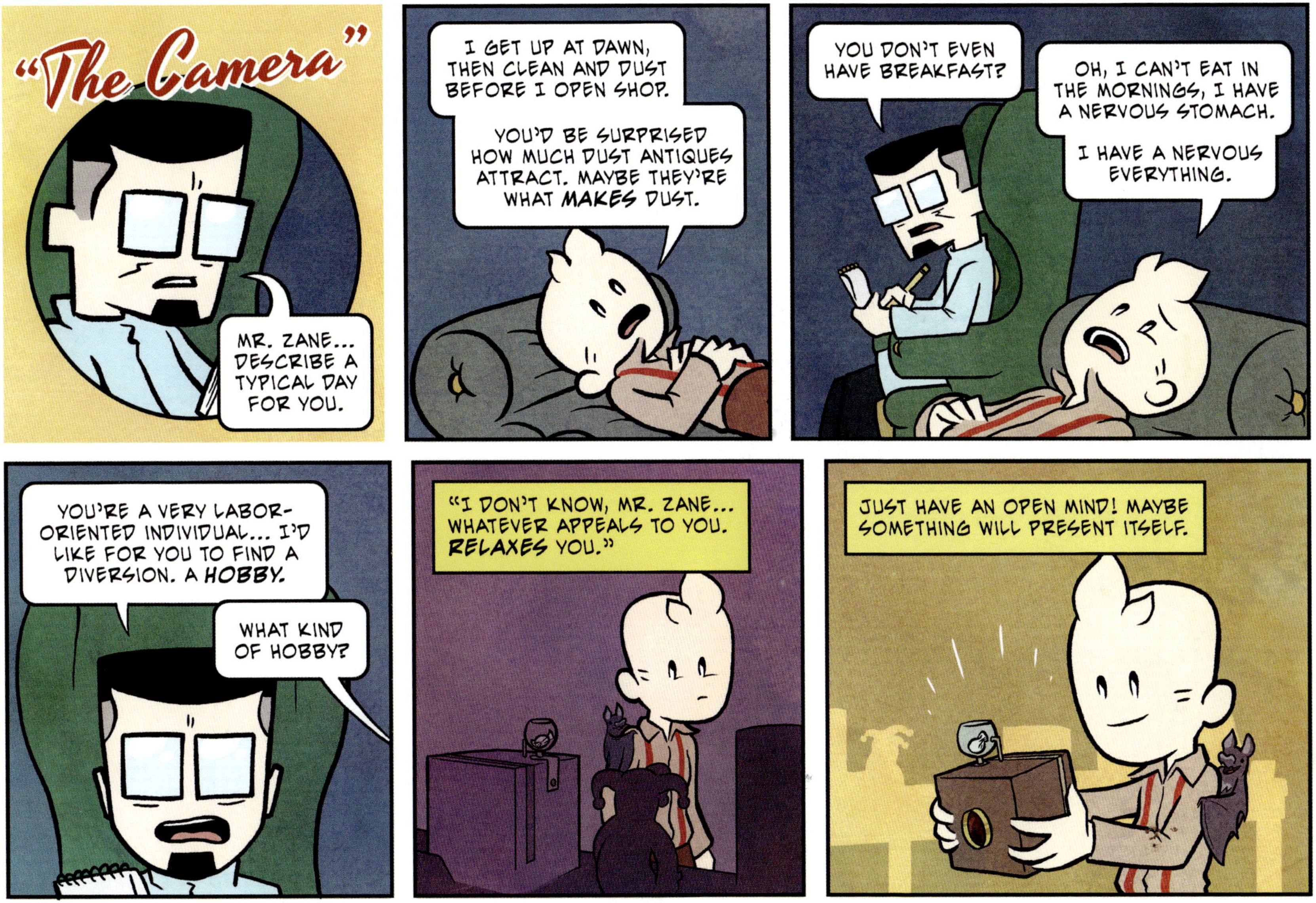
"The Camera"
MR. ZANE... DESCRIBE A TYPICAL DAY FOR YOU.
I GET UP AT DAWN, THEN CLEAN AND DUST BEFORE I OPEN SHOP.
YOU'D BE SURPRISED HOW MUCH DUST ANTIQUES ATTRACT. MAYBE THEY'RE WHAT **MAKES** DUST.
YOU DON'T EVEN HAVE BREAKFAST?
OH, I CAN'T EAT IN THE MORNINGS, I HAVE A NERVOUS STOMACH.
I HAVE A NERVOUS EVERYTHING.
YOU'RE A VERY LABOR-ORIENTED INDIVIDUAL... I'D LIKE FOR YOU TO FIND A DIVERSION. A ***HOBBY.***
WHAT KIND OF HOBBY?
"I DON'T KNOW, MR. ZANE... WHATEVER APPEALS TO YOU. ***RELAXES*** YOU."
JUST HAVE AN OPEN MIND! MAYBE SOMETHING WILL PRESENT ITSELF.

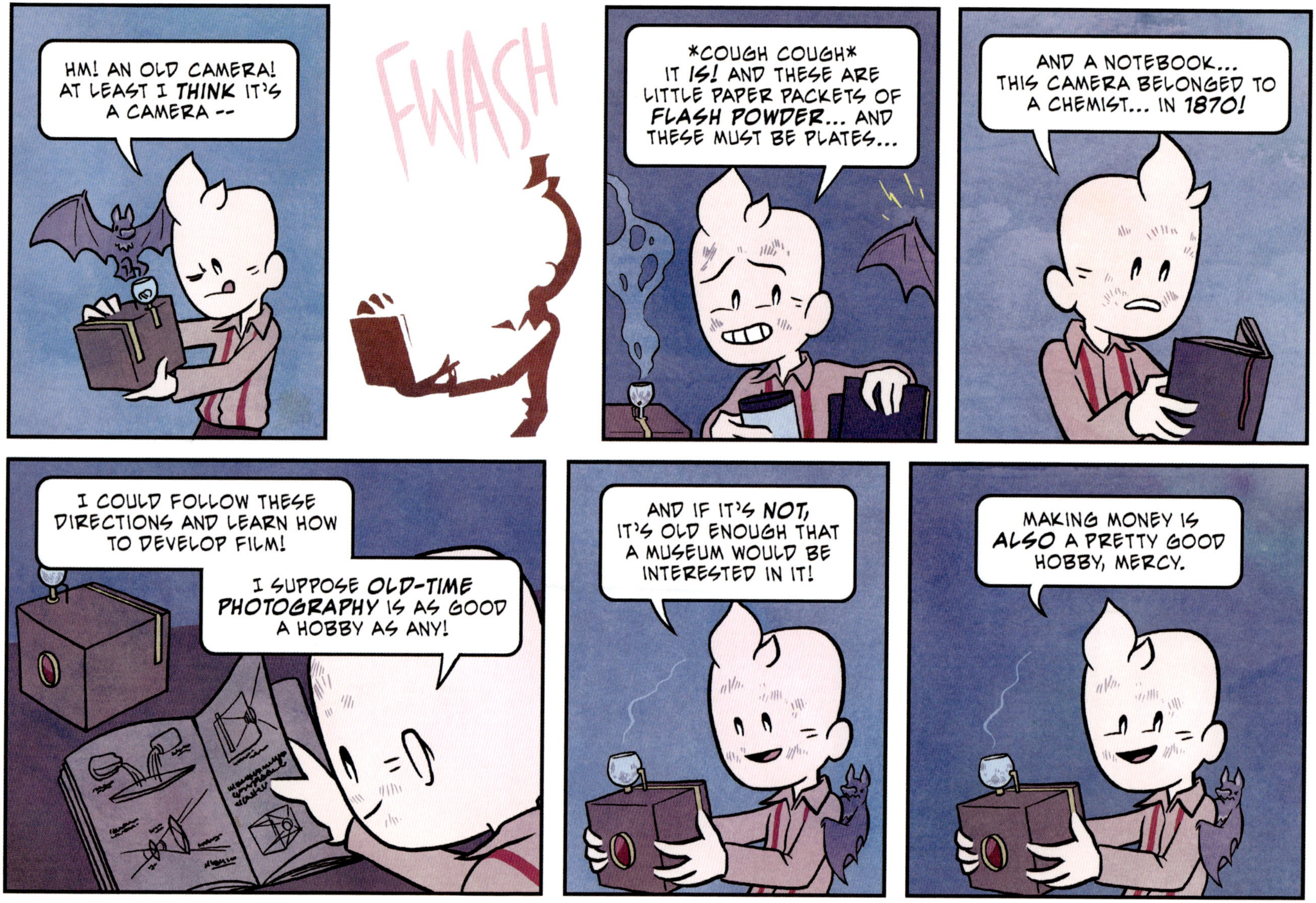
HM! AN OLD CAMERA! AT LEAST I THINK IT'S A CAMERA --
FWASH
COUGH COUGH IT IS! AND THESE ARE LITTLE PAPER PACKETS OF FLASH POWDER... AND THESE MUST BE PLATES...
AND A NOTEBOOK... THIS CAMERA BELONGED TO A CHEMIST... IN 1870!
I COULD FOLLOW THESE DIRECTIONS AND LEARN HOW TO DEVELOP FILM!
I SUPPOSE OLD-TIME PHOTOGRAPHY IS AS GOOD A HOBBY AS ANY!
AND IF IT'S NOT, IT'S OLD ENOUGH THAT A MUSEUM WOULD BE INTERESTED IN IT!
MAKING MONEY IS ALSO A PRETTY GOOD HOBBY, MERCY.

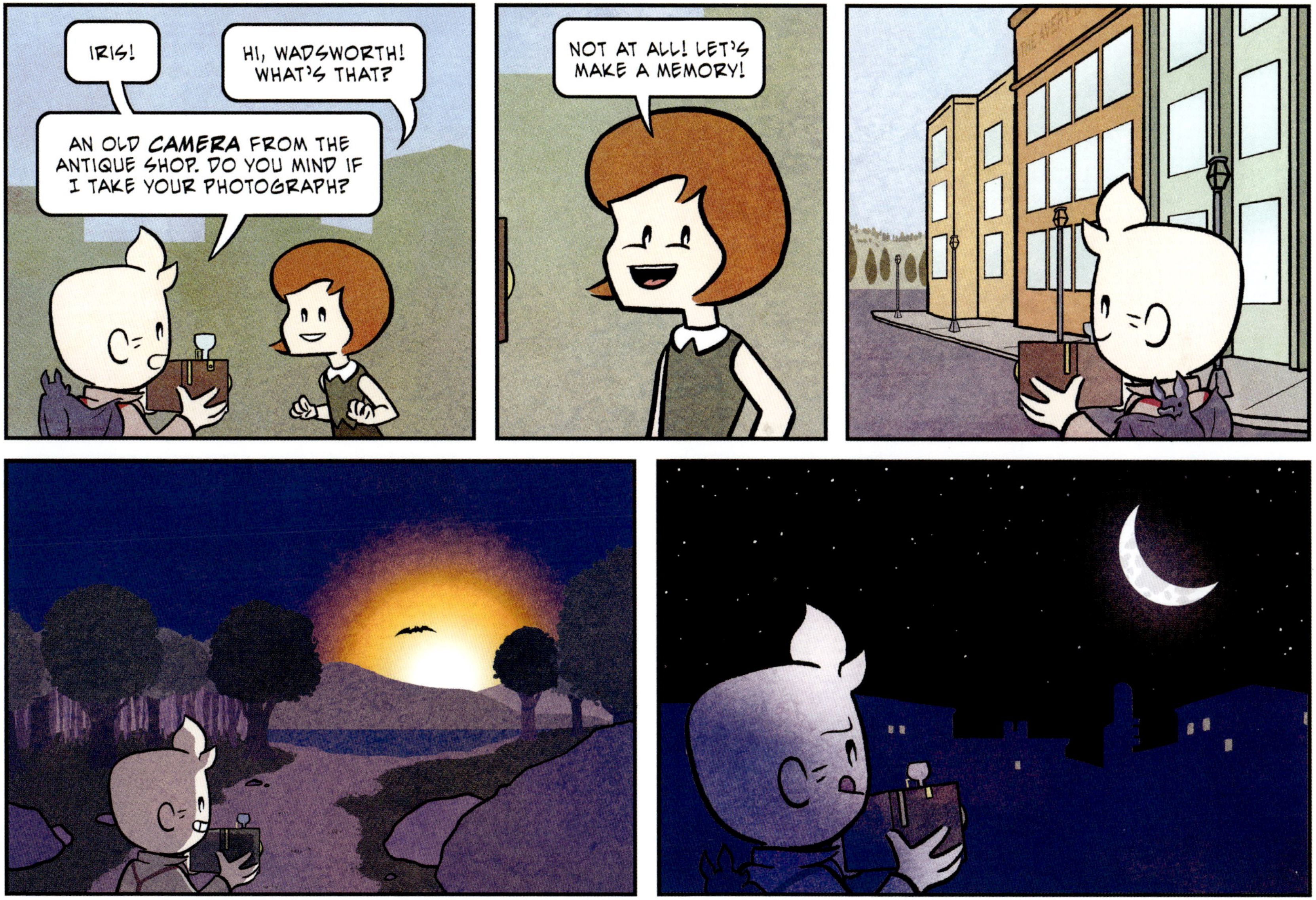
IRIS!
HI, WADSWORTH! WHAT'S THAT?
AN OLD CAMERA FROM THE ANTIQUE SHOP. DO YOU MIND IF I TAKE YOUR PHOTOGRAPH?
NOT AT ALL! LET'S MAKE A MEMORY!
THE AVERY

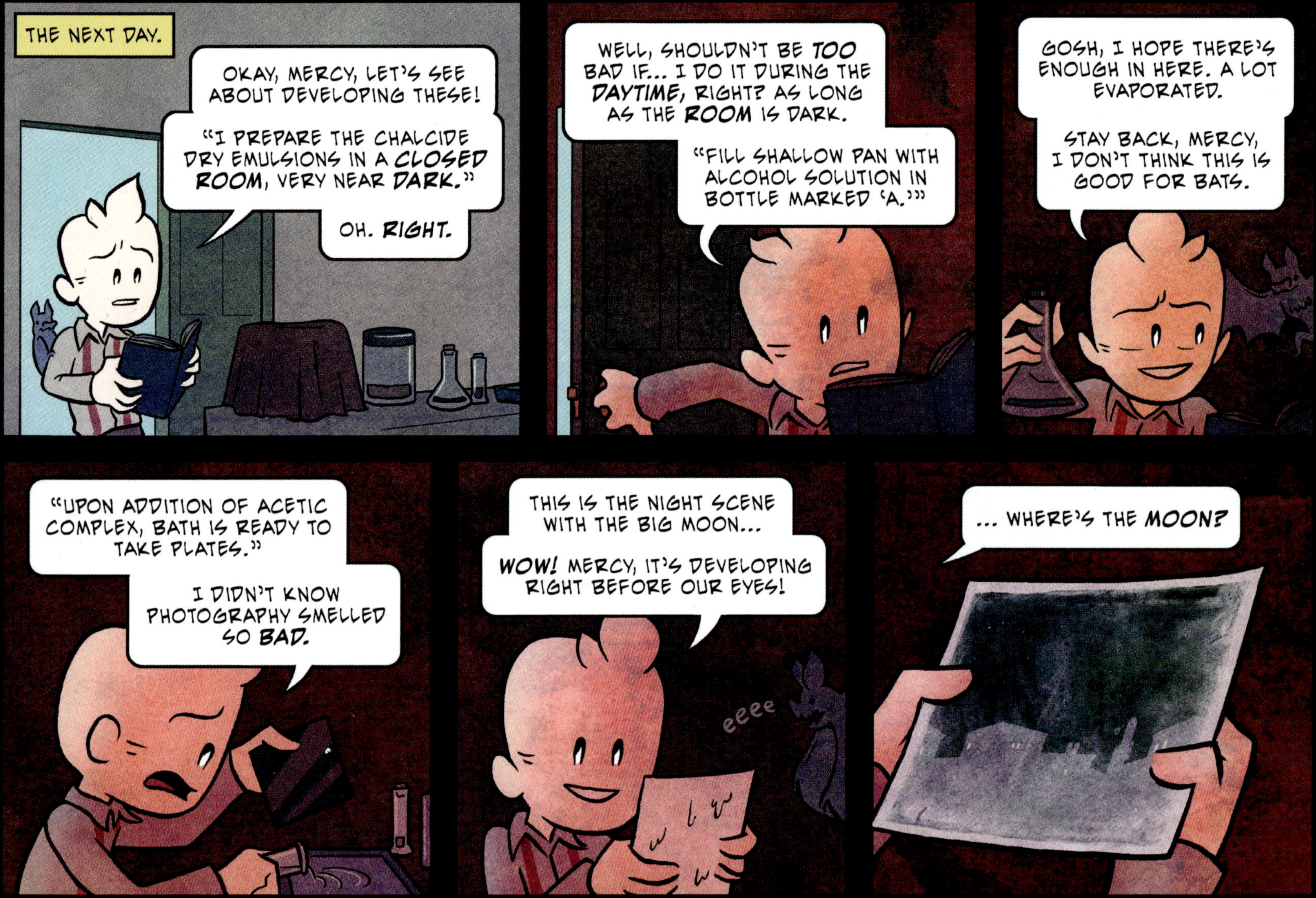
THE NEXT DAY.
OKAY, MERCY, LET'S SEE ABOUT DEVELOPING THESE!
"I PREPARE THE CHALCIDE DRY EMULSIONS IN A CLOSED ROOM, VERY NEAR DARK."
OH. RIGHT.
WELL, SHOULDN'T BE TOO BAD IF... I DO IT DURING THE DAYTIME, RIGHT? AS LONG AS THE ROOM IS DARK.
"FILL SHALLOW PAN WITH ALCOHOL SOLUTION IN BOTTLE MARKED 'A.'"
GOSH, I HOPE THERE'S ENOUGH IN HERE. A LOT EVAPORATED.
STAY BACK, MERCY, I DON'T THINK THIS IS GOOD FOR BATS.
"UPON ADDITION OF ACETIC COMPLEX, BATH IS READY TO TAKE PLATES."
I DIDN'T KNOW PHOTOGRAPHY SMELLED SO BAD.
THIS IS THE NIGHT SCENE WITH THE BIG MOON...
WOW! MERCY, IT'S DEVELOPING RIGHT BEFORE OUR EYES!
eeee
... WHERE'S THE MOON?

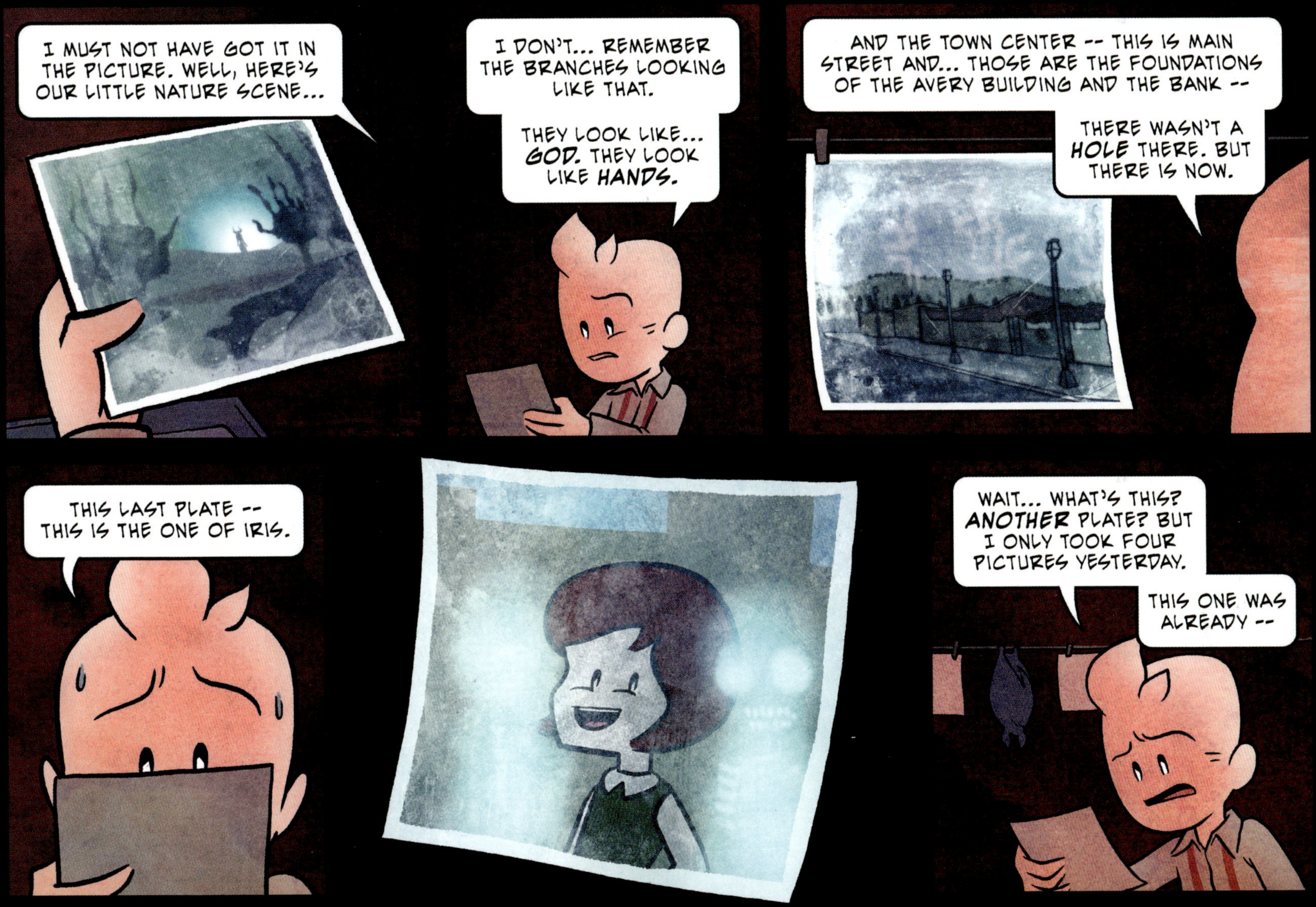
I MUST NOT HAVE GOT IT IN THE PICTURE. WELL, HERE'S OUR LITTLE NATURE SCENE...
I DON'T... REMEMBER THE BRANCHES LOOKING LIKE THAT.
THEY LOOK LIKE... GOD. THEY LOOK LIKE HANDS.
AND THE TOWN CENTER -- THIS IS MAIN STREET AND... THOSE ARE THE FOUNDATIONS OF THE AVERY BUILDING AND THE BANK --
THERE WASN'T A HOLE THERE. BUT THERE IS NOW.
THIS LAST PLATE -- THIS IS THE ONE OF IRIS.
WAIT... WHAT'S THIS? ANOTHER PLATE? BUT I ONLY TOOK FOUR PICTURES YESTERDAY.
THIS ONE WAS ALREADY --

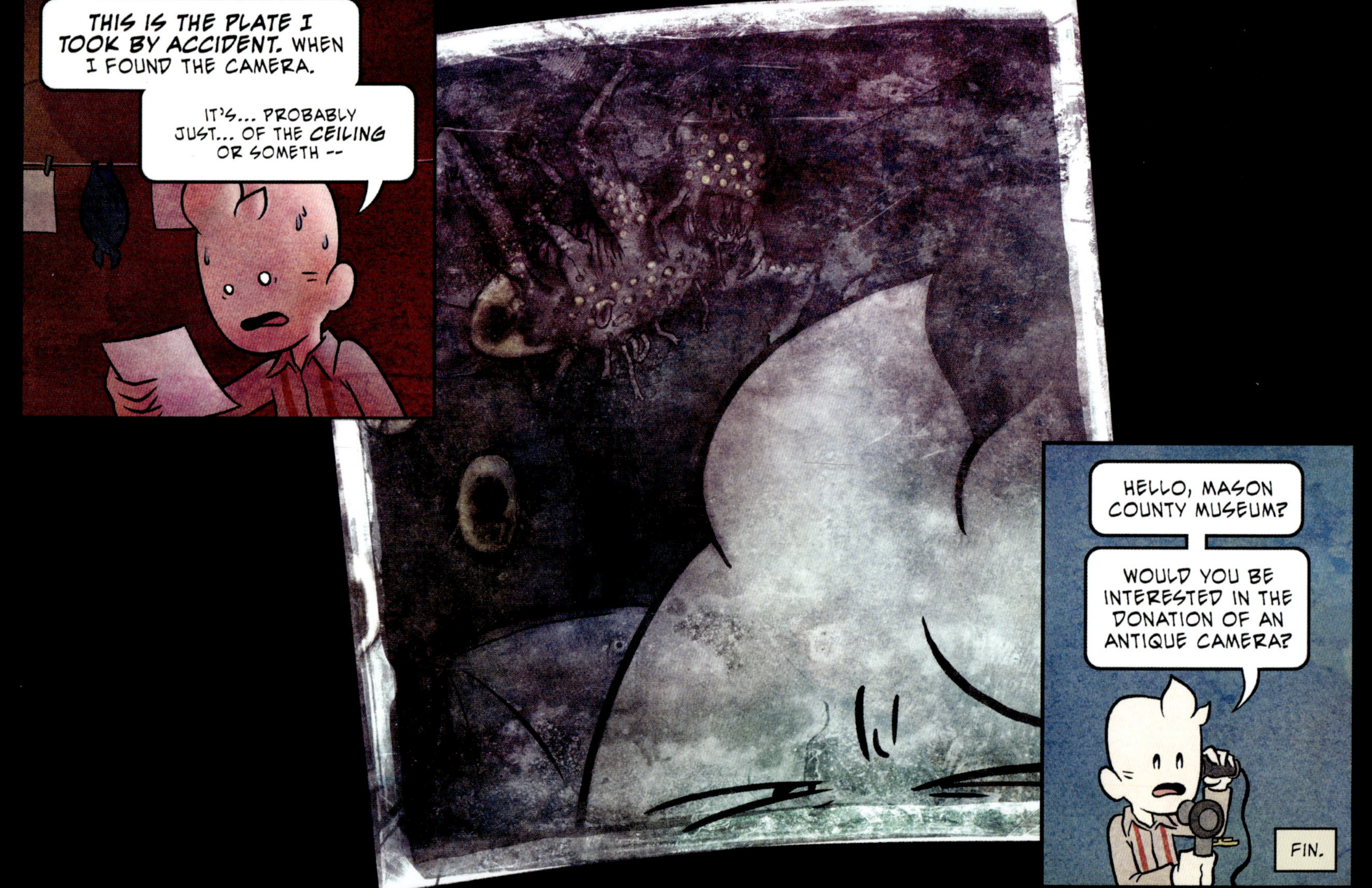
THIS IS THE PLATE I TOOK BY ACCIDENT. WHEN I FOUND THE CAMERA.
IT'S... PROBABLY JUST... OF THE CEILING OR SOMETH --
HELLO, MASON COUNTY MUSEUM?
WOULD YOU BE INTERESTED IN THE DONATION OF AN ANTIQUE CAMERA?
FIN.

Kris Straub has been a cartoonist since 2000, and has been afraid of the dark since *2001: A Space Odyssey* on Betamax.

He lives with his wife in Seattle, Washington. He is believed to be alive at the time of this writing.